CONTEMPORARY SOCIAL RESEARCH SERIES
General Editor: MARTIN BULMER

1

Social Measurement and Social Indicators

To Julia

Social Measurement and Social Indicators

Issues of Policy and Theory

MICHAEL CARLEY

London
GEORGE ALLEN & UNWIN
Boston   Sydney

GEORGE ALLEN & UNWIN LTD
40 Museum Street, London WC1A 1LU

© Policy Studies Institute, 1981

British Library Cataloguing in Publication Data

Carley, Michael
   Social measurement and social indicators. –
   (Contemporary social research series; 1).
   1. Social indicators   2. Social sciences –
   Statistical methods
   I. Title   II. Series
   300'.7'2   HN25   80–41674

   ISBN 0-04-310009-0
   ISBN 0-04-310010-4 Pbk

Set in 10 on 11 point Times by Fotographics, Bedford
and printed in Great Britain
by Billing and Sons Ltd., Guildford, London and Worcester

Contents

Editor's Preface

The structure of the social sciences combines two separate elements, theory and empirical evidence. Both are necessary for successful social understanding; one without the other is barren. The *Contemporary Social Research* series is concerned with the means by which this structure is maintained and kept standing solid and upright, a job performed by the methodology of social research.

The series is intended to provide concise introductions to significant methodological topics. Broadly conceived, research methodology deals with the general grounds for the validity of social scientific propositions. How do we know what we do know about the social world? More narrowly, it deals with the questions: how do we actually acquire new knowledge about the world in which we live? What are the strategies and techniques by means of which social science data are collected and analysed? The series will seek to answer such questions through the examination of specific areas of methodology.

Why is such a series necessary? There exist many solid, indeed massive, methodology textbooks, which most undergraduates in sociology, psychology and the other social sciences acquire familiarity with in the course of their studies. The aim of this series is different. It goes beyond such texts to focus upon specific topics, procedures, methods of analysis and methodological problems to provide a readable introduction to its subject. Each book contains annotated suggestions for further reading. The intended audience includes the advanced undergraduate, the graduate student, the working social researcher seeking to familiarise himself with new areas, and the non-specialist who wishes to enlarge his knowledge of social research. Research methodology need not be remote and inaccessible. Some prior knowledge of statistics will be useful, but only certain titles in the series will make strong statistical demands upon the reader. The series is concerned above all to demonstrate the general importance and centrality of research methodology to social science.

The topic of Michael Carley's *Social Measurement and Social Indicators* is significant politically, substantively and methodologically. Governments increasingly look to social scientists to provide them with so-called 'social indicators', regular, concise and comparable statistical summaries of the state of society, in fields as diverse as health, education, crime or job satisfaction. Michael Carley considers in detail the problems that such attempts entail, the pitfalls in the way of the incautious statistician, and the political assumptions of indicator construction. His book is an illuminating case-study of the uses and limitations of social measurement.

MARTIN BULMER
The London School of Economics and Political Science

Author's Preface

The pioneers of social indicators were inspired by their early recognition of the tremendous need for an improved flow of cogent social information to an increasingly complex public sector decision process. They responded with a ready and admirable enthusiasm and soon their efforts became a virtual 'movement'. The possibilities for doing social good by developing tools of social measurement seemed endless, and the social indicator movement grew rapidly in scope and stature.

Now, fifteen years later, the mood is somewhat changed. The high hopes held out for social indicators remain for the most part unfulfilled, especially for the data needs of policy-making. Administrators have become guarded, if not pessimistic, about the usefulness of social indicators, and many researchers have turned from a concern for enlightening the policy process to a narrower, and often misunderstood, emphasis on detailed statistical manipulation. This change in mood (with hindsight) was caused in part by the fact that the almost flamboyant optimism of the social indicator movement fostered naive expectations as to the development time for policy-useful social indicators. This was related to an underestimation of the severe difficulties to be faced in attempts at social measurement.

These difficulties reflect both policy-related and methodological issues, and this book is about those issues. It is not a 'how to' guide on the construction of social indicators, but rather a critical but optimistic review of the important practical and theoretical issues in the field, as embodied in the literature and in collections of social indicators. Such a review also provides a forward-looking agenda of important problem areas which must be addressed if the social indicators movement is to fulfil its twofold ambitions of contributing to social knowledge and providing useful and relevant information to the policy-making process. The book also suggests some compelling reasons why we must not abandon our attempts to develop and refine policy-relevant social indicators.

Given its attention to issues, this book is aimed at a wide cross-disciplinary audience in government and university. For students, it not only provides a critical examination of these important issues, but can serve as a compact and useful introduction to a broad field of social scientific endeavour loosely grouped under the banner of social indicators. For administrators, it explores the philosophical and measurement problems in social indicators, and suggests broad criteria useful for interpreting social indicator reports. For researchers, and indeed for anyone with interest in the field, it places social indicator efforts into a wider policy-analytic perspective with its inescapable political, value-judgemental and bureaucratic aspects. Such a perspective suggests why some social indicator efforts have been less than satisfactory from a policy-making point of view, and suggests new avenues of research for the field. In every case, the book is jargon-free in an attempt to enlighten not only those within the field, but especially those in other fields who must deal with social indicators, although they may never actually construct one.

Chapter 1 looks at the relatively simple concept of a social indicator and explores the spectrum of activity constituting the social indicator movement. The historical antecedents of social indicators are identified as are the important early landmarks in the movement. The basic problem areas in social measurement are contrasted with the compelling need for reliable social information. Chapter 2 goes on to examine the definition problems which have plagued social indicator research since its inception, and then draws out the most useful components of the best definitions, organised according to policy use and statistical sophistication. Various dimensions of social indicators are examined, including subjective indicators and quality-of-life studies. Chapter 3 suggests that systems of social indicators can be best understood by the way they are structured, and goes on to examine a number of such systems being developed, and in use, in different countries and by international agencies.

Chapter 4 explores the critical relationship between social indicators and social theories and models, and examines the major difficulties which impede the development of causal and predictive social indicator models. A simple conceptual framework is proposed for orienting and integrating research efforts. Chapter 5 examines social indicators in the policy-making process, and argues that for policy-relevant indicators the role of social scientific method must be considered in the light of the basic elements of the policy process: value-conflict, bureaucratic maintenance and analytic rationality. Policy constraints on social indicators are associated with non-use, misuse, quantification, value-judgements, distributional equity and value-weighting schemes. Means for overcoming political dilemmas and constraints are discussed.

Chapter 6 looks at the field of national social reporting, with special emphasis on the audience, the problems and the prospects for social reports in the UK and the USA. Chapter 7 explores in detail three different applications of social indicators to urban analysis: for classifying neighbourhoods within cities, for comparisons among cities and counties and for assessing performance in the delivery of urban services. Examples are drawn from both North American and UK experiences. Chapter 8 sums up the critical issues and arguments of the book and looks to the future of social indicators. An appendix suggests the most useful, and most approachable, further references in the literature.

The initial research for this book was undertaken at the London School of Economics, while the author was in grateful receipt of a fellowship from the Central Mortgage and Housing Corporation of the Government of Canada. Other research time was kindly funded in part by the Social Science Research Council (UK) and in part by the Policy Studies Institute in London. I am indebted to Martin Bulmer of the LSE for his very constructive criticism of the draft manuscript. Denis F. Johnston, Senior Advisor on Social Indicators at the US Department of Commerce, also subjected the manuscript to a detailed and valuable critique. Muriel Nissel, first editor of *Social Trends*, and Alex C. Michalos, editor of *Social Indicators Research*, both gave lively discussion and advice. Susan Johnson and Stephanie Maggin at PSI provided excellent library, typing and editorial services.

MICHAEL CARLEY
Policy Studies Institute,
London, 1980

Acknowledgements

The author and publishers gratefully acknowledge permission given by the following to reprint or modify copyright material.

Her Majesty's Stationery Office for Figures 1.1, 1.2, 1.3, 1.5, 6.1, and Tables 7.1, 7.2, 7.4; the World Bank/International Bank for Reconstruction and Development and Oxford University Press for Table 1.1; the Superintendent of Documents, US Government Printing Office, for Figures 1.4, 6.2, and Tables 7.7. 7.8, 7.9; D. Reidel Publishing Company for Figure 2.4, and Tables 3.1, 4.1; John Wiley & Sons for Table 2.1; Plenum Press for Figures 2.2 and 2.3; Dr Paul L. Knox for Table 2.2; the Chartered Institute of Public Finance and Accountancy for Table 3.2; the Organisation for Economic Co-operation and Development, Paris, for Table 3.3; the Academic Press for Figure 3.1; the *International Journal of Social Economics* for Figure 4.1; the Centre for Environmental Studies for Table 7.3; the *American Journal of Economics and Sociology* for Tables 7.5 and 7.6.

Portions of Chapter 3 first appeared in *European Research,* vol. 7 (1979), the journal of the European Society for Opinion and Marketing Research, Wamberg 37, 1083 C. W. Amsterdam, The Netherlands. The society has given its permission to use the material. Portions of Chapter 4 appeared in a previous article by this author, in a modified form, in the *International Journal of Social Economics.* I am grateful for the permission to incorporate that material.

1

Introduction to the Scope
of Social Indicators

> There seems to be no question but that measurement
> problems constitute one of the most important roadblocks
> to the advancement of social science.
>
> (Blalock, 1975)

> Waco [Texas] announced plans to reduce its crime rate by
> neglecting to report some of its violent crimes to the FBI.
>
> (*Texas Monthly,* January 1980)

In the mid-1960s a growing dissatisfaction with the amount and quality of social information available to government decision-makers spawned what came to be known as the 'social indicators movement'. Initially this was a reaction against what was perceived as an overemphasis on measures of economic performance as indicative of social well-being. Within a few years the term social indicators came to encompass a wide variety of diverse attempts to specify indicators of socioeconomic well-being, from very specific measures, such as those of housing quality, to broad measures of the quality of life. At present the research impetus begun by the social indicator movement has dispersed throughout the social sciences in a wide variety of guises and efforts. Some are concerned with particular social measures themselves, others with an analytic framework or system for comprehensive measurement, and others with the direct policy relevance of the measures. All, however, are concerned with the improvement of social measurement as a contribution to knowledge and as an ultimate aid to government decision-making.

The social indictor movement has grown rapidly. In 1972 an annotated bibliography by Wilcox *et al.* listed over 1,000 entries related to social indicators and by now this number would probably be ten times that. And while this great outpouring of articles and books points to considerable activity in this fledgling field it does not imply that even now there is anything approaching a consensus on what a social indicator is or should be. Horn (1978), for example, has shortlisted ten definitions of the term social indicator, and then thrown in a couple of definitions of social statistics for good measure, all of which give different shadings of meaning to similar terms. A later chapter will examine a number of recent government publications with the words 'social indicators' in their titles which some people argue do not contain social indicators at all. Such debates show little signs of subsiding.

What, then, is a social indicator? It is perhaps worthwhile to begin in the simplest terms. In everyday life we use certain kinds of symptoms or tokens as indications of less visible yet important states of being or situation. The colour of a person's face or the temperature of his forehead tells us something about his health, based on our experience. Colour or temperature, therefore, may be crude indicators of health. In the field of social policy or government we can assume that such policy or action of government (usually) exists to maintain or improve the well-being of individuals or society as a whole. If we accept this, then for either policy development or programme evaluation the government needs some way to ascertain that maintenance of or improvement in well-being is taking place. That is, measurements are needed, unless intuitive assessments are to be relied on. Unfortunately we are unable to measure well-being directly, since neither individuals nor countries carry convenient gauges of well-being. So surrogates for more direct measures of well-being are required. These surrogates may be termed social indicators – which are measures of an observable trait of a social phenomenon which establishes the value of a different unobservable trait of the phenomena.

This points up two important characteristics of social indicators: they are *surrogates* and they are *measures*. As surrogates, social indicators do not stand by themselves. Rather than translate abstract or unmeasurable social concepts, like 'safe streets', into operational terms that allow consideration and analysis of the concept, like 'number of crimeless days'. A social indicator must always be related back to the unmeasurable concept of which it is a proxy. And as 'measures' social indicators are concerned with information which is conceptually quantifiable, and must avoid dealing with information which cannot be expressed on some ordered scale. In the next chapter we consider the question 'what is a social indicator?' in detail, and Chapters 4 and 5 take up some of the knotty problems associated with the fact that social indicators are, by nature, surrogates and measures.

Social indicators – a spectrum of activity

Just as there are multifold definitions of social indicators, so there is an enormous diversity of activity being carried out, in and out of government, under the banner of 'social indicators'. It is worth looking at the range of these activities to begin to grasp, if only unsystematically, the breadth of the field.

One of the most recognised forms of social indicator effort involves the assembly or collection of social measures. The best-known of these collections are the national social reports now issued by no fewer than thirty countries. These social reports, like *Social Trends* in the UK and *Social Indicators* in the USA, are usually large compendia of tables, charts and textual material dsigned to tell, in a broad way, what is happening to social conditions and trends in a country at the national level. Figure 1.1, for example, is two graphs from *Social Trends* showing the general availability at a national level of medical and dental services in the UK for the years 1971–8 (Thompson, 1979). Such social measures as the infant mortality rate, or numbers enrolled in primary school, are now also an important part of reports of international agencies, such as the World Bank. Table 1.1 shows some health-related indicators for some of the poorest and some of the richest countries in the world (World Bank, 1979).

Such social reports provide background data on social change, and for many people are the most visible manifestation of social indicator activity. Some people argue, however, that they only contain social *statistics* rather than indicators because the information they provide does not directly represent cause-and-effect social relationships. The reasons for such an assertion are examined in Chapter 4. Whatever stance one accepts, however, social reporting is far too important to ignore in any consideration of social indicators. Social reporting is examined in detail in Chapter 6.

A second important social indicator activity involves those indicators being developed, refined and in use directly to assist or guide government decision-making. These can be roughly divided into macro or national level indicators and micro, or local, or programme level indicators, with regional indicators somewhere in between. An example of a macro indicator is the unemployment rate which, as we know, figures heavily in government decision-making and in political debate in many countries. This rate is considered important as an indicator of national well-being and potential socioeconomic problems, and numerous social and economic policies are considered in the light of it. Figure 1.2 shows total 'unemployment by duration' in the UK for the years 1971–8. Figure 1.3 shows the unemployment rate for eight Western countries for the years 1971–8, adjusted to US concepts as a common basis for comparison (Thompson, 1979). Similarly, the retail price index is an important and time-honoured macro indicator of the level of inflation in the UK. There was considerable furore when Mrs Thatcher's government attempted to replace it with a new standard-of-living index, calculated on a different basis.

An example of a macro indicator used in the USA is the FBI's 'uniform crime index' which is often cited in arguments for allocating

Table 1.1 Health-related indicators from some low-income and some industrialised countries

| | Population per: | | | | Percentage of Population with Access to Safe Water | Daily Per Capita Calorie Supply | As Percentage of Requirement |
| | Physician[a] | | Nursing Person[a] | | | | |
	1960	1976	1960	1976	1975	1974	1974
Low-Income Countries (w)	—	—	—	—	—	2,036	91
1 Bhutan	18,700	10,300	—	9,720	28	2,078	94
2 Cambodia	—	—	—	—	—	1,894	85
3 Bangladesh	—	11,350	—	53,700	53	2,024	92
4 Lao PDR	—	—	—	—	—	2,090	93
5 Ethiopia	91,000	84,850	—	25,670	6	1,914	82
6 Mali	39,000	32,460	4,990	3,040	9	1,774	75
7 Nepal	72,000	38,650	—	52,770	9	2,088	95
8 Somalia	30,000	—	2,010	—	33	1,822	79
9 Burundi	63,000	45,430	—	6,240	—	2,307	99
10 Chad	—	41,160	—	4,820	26	1,781	75
11 Rwanda	144,000	39,350	11,680	16,000	35	2,086	90
12 Upper Volta	100,000	61,800	—	4,890	25	1,859	78
13 Zaire	63,000	—	—	—	16	1,885	85
14 Burma	9,900	5,410	—	6,120	17	2,223	103
15 Malawi	—	48,500	—	4,370	33	2,397	103
16 India	5,800	3,140	9,610	6,320	33	1,976	89
17 Mozambique	20,000	42,970	4,660	—	—	1,975	84
18 Niger	71,000	—	8,800	8,220	27	1,827	78
19 Viet Nam	—	5,340	—	880	—	2,397	111
20 Afghanistan	40,000	28,290	32,030	35,680	6	2,022	83

Industrialised Countries (w)	820	630	440	210	100	3,342	130
93 Ireland	*950*	830	*180*	200	—	3,545	141
94 Italy	*610*	490	*920*	*330*	—	3,524	140
95 New Zealand	700	730	—	200	—	3,551	133
96 United Kingdom	960	670	*420*	180	—	3,349	133
97 Japan	920	850	*460*	290	—	2,835	121
98 Austria	*550*	440	*600*	270	—	3,450	131
99 Finland	1,600	670	*220*	110	—	3,204	118
100 Netherlands	900	600	—	300	—	3,350	124
101 France	930	680	—	200	—	3,411	135
102 Australia	860	—	—	—	—	3,310	124
103 Belgium	780	500	—	*250*	—	3,713	141
104 Denmark	810	510	*270*	170	—	3,407	127
105 Germany, Fed. Rep.	690	500	*450*	270	—	3,432	129
106 Canada	910	580	*300*	*130*	—	3,377	130
107 United States	780	600	*340*	150	—	3,504	133
108 Norway	840	560	*330*	120	—	3,213	120
109 Sweden	1,100	*580*	—	*140*	—	3,064	114
110 Switzerland	740	520	*390*	230	—	3,439	128

Notes:
a Figures in italics are for years other than those specified.
w Weighted average.
Source: World Bank, 1979.

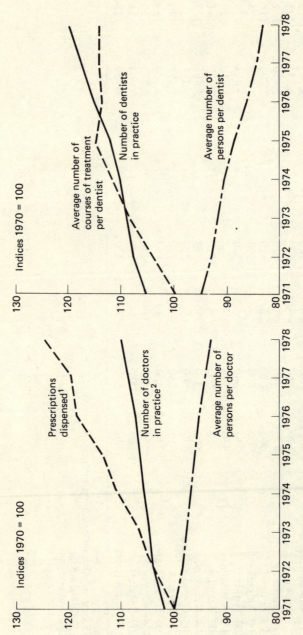

Figure 1.1   General medical, pharmaceutical and dental services for the United Kingdom.
Source: Thompson, 1979.

[1] Prescriptions dispensed by general medical practitioners are not included.
[2] Unrestricted principals only

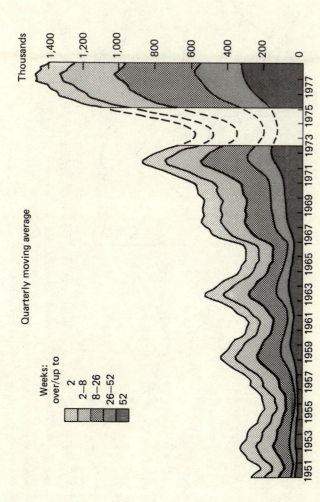

Figure 1.2 *Unemployment by duration for Great Britain.*
Source: Thompson, 1979.

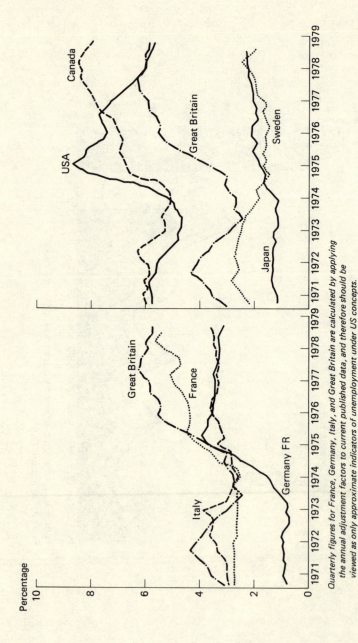

Quarterly figures for France, Germany, Italy, and Great Britain are calculated by applying the annual adjustment factors to current published data, and therefore should be viewed as only approximate indicators of unemployment under US concepts.

Published data for Sweden, Japan, and Canada require little or no adjustment.

Figure 1.3   *Unemployment rates adjusted to US concepts: international comparisons.*
Source: Thompson, 1979.

resources to various police forces to 'fight crime'. Figure 1.4 graphs nationally four of the seven index crimes for the years 1960–78 (US Department of Commerce, 1977). The other three index crimes (larceny, burglary, motor vehicle theft) are graphed separately as their occurrence is proportionally higher per unit of population. Many authors have argued that the uniform crime index is open to manipulation and distortion, for example, by increased reporting of crime which often results in apparent rises in the crime rate, and vice versa.

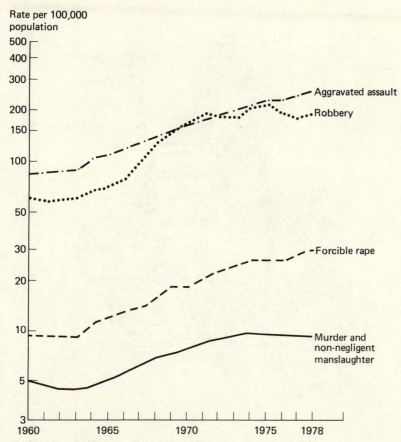

Figure 1.4   Violent crime by type, 1960–75, United States.
Source: US Department of Commerce, 1977.

At the regional level the EEC uses a series of indicators to determine the eligibility of regions within Europe for industrial financial assistance. Similarly a complex formula was developed in the UK to allocate health service resources among competing regions. Developed by the Resource Allocation Working Party (RAWP, 1976), this quantitative approach made use of a series of indicators of 'need' or demand on the health services, such as numbers of elderly, and indices of mortality in different regions. Figure 1.5 shows one of these social indicators of need, the standardised mortality ratio*, overlaid on a map of England divided into regions. Like the uniform crime index, the RAWP formula proved contentious when used as a means of determining government expen-

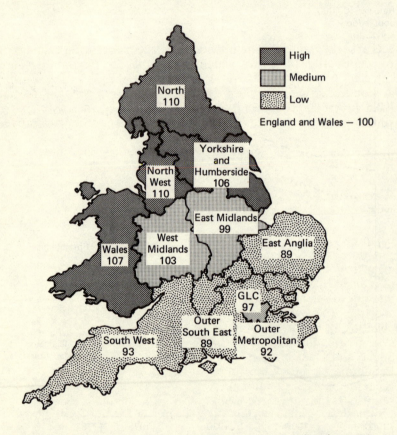

Figure 1.5 *Standardised mortality ratios for England and Wales, 1972.*
Source: Resource Allocation Working Party, 1976.

*Standardised, in this case, by setting the national average at 100 and comparing the regions with that figure.

diture. This contentiousness is generally the case for all social indicators used to allocate resources and this issue is examined in Chapter 5.

At the micro level are social indicators used to delineate territorial need or to evaluate the quality of government programmes designed to meet need. In the UK there has been considerable development of indicators useful for identifying geographical areas or population subgroups towards which policy might be directed. Some claim to be neutral, that is, they do not take a stance on what constitutes need; rather, they simply identify like neighbourhoods across a range of social indicators. An example of this is the complex system of the Planning Research Applications Group (PRAG) which has the capacity to classify residential neighbourhoods across Britain. Other sets of social indicators are intended to identify areas of special need, or deprivation, towards which governmental programmes are directed. An example of such a programme in the UK is the Housing Action Area which offers residential improvement grants and special local government powers to improve the physical environment. A similar programme in Canada is called the Neighbourhood Improvement Programme. In the USA considerable attention has been directed to developing useful and appropriate social indicators which might help evaluate the efficiency or effectiveness of specific government actions in meeting need. For example, the Urban Institute in Washington has done considerable work in developing measures of performance in the provision of local government services. These kinds of micro level social indicators are examined in detail in Chapter 7.

A third type of social indicator activity involves attempts to move away from the more *ad hoc* collections of indicators towards systems of indicators with an integral structure and rationale. Such systems attempt to offer a multiple or comprehensive, and systematic, perspective on social phenomena by the use of many social indicators covering a wide variety of important human activities. Some of these systems are international in scope, for example, the UN's System of Social and Demographic Statistics (SSDS) or the Organisation for Economic Co-operation and Development's (OECD's) elaborate scheme. Others are national like the German SPES system (Social-politisches Entscheidungs und Indikatorensystem).

Other social indicator systems are local or municipal in scope. In the US, for example, the Socio-Economic Accounts System (SEAS) comprises no fewer than 477 community level indicators. In the UK the Chartered Institute of Public Finance and Accountancy (CIPFA) publishes social indicator data for UK communities which are designed to help local authority decision-makers. Finally, some social indicator systems are still at a very theoretical stage. In the USA for example, Fox (1974) has attempted to integrate theoretical concepts from a number of the social sciences as the basis for a social indicator system. These systems of social indicators are explored in detail in Chapter 3.

A fourth and last type of social indicator activity involves attempts to find new ways to measure important, but hard-to-quantify, information. For example, a number of researchers are directing their attention to measures which might accurately reflect an individual's health status. This requires attention not only to physical health but also to psychological health, and the biggest of the 'hard-to-quantify' research efforts is in the field of quality-of-life measures, or what are often called subjective social indicators, to distinguish them from other 'objective' indicators. This terminology is confusing but very widespread. Objective indicators are based on counting the occurrence of an event or activity, while subjective indicators are based on reports or descriptions from individuals on their feelings and perceptions about themselves and the world around them. The most notable example of subjective social indicator research is the work being carried out at the Institute for Social Research at the University of Michigan. Subjective social indicators are discussed in Chapters 2 and 4.

This, then, is a rather unsystematic tour of the activities carried out in the name of social indicators. In some cases people engaged in one type of activity may be unaware that other types of activity also involve social indicators in some form. In other cases disputes may arise as to whether certain activities can properly be termed 'social indicators' work or work in the more general area of social statistics. This book does not take sides but it does suggest a variety of systematic dimensions and characteristics of social indicators which can help the interested reader make some sense of the welter of diverse activities which seek to develop or make use of such indicators. In addition a variety of problems associated with social indicators are explored, some unique to particular activities, like social reporting, and others germane to all attempts at social indicators. Before going on to put the social indicator movement in a historical perspective it is useful to look briefly at two of the main problem areas in social indicators, by way of continuing this introduction to the field.

First problems with social indicators

One of the most common criticisms of social indicators, and indeed social science in general, is that researchers are technocrats or philistines who would like nothing better than to reduce the quality of life to mere numbers (Miles, 1975). The next step in this nefarious plan of such technocrats is, of course, to convince people that the numbers represent reality, since these technocrats 'control' the numbers. And even when such 'quantificationism' is not intentionally maladroit, there is always the danger that researchers will become enamoured of their statistical procedures and models and lose sight of the complex political reality of policy problems.

On the other hand, there is always the possibility that social indicators will be used to advance particular political stances, or will be distorted by bureaucratic wrangling or poorly provided data. Indicators can be used to hide problems, to make past policies look more or less successful, or to manipulate public debate in a particular direction. If they are accurate they may cause acute embarrassment to those identified as inept or inefficient and they can be threatening to politicians in power. Social indicators might identify unwanted political skeletons in closed closets. For example, there is constant debate over social indicators of poverty in society. In the UK the government has been accused of suppressing such data even while the number of families in poverty is increasing (Pond, 1979). In the USA some researchers argue that there is a considerable gap between official measures of poverty and other more independent estimates (Danziger and Plotnick, 1979). The reality of the political and value-judgemental aspects of social indicators is then a first important problem area to be considered.

The second problem area is methodological: if indicators are quantified surrogates for other *unmeasurable* phenomena, it can be very difficult to establish a correlation between the measured and the unmeasured. This problem prompted the rise in interest in judgements on quality of life, or subjective indicators, which, it was thought, might help establish some validity for other objective indicators. At this point one might wonder: why not use such subjective judgements themselves to make policy? But in turn the issue is about whose judgements are used and by what method those judgements are aggregated. And while such subjective judgements may help highlight social problems and concerns, they are seldom accurate enough to use to allocate scarce resources among competing needs. What is obviously called for is some combination of objective measures with indicators of perceptions in a rigorous and systematic framework. Unfortunately, as we shall see, the social indicators movement grew in an *ad hoc* fashion out of specific demands for information required for specific decision-making problems, and not out of any systematic framework based on social theories and established cause-and-effect relationships. This *ad hoc*ness is reflected in the confusion over what social indicators are, and what they are supposed to do. It is also reflected in the fact that obviously tenuous cause-and-effect relationships in some social indicator presentations have caused them to be dismissed as useless and, worse, misleading, by those who might find them most useful – politicians and administrators allocating resources. This a-theoretical and unsystematic approach to much social indicator activity constitutes a second important problem area in social indicators.

This book will examine both these important problem areas in relation to the field generally, and to specific social indicators applications. It will argue that neither political nor methodological problems can be ignored and that they are best considered as complementary issues which, when thought through, give a clearer and more complete understanding of social indicators than is possible from a single perspective. On the methodological side, which is especially considered in Chapter 4, attention is concentrated on the need for rigorous examination of social indicators in the framework of social models. On the political side, Chapter 5 looks at the relationship between indicators and the policy-making process, and pays special attention to the problems of quantification, and the essential and inescapable role of value-judgements in the policy process. Both chapters take up the issues surrounding the aggregation of indicators, which poses both political and methodological dilemmas.

The antecedents of modern social indicators

Before moving on to a look at different, and often competing, definitions of social indicators, it is worthwhile to put the field into a historical context. Statistical information on social topics has been collected since at least the seventeenth century and even in the sixteenth century mortality figures were collected irregularly. Such information became of use as trade and commerce began to flourish, and the state assumed an increasing role in such fields as national defence and environmental health. The word 'statistics' itself comes from the same root as the German word for 'state' and statistics originally meant, in broad terms, the study of the state (Hope, 1978). In Germany at this time Conring urged the collection of data about the state interests in such fields as the military, trade, population and finance. This was to be a unifying factor among the 300 small principalities which made up the German state.

In England in the middle of the seventeenth century William Petty introduced the concept of 'political arithmetic' and argued for the use of statistical data in government for such purposes as devising a taxation system, or assessing military strength. Around the same time in London a merchant named Graunt introduced the first tables of life expectancies for people in different age-groups. These tables showed that there were patterns and seasonal variations in mortality, and differences in life expectancies between the city and country. The astronomer Halley extended these life-tables and argued they had practical uses for the state, such as estimating the numbers of soldiers that might be available from a given population (Shaw and Miles, 1979).

This movement towards collection and organisation of social, economic and demographic data continued in the eighteenth and nineteenth centuries. Notable in this period is the work of the Belgian astronomer Quételet who published a statistical handbook on Belgium, and whose efforts Lazarsfeld (1961) credits as the beginning of modern efforts at social quantification. In the USA the decennial census, the first of which was held in 1790, incorporated an increasing amount of social data, and Hauser (1967) speaks of the early census as offering the possibility of a crude form of 'social accounting'. In England the collection of statistics became increasingly institutionalised. In 1832 a Statistical Department of the Board of Trade was organised, in 1836 a General Register Office was set up for vital social statistics, and in 1854 the first official *Statistical Abstract* appeared (Shaw and Miles, 1979).

In the early twentieth century the Italian Niceforo published a book on 'the measurement of life'. A few years later he published what might be the first-ever social report, entitled *Les Indices numériques de la civilisation et du progrès*. In this work Niceforo attempted to develop key indicators for various dimensions of his concept of civilisation (David, 1973). At the same time various social reform movements in England, like the Fabians, made increasing use of social data to argue their case. At the same time the word 'statistics' was undergoing a change in meaning from 'numerical facts' to that of analytical techniques for interpreting data.

This brings us to the twentieth-century antecedents of the social indicator movement, of which two are especially important. The first, and less obvious, is the work of the British economist A. C. Pigou (1924) who argued in *The Economics of Welfare* that neo-classical economics could no longer ignore the concept of social costs which might cause public welfare to differ from private welfare. This difference reflected an imperfect working of the market economy and a role for state intervention in the workings of that economy.

Pigou went on to point out that overall public welfare could be lessened by those social costs, or disservices, which exceed the private costs of production. He gave examples: the lessening of the amenity of residential neighbourhoods by factory construction, or the cost of police services related to liquor sales, neither of which would be the concern of factory-owners or distillers in their corporate balance sheets. He argued that these types of social costs had to be quantified to determine their impact on the net social product.

Pigou's arguments on social cost had little effect until the 1950s when the concept was incorporated into welfare economics, and especially cost-benefit analysis, as what the economists now call 'externalities'. The social cost concept explicitly argued that a consideration of these externalities was essential to good decision-making, and this suggested a whole variety of social factors which needed to be measured. This concept of social cost is not only an important dimension of the social indicator movement but also of some related fields, like social impact assessment, which make use of social indicators. The common basis of social indicator thought and modern welfare economics also suggests one reason why it turned out to be almost impossible to draw a fine distinction between economic and social indicators of well-being.

A second, and widely recognised, source for the social indicator movement was the work of sociologist William F. Ogburn and his associates at the University of Chicago. One of Ogburn's broad interests was promoting the role of social research in government decision-making. In 1922 he published a theoretical volume, *Social Change,* which became a widely read sociological text. In it he argued that social change was best explained by the development and evolution of culture, and that this could be studied by developing reliable measures of change. The best measures of social change were to be actual quantitative descriptions in the form of statistical time series, if possible, and if not, then carefully described observations (Land, 1975a).

Ogburn was associated with two important works containing social statistics. One was the by now almost classic *Recent Social Trends.* This volume was the result of the setting up of a President's Committee by US President Hoover in 1929. This committee was to prepare reviews of social trends in a variety of sectors of American life. Ogburn was an influential member of the Committee and directed the research staff. One of his objectives was to establish statistical series which 'would improve the methods of extrapolation and correlation as a means of predicting the future' (Bell, 1969, p. 75).

In the introduction to *Recent Social Trends* President Hoover wrote that the volume 'should help all of us to see where the social stresses are occurring and where the major efforts should be taken to deal with them constructively' (President's Committee, 1933). The basic concept behind the volume was that the dynamic of social change could be captured in an array of quantitative measures. Thirty-two topics were investigated in this report including education, the arts, race and ethnic groups, recreation and leisure, health and environment, rural trends, women, occupations, the family, crime and punishment, religion and others. Ogburn was especially interested in hitherto unexplored interrelationships among these rather disjointed topics, the study of which he hoped would give a more holistic view of American society. A product similar to the *Recent Social Trends* report was an annual issue of the *American*

Journal of Sociology, edited by Ogburn, and devoted to social change during the period 1928-34. The 1934 issue was the last, and the depression and subsequent war put an end to Ogburn's hopes for an annual publication of this sort.

Ogburn is now criticised by a few people (with the benefit of hindsight) for his belief in continuous, incremental and technologically led social change (Miles and Irvine, 1979). While there is some case for this, it does not diminish his important contribution to the idea of an organised data system for monitoring social change. His influence is now reflected in the spate of national compendia of social statistics, for example, in *Social Trends,* the British namesake of his earlier volume.

The social indicators movement

The rise of what Otis Dudley Duncan (1969) termed the 'social indicators movement' in the 1960s is related both to the success of economic indicators *and* to the apparent limitations in those indicators. In the early 1960s economists using indicators and econometric models were able to advise governments to take various actions, like cutting tax, which had the intended result of reflating the economy as measured by the gross national product (GNP), by about the predicted amount (de Neufville, 1975). In addition to GNP, such economic indicators included measures of gross domestic product, prices, earnings, inflation, and so on. The relative usefulness and success of these indicators in guiding economic policy suggested to some social scientists that an analogous series of 'social' indicators, or social accounts, might be just as effective in the manipulation of social policy.

In addition, the more successful economic indicators became, the more obvious were their limitations in evaluating wider social welfare considerations, such as qualitative aspects of life, equity and the side-effects, or externalities, of economic prosperity, like environmental pollution. Many felt that the very success of economic indicators led to an overemphasis on those monetary measures at the expense of other important social considerations – what Gross (1966) calls 'economic philistinism'. Some of the more specific criticisms of economic indicators, or the GNP approach, are that:

(1) such measures cannot be equated with psychological satisfaction, happiness, or life fulfilment;
(2) the market valuations of goods and services is not necessarily related to their welfare content;
(3) non-marketed activity tends to be excluded from consideration;

(4) GNP measures often obscure important distributional effects by
     averaging. (Encel *et al.,* 1975)

Such criticisms prompted either of two prescriptions: (1) ignore
GNP and develop alternative measures or (2) alter GNP to reflect
social welfare considerations. Neither turned out to be very practical.
The former prescription faced the difficulty that economic variables
do play a very obvious and important part in overall quality of life
and can hardly be excluded from any such consideration. As to the
latter approach, economists were quick to point out that GNP was an
economic measure, and not designed to be an overall measure of
social welfare anyway (Okun, 1971). So the social indicators movement was set a task of evolving indicators complementary to the
useful, and inescapable, economic indicators, rather than attempting
to supersede them.

The impetus for the rise of interest in social indicators in the USA
came in 1962 when the American Academy of Arts and Sciences
undertook a project for National Aeronautics and Space Administration (NASA). The purpose of this project was to examine
the second-order effects of the space exploration programme on
American society. These second-order effects were seen as either
unintended or indirect consequences of the space programme and it
was soon found that many of these were social effects. These social
effects were very difficult to analyse as the necessary data did not
exist, nor did any framework or methodology for analysis (Land,
1975a). This caused the research team to turn their attention to the
more general issue of monitoring socioeconomic change. The result
was the influential book *Social Indicators,* edited by Raymond Bauer
(1966), which discussed the development of social indicators, their
relationship to social goals and policy-making, and the need for
systematic social accounts and improved satistical information. In
addition the book lent its title as a description of the new field it was
proposing.

At the same time ' as the NASA effort, another American
institution, the Russell Sage Foundation, provided support for a
series of studies exploring the conceptual and methodological
problems of monitoring large-scale social change, as first proposed by
the sociologists Sheldon and Moore in 1965. This effort is very much
in the vein of Ogburn's work of three decades earlier. Social change
was to be monitored in five major areas: (1) demographic base, including distribution of population, (2) structural components, including
production of goods and services, the labour force and the family, (3)
distributive features including health, education, recreation and
leisure, (4) aggregative features such as social stratification, mobility
and cultural diversity and (5) measurements of welfare (Land, 1975a,

p. 10). Two major publications arose out of this work. The first was *Indicators of Social Change: Concepts and Measurements* edited by Sheldon and Moore (1968), with fourteen essays on social change organised according to the above categories. The second was the volume *Human Meaning of Social Change* by Campbell and Converse (1972) which was commissioned by the Russell Sage Foundation as a companion piece to the Sheldon and Moore book. Where the former volume was concerned with sociostructural, objective indicators, Campbell and Converse were concerned with psychological, or subjective, indicators of attitudes, expectations, aspirations and values. In subsequent publications the Russell Sage Foundation emphasised social measurement, the analysis of accumulated data and the development of social models (Ferriss, 1979).

A third effort which helped give form to the social indicators movement in the USA was the publication in 1969 of *Towards a Social Report* by the Department of Health, Education, and Welfare. This was another collection of essays which considered a wide variety of measures for monitoring changing social conditions in such areas as health, family life, the environment, distribution of income, fertility patterns, public safety, race relations and social cohesion. The purpose of this effort was to set out the parameters and requirements for the development of a comprehensive social report. We have noted that the publication of such social reports, of varying comprehensiveness, is now a major effort in the social indicator field. The first to appear was the UK's *Social Trends* in 1970. The US volume followed three years later, as did the French *Données sociales*. The German *Gesellschaftliche Daten* and the Japanese *White Paper on National Life* also appeared in 1973. Within six years thirty countries had issued social reports.

Social indicators for policy-making

The rise of the social indicator movement in the 1960s and early 1970s was marked, then, by a kind of boundless enthusiasm which envisioned dramatic progress in social measurement and social accounting, translated into almost utopian social planning for new and improved quality of life. A journal of *Social Indicators Research* was established, and the Social Science Research Councils in the USA and the UK set up research units to delve into social indicators. As Brand (1975, p. 78) noted, social indicators became 'very big business these days'. For example, the National Science Foundation provided the University of Michigan with more than a million dollars for social indicator research in 1971–2 alone (Meehan, 1975). The possibilities for doing social good via social measurement seemed endless.

By the late 1970s the mood had changed. The promises held out for social indicators remained for the most part unfulfilled, especially for the data requirements of policy-making and planning. In some cases the information presented under the 'social indicators' rubric was dismissed as useless, or even misleading, by bureaucrats and administrators. Many academics had turned from a wide concern for social information for government decision-making to a narrower perspective represented by highly elaborate, and often misunderstood, statistical manipulations. Many people became guarded, if not downright pessimistic, about the potential for social indicators. What caused this somewhat sudden change in mood? First, and most simply, it was that the social indicator movement, in its rapid growth, fostered naive expectations as to the development time for social indicators useful for policy-making. This, in turn, certainly reflected an underestimation of the severe policy-related and methodological difficulties which social indicators had to overcome.

One of the main barriers to the rapid development of social indicators is the fact that social theorising is also at a very early stage of development. It has been noted how social indicators involved an unmeasurable concept and a quantitative surrogate for that concept. Unfortunately the often pressing need for social indicator data for policy-making frequently meant that *ad hoc* information was presented to decision-makers in which the relationship between concept and surrogate was implicit, unstable, or poorly or even wrongly articulated. From a methodological point of view this meant unreliable indicators of the overall concept.

An equal problem is that for social indicators to be policy-relevant changes in the indicators have to be clearly related to the concept in the form of policy objectives. These relate in turn to social goals. This means asking two related questions. How does the social change relate to an explicit policy objective and in what direction should change occur? The answers to such questions almost always involve political value-judgements. Unfortunately too much social indicator research has been based on an implicit, and often misguided, understanding of policy objectives. And it has not been unusual for academic researchers, pursuing knowledge for its own sake, simply to assume certain policy objectives which in fact reflect no more than their own particular value-sets. While such approaches may be interesting, they have not generated many social indicators directly useful for policy-making. Policy-relevant social indicator research is more likely to come about when undertaken in the context of a policy model in which political value-judgements are an essential component.

Do these very difficult problems suggest that efforts at social indicators are best abandoned? On the contrary, although the expectations for social indicators may have been excessive, and the claims of their proponents overconfident and ill-timed, those expectations arose from a very real need for an improved flow of cogent social intelligence to a decision-making process becoming ever more complex. That need has not gone away, nor is it likely to. The demand for reliable socioeconomic indicators grows unabated, even if expectations are not met, and economists and other social scientists must continue to seek social indicators as useful *complements* to economic measures. Policy-making continues to require that the relative merits, and potential outcomes, of various resource expenditure patterns be assessed in terms of very complex sets of socioeconomic variables, and that there are some means of consistently evaluating ongoing resource commitments. For example, proposals for cancer research should be weighed against proposals for health education, and even against defence or road-building expenditures, and it is almost a truism that more reliable information means better resource allocation decisions. Econometrics, always open to political debate, took forty to fifty years to develop into a useful art and science. Social indicators, which will *always* be equally open to political debate, will no doubt require the same gestation period, if not longer. For anyone committed to improved policy-making, it is a few decades too early to abandon social indicators.

2

Definitions and Dimensions of Social Indicators

> Quality of life is a vague and ethereal entity, something
> that many people talk about, but which nobody knows
> very clearly what to do about.
> > (Campbell, Converse and Rogers, 1976)

> The terms social indicators, social accounting, social
> reporting . . . have been bandied about in the literature to a
> considerable extent.
> > (Henderson, 1974)

This chapter explores the evolution of definitional thinking on social indicators, and makes note of some of the most useful elements in the best definitions. Such an examination is interesting because it sheds light not only on the obvious question 'what is a social indicator?', but also on the more important underlying issues of 'what role should a useful social indicator fulfil?' and 'what is possible in the way of social indicator measurement?'. The arguments here reflect to a certain extent a tension between these last two questions. The chapter goes on to explore a variety of dimensions and issues in social indicator research which help us differentiate and critically examine the wide variety of efforts to develop social indicators.

Early attempts at defining social indicators

Probably the most publicised early definition of social indicators was given in a US Department of Health, Education, and Welfare (HEW) document, *Toward a Social Report*. This publication argued that the development of indicators would be useful in setting social goals, studying well-being and evaluating programmes. It went on to define a social indicator as a

> statistic of direct normative interest which facilitates concise, comprehensive and balanced judgement about the condition of major aspects of a society. It is, in all cases, a direct measure of welfare and is subject to the interpretation that if it changes in the 'right' direction, while other things remain equal, things have gotten better, or people are better off. Thus, statistics on the

numbers of doctors or policemen could not be social indicators, whereas figures on health or crime rates could be. (US Department of Health, Education, and Welfare 1969, p. 971)

The two most important concepts in the HEW definition are its emphasis on the normative nature of indicators, and on output, not input, measures. The normative emphasis meant that indicators would measure 'things getting better', which meant that someone had to decide what 'getting better' meant, and by how much better. In other words, social indicators were not simply value-free descriptions of reality, but measured increases or decreases in worthwhile or detrimental social effects. The emphasis on output measures reflected the important feeling that input measures had too long held sway in governmental decision-making and were too often based on untested assumptions of cause and effect. Such input measures, like the ratio of numbers of doctors to numbers of population, or number of hospital bed spaces, implicitly assumed that improved health was somehow directly related to these numbers, rather than indirectly related along with a host of other environmental and personal factors like income level, pollution, diet, smoking, and so on – all of which might have substantial effects on 'better' health. And indeed some people, like Ivan Illich (1975), even argued that more doctors meant worse health. The HEW definition made the important point that the volume of resources applied to health problems should *not* be taken as a suitable proxy for the concept of 'good health'. Rather, a proper output measure might be something like 'number of days in good health'. These arguments about the normative nature and input/output dimensions of social indicators permeate the literature.

Critics were quick to seize on the treatment of these basic concepts in this definition. First, the position that indicators must be of normative interest was felt to be restrictive because what is a norm today may change over time. Secondly, the requirement that indicators need to measure welfare directly would restrict the number of variables that might be relevant to an understanding of a social situation. For example, statistics on the number of doctors might help in understanding changes in morbidity rates over time. Sheldon and Freeman (1970) argued that there is little agreement on the definition of social indicators beyond the idea that they are, first, time-series data that allow comparison over an extended period and, secondly, statistics which can be cross-classified or disaggregated by other relevant characteristics.

Other authors criticised the HEW definition in a different vein. One argued that:

in all cases the reader is left with the notion that the general goal of researchers . . . is to find those indexes which are most representative of the quality of life. And therein lies the rub. On the basis of whose value is quality to be judged? (Palys, 1973, p. 7)

This raises the issue of the correlation between certain social indicators and quality of life, and the question of value-judgements and indicators, two important and related issues. Another issue ignored in the HEW definition was whether indicators should measure phenomena amenable to manipulation by policy change. Some authors stressed that this was certainly the case (Campbell and Converse, 1972) but we will see later in this chapter how some branches of social indicator research ventured far from policy-oriented measurement. Finally, the critics of the HEW definition did not escape unscathed either. An American sociologist, Kenneth Land (1971), for example, warned against unrestrictive definitions which made it impossible to distinguish between social indicators and all other social statistics, such as might be used for administrative purposes.

Such arguments raised four important points about social indicators – they might be normative, measure input or output, be amenable to policy manipulation (or not) and, finally, they are generally not value-free. Questions of policy and value-judgements are taken up in detail in Chapter 5. Before going on, it is worth exploring briefly here what is meant by the normative and input-output aspects of social indicators.

Descriptive and evaluative indicators
Descriptive social indicators consist of collections of apparent fact – they are not based on any explicit model of cause and effect, on any means–end relationships, or on any prospective theory about the allocation of resources (Davies, 1977). Normative, or evaluative, social indicators, on the other hand, are usually based on a model and either draw a conclusion on the relationship of two or more factors in the past (evaluation) or attempt to predict the relationship between two or more factors in the future. Normative indicators often suggest that some social effect is good or bad, better or worse, or may indicate a potential allocation of resources. Such normative indicators have also been called analytic (Clark, 1973) or diagnostic (Hakim, 1978a). For example, the use in the UK of complex social indicators as part of the rate support grant (used to allocate funds from central government to local authorities) is normative in that this is based on a preconceived model and results in resource allocation decisions. On the other hand, social reports, like the USA's *Social Indicators 1976,* are descriptive – no conclusions are drawn and the data represents no

more than a collection of apparent fact (Chapter 6 suggests why the facts may be 'apparent').

Input, throughput and output measures
Social indicators may be measures of input, throughput, or output. Input measures are the resources available to some process affecting well-being in the social environment, for example, number of doctors per unit of population or amount of money available to cleanse streets. Secondly, 'throughput' indicators are usually based on workload or caseload measures – number of doctor visits for flu shots or tons of refuse collected per man-hour, for example. Thirdly, there are intermediate output indicators which are measures of the results of specific activities performed, for example extension of life expectancy, reduction in morbidity, or infant mortality, or degree of street cleanliness. These constitute some of the most policy useful social indicators. They do, however, represent *quantity,* not quality, of life and so lastly, there are final output measures of such concepts as a 'healthy' population or a 'better' environment. The latter are often measured by subjective social indicators, and most objective social indicators are of the input, throughput, or intermediate output variety.

Defining social indicators by their policy use

While early definitions of social indicators suggest useful issues they are not embracing enough – too much is controversial and too much is excluded. Better definitions are available and this section compares the best two. In his 1971 definition of indicators, Land took the important step of introducing the concept of social system models into the social indicator discussion. He states that 'the term social indicators refers to social statistics that are components in a social system model (including sociopsychological, economic, demographic and ecological) . . .' (p. 323). By social system models, Land means conceptions of social processes, which can be formulated verbally, logically, mathematically, or by simulation. He stresses that what distinguishes a social indicator from a social statistic is its information value, which derives from being empirically verified as part of a social system model. He expands on this in later work where he distinguishes between indicators relating to social policy and indicators relating to broad social change. The policy indicators are concerned with output, and amenable to policy manipulation (as in Campbell and Converse's criteria), while social change indicators make attempts at broad theoretical analysis (Land, 1975a).

Land delineates among three types of social policy indicators, the first two being variations of a similar concept. These are (1) output descriptive indicators, that is, measures of the end-products of social processes and related directly to social policy, in other words, true output measured by subjective indicators; (2) other descriptive indicators which provide background to policy decisions by way of measures of the social conditions of human existence, in the form of input, or throughput measures; and (3) analytic indicators which are components of explicit conceptual models of the social processes which result in the values of the output indicators. This last category involves social indicators specifically developed as components of social system models which attempt to identify and isolate causal relationships in society. Other authors also make note of the problem of relating indicators to social models and social theory and this important relationship is examined in detail in Chapter 4.

There are numerous other definitions of social indicators, many not very rigorous. A very complete definition, however, remains that of Carlisle. She has defined a social indicator as 'the operational definition or part of the operational definition of any one of the concepts central to the generation of an information system descriptive of the social system' (Carlisle, 1972, p. 25). The two most important elements in this definition are first, that social indicators are the result of *operationalising* abstract concepts, like health, by translating them into measurable terms in the form of proxies like 'number of days without sickness'. It is this process of operationalising which of course is the simple root of all methodological, or measurement, problems in social indicators. Secondly, social indicators are part of an *information system* which is used by policy-makers to understand and evaluate those parts of the social system over which they exert some power. This information system must satisfy, therefore, not only analytic requirements for making resource-maximising decisions, but equally important political and bureaucratic needs.

In Carlisle's definition the central concepts to be operationalised are categorised as system components, system goals, social problem areas and policy goals and objectives. The system components in total represent the interrelated structure of society, broken down into whatever particular subsystems are of interest, for example, that of education or of health. The interrelationships between various components are measured as a means of providing information useful for considering achievement of present social objectives or goals, which are states of affairs considered desirable by (some) members of society (analogous to Land's analytic indicators). Operationalised social problem areas provide one-time background information on specific social problems, like the problem of 'the aged' (Land's descriptive indicators). Operationalised policy goals give indicators of the performance of specific social policies (Land's output descriptive indicators).

In Carlisle's scheme social indicators are then classified according to their policy use, and we illustrate each type of indicator by reference to a hypothetical policy problem involving teenagers' use of urban recreational facilities:

(1) *Informative indicators* – which are intended to describe the social system and the changes taking place within it. These are social statistics subject to regular production as a time-series and which can be disaggregated by relevant variables. For example, data on recreational facility use, disaggregated by age-groupings, provides important background information to our policy problem.

(2) *Predictive indicators* – which are informative indicators fitting into explicit formal models of subsystems of the social system. For example, a model consisting of a series of indicators of various environmental factors (family income levels, urban recreational facility location, spare time usage) might be variables in a model which attempts to predict potential levels of juvenile crime in particular neighbourhoods.

(3) *Problem-oriented indicators* – which point towards policy situations and actions on specific social problems, like measures of high juvenile crime rates in areas with, among other factors, little or no recreational facilities.

(4) *Programme evaluation indicators* – which are operationalised policy goals to monitor the progress and effectiveness of particular policies. For example, a policy may be instituted which actively seeks to increase recreational facility use by teenagers in certain neighbourhoods. The success of such a programme would be evaluated by reference to increases in the number and type of user.

To these four indicator types it is helpful to add a fifth which might be called 'target delineation' indicators, and which are variables describing demographic, environmental, pathological, or service provision characteristics, and useful for identifying geographical areas or population subgroups towards which policy is directed (Edwards, 1975). To carry on the above example, a target delineation indicator might be used to identify particular types of neighbourhoods in which juvenile recreational facilities are to be brought up to a minimum standard. Finally, a last useful definition, similar to Carlisle's but very concise, is Zapf's (1975, p. 479), which states 'by systems of social indicators, I understand primarily all attempts to operationalise and measure the components of a multi-dimensional conception of welfare'. The concept of systems of indicators is taken up in the next chapter.

Social indicators in a statistical hierarchy

A useful classification of social statistics is according to a hierarchy of statistical sophistication. The Conference of European Statisticians suggests the following classification of statistical series which may or may not be termed social indicators (Fanchette, 1974, p.8):

(1)   raw statistical series, that is, basic data;
(2)   key series – commonsense attempts to pick out interesting series of statistics, as is done in national social reports;
(3)   comprehensive systems of statistics, like the UN's System of Social and Demographic Statistics, discussed in the next chapter;
(4)   composite indices derived from combining individual series. This is often called an index, for example, the retail price index;
(5)   synthetic representative series derived by multivariate techniques, such as discriminant analysis;
(6)   series which fit explicitly into social models.

This classification is of special interest because each of the categories 2 to 6 has been termed social indicators at some point in time. Some researchers make use of all types 2 to 6 as social indicators and term them so (Fitzsimmons and Lavey, 1976). Other researchers argue that only categories 4 to 6 can be social indicators, which require a summation or aggregation of data, as distinguished from 1 to 3 which are social statistics and are only the raw material for social indicators (United Nations, 1976). Still others argue cogently that the term social indicator should be confined to category 6 – fitting explicitly into a social model (Bunge, 1975).

Although this latter argument has a certain attractiveness to it, and can be seen as a worthwhile ideal for social indicators, it is a requirement far beyond the state of the art. It would also severely limit the usefulness of social indicators to policy-making, where decision-makers often require quick and inexpensive information – something complex social modelling exercises are not yet able to supply.

As for arguing that only aggregated data constitute social indicators, there is little logic to that. Instead it is useful to accept any usage from 2 to 6 under the term social indicator – not because there is any inherent benefit in doing so, although it does conform to much common practice, but rather because we will find there is no especially useful purpose in trying to make limiting distinctions. Rather it is helpful to be mindful of both of the above two classification systems, one based on a hierarchy of statistical sophistication, the other describing the policy use of indicators.

These certainly describe most attempts at social indicator research and it is worthwhile to remember that the field is that broad.

Is a definition of social indicators worthwhile?

It has been noted that some people feel that publications like *Social Indicators 1976* do not contain social indicators but only social statistics, and this kind of definitional debate shows no signs of subsiding. The question, however, may end up being more academic than real, at least until substantial advances are made in the construction of social theories. The social indicator movement itself, in its early days, was certainly not about social theorising, at least not in the 1960s. Rather the field arose in the fervent desire that better information about social factors in life would aid better decision-making. And as new information needs were perceived, sets of social indicators were put forward, sometimes naively, and most often on an *ad hoc* basis, and tailored to the perceived information need. The field is therefore characterised by persistent terminological confusion which stems in large part from the lack of a strong conceptual framework based on theory. This state of affairs accounts for much of the confusion surrounding this issue of definition.

So is one universally accepted definition possible, likely, or even worthwhile? Most certainly it is worthwhile, and definitely possible, but hardly likely. The point is not that *a* definition is essential but rather that the definitional *process* causes a critical examination and re-examination of the essential concepts in social indicators, and thereby causes the incremental advancement of knowledge. It was partly this process of critical examination which led many people to revise downward their initial optimism about social indicators to a more practical perspective. This process of definition and critical examination is of course the essence of the validation process in most descipline research. The overly high expectations in the social indicator field stemmed not so much from delusions of grandeur on the part of advocates (as some critics would like us to believe) as from the real information needs in and out of government. And while the social indicator field may not yet have met those needs, it will hardly do to dismiss it for its partial failure. The need is still there and remains to be met, and if the problem is that the policy task is more difficult, and the methodological tools need more refining, than was originally conceived, this does not mean that the task should be abandoned.

This suggests that all good social indicator research must be concerned with two things. First, it must consist of methodologically appropriate techniques, that is techniques which do not ignore the important social scientific criteria by which discipline research is evaluated. Such criteria include attention to the problems of quantification, prediction, causality, aggregation and value-judgements internal to the analysis. This can be described succinctly as the internal logic of social indicators.

The second important aspect of good social indicator research involves an understanding of the process of policy formation with its essential, and sometimes paramount, emphasis on such factors as political value-judgements, value manipulation and bureaucratic maintenance. This dimension reflects an iterative cycle in which the policy formation process may be informed by various social indicator studies (each with its own particular methodology or technique). In turn, the contingencies of the policy-making process must serve to establish some of the parameters which define the individual social indicator efforts. Other parameters are of course defined by the social scientific criteria of discipline research. This consideration of the policy formulation process can be described as the logic of the mode of production of policy decisions. The need to consider this logic is sometimes used to distinguish policy analysis from pure discipline research.

Good social indicator research reflects some combination of the above two aspects – the mix according to policy needs and the intent of the researchers. Either aspect is ignored at great peril. Early efforts overemphasised the immediacy of policy information needs at the expense of attention to methodology, and the result was reports based on implied causation, which were later rightly dismissed when it became apparent that the social causes and effects implied simply were not true. If some of the high hopes of the movement were dashed by this lack of attention to methodology, so be it. But it will not do to throw the policy information needs baby out with the methodologically muddy bathwater. Good social indicator research is simply about two things: it aids decision-making and policy formation, and it attempts to contribute to improved social knowledge, which indirectly aids decision-making. This theme is taken up again in Chapter 5.

Other terminology in social indicators

There are a few common terms which have not been adequately dealt with yet. First, social indicator research can have an *ex post* or *ex ante* dimension in so far as it may involve studying time-series data, which either describe the past, or may be used to predict certain relationships between phenomena in the future. In addition, research using subjective social indicators may involve asking people about their feelings in the past, or potential reactions to postulated future events.

This of course suggests that social indicators are *objective* or *subjective.* Objective indicators are the occurrences of given phenomena, such as environmental stimuli and behavioural responses, which are measurable on an interval or ratio scale, and amenable to the usual methods of data analysis. In Chapter 1 a number of such objective indicators were reproduced, and the vast majority of the social statistics and indicators we are all familiar with consist of objective data, by this definition. Subjective indicators, on the other hand, are those based on reports from individuals on the 'meaning' aspects of their reality and as such represent psychological variables which are usually presented on an ordinal scale. Questionnaires, interviews and opinion polls elicit this subjective information. As an example, time-series arrest statistics, or money-income levels, are objective social indicators, while feelings and perceptions of individuals about street safety, or relative deprivation, are subjective social indicators. The specific study of well-being as defined by subjective social indicators is often called rather vaguely 'quality-of-life' research. This is discussed in more detail in the next section.

A few authors (Henderson, 1974; Mindlin, 1974) have used the terms quantitative and qualitative indicators instead of objective and subjective respectively. Their motivation for this is understandable but the terms themselves are confusing, for subjective ordinal rankings are often manipulated in a quantitative, statistical manner. Further, as Bunge (1975) points out, in part this distinction may reflect more on the backward state of the field of social indicator research than on the actual subjectivity of the conditions being investigated. For it may be that one day psychologists will develop indicators which will give 'objective' assessments of the quality of life in terms of psychological variables.

Groups, sets, or systems of social indicators are also described as *composite* or *simple.* A composite indicator is a composite of several indicators formed into a summary figure. The argument is that this summary figure is more useful than a host of individual indicators because it combines into a more meaningful whole. This composite indicator requires that unlike measures be transformed into a common scale so they can be added together. This procedure is sometimes accompanied by the value-weighting of indicators in an attempt to express differences in the relative importance of the individual phenomena indicated within a composite indicator. A simple, or non-aggregated, indicator system, on the other hand, is simply a grouping of separate indicators. As we shall see later, overemphasis on aggregation, with all its pitfalls, leads to some rather dubious social indicator exercises, where, for example, the quality of life in a city is summed up by a single composite indicator.

One other distinction is found in the UK's literature on the identification of geographically based deprived urban areas. This is drawn between indicators which are *sufficient* to indicate adverse social conditions and indicators of factors which may *aggravate* adverse social conditions (Craig and Driver, 1972). For example, income level might be a sufficient indicator of poverty while family size might be an aggravating indicator. Other authors have used the terms direct and indirect for sufficient and aggravating (Hatch and Sherrott, 1973). Aggravating indicators cannot be, in themselves, proof of deprivation of any sort. They only help identify areas or groups which may have a tendency toward deprivation. This distinction is of important conceptual value when examining specific indicators within a system of indicators and as a first step toward selection of indicators for testing of causality. Most social indicator research consists of a mix of sufficient and aggravating indicators, unless only a very few indicators are specified.

Social reporting and social accounting

There are two terms related to social indicators which are used in a variety of ways. Social accounting involves the development of integrated sets of statistical accounts which describe the social welfare of a country (SSRC, 1979). Social accounts complement economic accounts. Social accounting has also been described as a full quantitative description of the social system, based on well-specified social theory utilising formal accounting techniques (Henderson, 1974). This latter concept of social accounting is expanded by Gambling (1974) who argues that classical accounting theory should be redefined to serve as a data base for all aspects of social measurement and policy. He goes on to describe a possible framework for such an approach to accountancy. The UN's system for social accounting is described in the next chapter.

Social reporting, on the other hand, has been defined as descriptions and conclusions about the state of society drawn from both quantitative and qualitative measures of various aspects of the social system (Henderson, 1974). We have noted, however, that collections of national level objective indicators are commonly called national social reports, although in fact they almost never draw any conclusions about the state of society or make explicit cause-and-effect linkages.

The terms social accounting and reporting are also used in a very different context to describe *corporate social audits.* These are extensions to individual corporations' more usual financial statements and seek to include social costs and benefits in the final balance sheet. External benefits (such as wages) and external diseconomies (such as pollution) are included to describe the company's relationships both with people and the environment. As such it is very similar to the usual social cost-benefit analysis calculations. Table 2.1 shows such a sample balance sheet. The inducement to undertake such a corporate audit is suggested as 'corporate social responsibility', although it is not likely to be undertaken to any great extent except where public pressure is great, or it is profitable for companies to do so (Grojer and Stark, 1979). In any case, the terms social reporting and accounting are generalistic, sometimes used in rather vague ways, and are not to be taken to mean too much out of specific contexts.

Table 2.1   *The corporate social report: balance sheet*

The Progressive Company
Corporate Social Report
for the Year Ended 31 December 1984

Social Benefits:

Products and services provided		$ xxx	
Payments to other elements of society –			
Employment provided (salaries and wages)	$ xxx		
Payments for goods and other services	xxx		
Taxes paid	xxx		
Contributions	xxx		
Dividends and interest paid	xxx		
Other payments	xxx	xxx	
Services to employees	—	xxx	
Improvements in environment		xxx	
Staff services donated to others		xxx	
Equipment and facility services donated		xxx	
Other benefits		xxx	
Total Social Benefits		—	$ xxx

Social Costs:

Human services used		$ xxx	
Raw material purchases		xxx	
Building and equipment purchases		xxx	
Other goods and materials used		xxx	
Payments from other elements of society –			
Payments to company for goods and services	$ xxx		
Additional capital investments	xxx		
Loans	xxx		
Other payments	xxx	xxx	
Environmental damage –	—		
Terrain damage	$ xxx		
Air pollution	xxx		
Water pollution	xxx		
Noise pollution	xxx		

Solid waste	xxx	
Visual pollution	xxx	
Other environmental damage	xxx	xxx
Public services used	—	xxx
Public facilities used		xxx
Work-related injuries and illness		xxx
Other social costs		xxx
Total Social Costs	—	xxx
Social Surplus (Deficit) for the Year		$ xxx
Accumulated Surplus (Deficit) for Company 31 December 1983		xxx
Accumulated Surplus (Deficit) for Company 31 December 1984		$ xxx

Standard Footnotes:
1 Significant secondary effects associated with inputs.
2 Significant secondary effects associated with outputs.
3 Environmental protection outlays and activities.
4 Employment and promotion of minorities and women.
5 Bases for measurements and estimates.

Source: Estes, 1975.

Subjective social indicators and the quality of life

In the early 1970s many politicians stressed their concern for the vague notion of 'quality of life' (QOL). Land (1975b) suggests this was due in large part to the convenient vagueness of the term with its lack of any reference to real policy issues. At the same time a few social researchers made (in retrospect, misguided) attempts to identify some sort of overall measure of quality of life *as a whole,* usually by aggregating a variety of objective measures – this was called, of course, quality-of-life research. One such effort, that of Forrester (1971), derived a QOL index from measures of pollution, crowding, and food and material standards of living. Miles (1975, p. 186) notes dryly that in this model QOL reached its zenith during the Second World War and would reach record levels again when the world population was zero. For most researchers, however, quality-of-life research means attention to subjective social indicators. These endeavours are based on the distinction between those aspects of a person's life which relate to its quality derived from sources external to the person, and those derived from a person's own perceptions of what is important to, and the level of, his quality of life (Ward, 1978, p. 10). This distinction, reflected in the objective and subjective indicators described earlier, is common in the literature.

Blalock, writing on measurement problems in the social sciences generally, suggests that on the one hand there are those researchers who rely primarily on objective indicators, such as environmental stimuli and behavioural responses, as data most suitable to statistical manipulation. On the other hand, there are sociologists and social psychologists who emphasise the subjective or 'meaning' aspects of reality and tend to reject objective behavioural kinds of measures as inadequate (Blalock, 1975, p. 359). Ben-Chieh Liu (1976a) puts these two different approaches in terms of quality of life which he defines as the output of a certain production function of two different but often independent input categories – physical inputs and psychological inputs. This is echoed by Angrist *et al.* (1976) who feel that to quantify quality of life, researchers must go beyond objective outputs and measure the 'reality' in which people live. Allardt (1977) sees the problem of assessing well-being in society as determining whether to rely on objective conditions or subjective evaluations.

Objective conditions are measured by counting the occurrences of a given phenomenon, and subjective evaluations are based on reports from individuals about their own perceptions, feelings and responses. The objective indicators are familiar as variations of one sort or another of time-series social statistics, which may or may not be displayed in a normative fashion. Subjective indicators are usually based on questionnaires composed of a series of rating scales which ask respondents to codify their satisfactions with, or evaluations of, a large variety of the aspects and circumstances of their lives (Cullen, 1978). This is often done by using a five or seven point Likert scale which involves a statement like 'my housing meets all my family's housing needs' presented in conjunction with a scale on which the respondent may (1) agree strongly (2) agree (3) be indifferent (4) disagree or (5) strongly disagree. These Likert scales give a relative intensity of respondents' feelings if not interval values. A complete set of such statements with attendant scales is used to elicit feelings as a basis for developing social indicators.

Techniques of even more sophistication have been proposed which yield interval data and force the respondent simultaneously to consider positive and negative aspects of particular feelings at the same time – a problem for simpler surveys. Such techniques like Clark's (1974) 'budget pies' for assessing citizen feelings about urban expenditure, or the use of priority evaluation games in the UK for evaluating preferences in environmental and transport planning (Hoinville and Courtenay, 1979), may be applied more generally to subjective social indicators in the future.

Activity in the subjective indicator field has its roots in the work of Hadley Cantril and of Abraham Maslow in the 1950s and early 1960s. Cantril and his associates interviewed a cross-section of people from various countries to determine what aspects of life they found important from positive and negative points of view, and where they scaled their personal standing in the present and future. This was done by presenting the respondents with a 'ladder of life' device, or the Cantril Self-Anchoring Striving scale (1965, p. 22), on which a person expressed perceived variations between his ideal situation and his actual condition. These variations were assessed on a scale ranging from zero for the worst to ten for the best possible actuation in any one of a number of life areas. Figure 2.1 shows the self-anchoring scale. This work, reported in *The Pattern of Human Concerns,* allowed Cantril to make a number of comments on the general aspirations of adults in different societies, for example, 'human beings continuously seek to enlarge the range and to enrich the quality of their satisfactions' (p. 316).

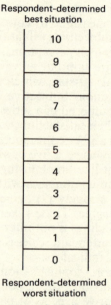

Figure 2.1   *Cantril's Self-Anchoring scale.*

In a similar vein to Cantril's work, and frequently cited, is the work of Abraham Maslow (1954, 1970) who proposed a hierarchical classification of five levels of human needs. The lowest level are the physiological needs for food, water, sleep, shelter, sex and so on. The second level is the need for security and safety for self and family. The third level is made up of various facets of the needs for 'belongingness' and love, and the fourth for independence and freedom. The highest level in this hierarchy is the need for aesthetic beauty and knowledge as ends in themselves.

There are two important points to this hierarchy. First, Maslow argues that needs must be met in some semblance of ascending order, that is, physiological needs must be met before any higher order needs can be met. Secondly, Maslow (1954, p. 91) argues that man is 'self-actualising', that is, what 'he can be, he must be'. Man's self-actualisation process then (his quality of life) can be helped or hindered by the nature of his society. This concept of self-actualisation implies a strong relationship between the more general nature of society and the environment, as often measured by objective indicators. Further, the concept of hierarchical human needs implies that relationships among areas of life satisfaction are as important as expressions of satisfaction with any one area. This means that careful attention must be paid to both the structuring and the interpretation of surveys from which social indicators are developed. For example, the inherent value of proximity to cultural or recreational facilities may be quite different for people whose housing situations vary from adequate to inadequate.

Beyond these early research efforts interest in subjective indicators is renewed in the 1970s, at least in part, by a lack of confidence in the correlation between objective indicators and life quality. For example, Schneider (1975, p. 508) warns, 'the use of objective measures alone as quality of life indicators is . . . highly suspect'. His research into over thirty objective indicators used in US urban areas showed no correlation between these common indicators and individuals' satisfaction with various aspects of their lives. He concludes: 'We have found no relationship exists between the level of well-being found in a city as measured by a wide range of commonly used objective social indicators and the quality of life subjectively experienced by individuals in that city' (Schneider 1975, p. 505). In another study Strumpel (1974) points out that his research into work satisfaction shows strong socioeconomic strata differences in the correlations between socioeconomic indicators and satisfaction.

Recent research in Canada points to similar conclusions. Kuz (1978) undertook a study in Manitoba based on twenty-one objective indicators and thirteen subjective measures. He concluded that quality-of-life research using only objective variables is highly suspect in that it provides only one aspect of a multidimensional problem and that the subjective realities are equally important to overall quality of life. Kennedy et al. (1978, p. 464) in a study of social indicators for Edmonton, Alberta, find similar results and suggest that 'the reasons for this low or lacking relationship between objective states and subjective perceptions lie in the fact that different individuals can be satisfied or dissatisfied by the same objective conditions'.

In other words, two important social processes are at work in human society. First is the fact that one objective condition (e.g. poor accessibility to public open space) can quite easily elicit very different

subjective responses from different individuals (e.g. strong dissatisfaction *v.* complete indifference). Secondly, and to compound
the situation, similar subjective responses can result from widely
differing objective situations. For example, people may experience
complete satisfaction with a small cottage as well as with a large
country estate. Given that both these processes will be simultaneously coexisting in society, and vary according to population
subgroups and even from individual to individual, it is not surprising
that researchers find a poor correlation between objective indicators
and subjective responses. Attention to subjective social indicators is
seen as a means of increasing this correlation between indicator sets
and the reality of well-being.

The broadest study in this field, and one very much in the spirit of
Cantril if not in the methodology, is that of Andrews and Withy on
Americans' perceptions of their quality of life. Their research
involved interviews with over 5,000 respondents and addressed the
following issues (1976, pp. 8–9):

● the significant general concerns of Americans;
● the relative strength of each concern vis-à-vis well-being;
● the relationship of the concerns to one another in terms of
  co-variation and distinction;
● the relationship of the perception of general well-being to
  particular concerns;
● the stability of evaluations of concerns;
● comparability between population subgroups;
● the costs and difficulties of doing this research.

The benefits of this type of research into what Andrews and Withey
prefer to call perceptions of well-being (rather than subjective social
indicators) are: that it provides a data base against which subsequent
measures can be compared and gives information on the distribution
of perceptions across society and on the structure and inter-
dependence of these perceptions. Further, it helps in understanding how people evaluate and feel about such areas of life as
family, job, housing, neighbourhood, and so on and how they
combine various feelings into an overall evaluation of the value of
life. The basic concepts in the Andrews–Withey model concern well-
being at several levels of specificity. The most general are global
indicators which refer to life as a whole. The next level is of 'concerns'
which are aspects of life about which people have feelings. These are
divided into 'domains' and 'criteria'. Domains are subject areas
(house, marriage, etc.) which can be evaluated in terms of the criteria
(privacy, comfort, security, etc.). A large subset of the domains turned
out to be the equivalent of a taxonomy of social institutions and

agencies and this, though unintended, is not surprising. In the next chapter we see why this is common in social indicator research.

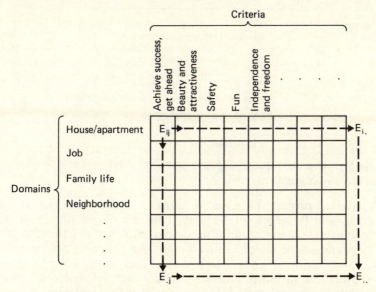

E_{ij} = Affective evaluative response to a particular domain with respect to a particular criterion

$E_{i.}$ = General affective evaluative response to a domain (across criteria)

$E_{.j}$ = General affective evaluative response to a criterion (across domains)

$E_{..}$ = General affective evaluative response to life-as-a-whole—i.e., perceived quality of life

Figure 2.2   *Two-dimensional conceptual model of domains and criteria.*
Source: Andrews and Withey, 1976.

Andrews and Withey propose a simple conceptual model of the relationship of domains to criteria combined in a two-dimensional matrix, with the combined measure termed an 'affective evaluation' (Figure 2.2). This term reflects the researchers' hypothesis 'that a person's assessment of life quality involves both a cognitive evaluation and some degree of positive and/or negative feeling, i.e. "affect" ' (Andrews and Withey, 1976, p. 18). Measurements were on a D–T scale (delighted–terrible!). This scale differs from the Cantril approach in that each category is explicitly labelled, and it extends beyond the five point scale because similar research (Campbell, Converse and Rodgers, 1976) had demonstrated a markedly skewed distribution towards the satisfactory in the simpler scale. Figure 2.3 shows a sample D–T scale.

I feel:

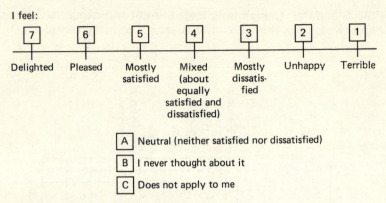

Figure 2.3   The 'delighted–terrible' scale.
Source: Andrews and Withey, 1976.

A similar project for nine Western countries is reported by Andrews and Inglehart (1979). They consider eleven life concerns and organise these in a 'multidimensional map' in which the strength and weaknesses of relationships among the concerns are demonstrated in terms of nearness/distance and association. Figure 2.4 shows a sample multidimensional map. Notice, for example, that evaluations of income are close to (i.e. relatively strongly related to) evaluations of standard of living, but distant from (weakly related to) evaluations of health. Not surprisingly the authors also found that European contries are more like each other than like the USA, and suggest that comparative research on well-being is feasible among European countries.

In the UK the work of Abrams and Hall was in a similar vein (Abrams, 1976, 1978). They defined quality of life as a function of the satisfaction felt by individuals and argued it was necessary to 'turn to subjective social indicators and to the problems of reliable quantification of states of mind and mood . . .' (Abrams, 1973, p. 36). In their study, respondents gave an overall evaluation of their life situation, and assessed twelve life domains from the viewpoints of satisfaction and importance. These domains included housing, health, neighbourhood, job, family life, financial situation and others.

Other interesting research in the UK is that of Knox (1976a) who, in one study, attempts to gauge whether there exists a clear order of priority preferences for different aspects (domains) of social well-being, and whether this varies by social class, age, region, or neighbourhood. Knox used an eleven point self-anchoring scale similar to that of Cantril to establish priority rankings. He finds that overall for Britain the rankings are health (most important), then family life, social stability, housing, job satisfaction, neighbourhood, financial situation, and so on. Table 2.2 shows a summary of domain ratings for the overall UK sample. The ranking of health first corroborates similar findings of an earlier study (Hall and Perry, 1974). Beyond an overall consensus on the importance of health, however, Knox finds considerable variations in preferences expressed by social, economic, demographic and geographic population subgroups. Especially noteworthy are the strong regional variations for the domains of educational attainment, leisure and social status.

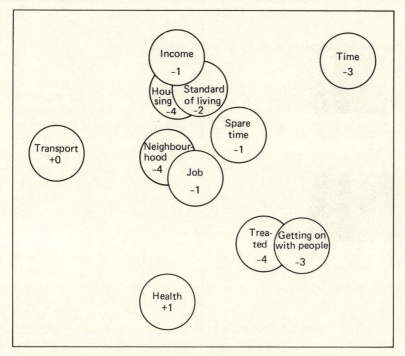

Figure 2.4 *A multidimensional map of life concerns in the UK.*
Source: Andrews and Inglehart, 1979.

A fairly complete definition of well-being in terms of subjective indicators has been developed by Levy and Guttman who attempt to define and manipulate a universe of items relating to well-being. They state 'an item belongs to the universe . . . if and only if its domain asks for [a type of] assessment of the . . . state of a social group in some life area and the range is ordered from "very satisfactory" to "very unsatisfactory", according to the normative criteria of the

Table 2.2 Priority preferences for domains of social well-being

	Per cent giving:											Mean	Rank
	0	1	2	3	4	5	6	7	8	9	10		
Housing conditions	0	0	0	1	2	5	4	9	21	14	43	8.49	4
Neighbourhood	1	0	1	1	2	5	7	12	25	15	28	7.91	6
Social status	6	4	4	4	6	16	11	9	17	9	13	6.11	10
Health	0	1	1	1	0	2	2	4	9	17	63	9.11	1
Job satisfaction	3	1	1	1	2	5	5	7	16	19	38	7.99	5
Family life	1	1	1	1	2	4	2	4	12	16	56	8.76	2
Leisure and recreation	3	2	4	4	5	12	12	14	19	11	13	6.55	9
Educational facilities and opportunities	4	2	3	3	3	7	5	7	16	16	34	7.56	8
Social stability	0	1	1	1	2	4	4	7	19	16	44	8.50	3
Financial situation	1	0	1	2	2	7	8	12	24	15	28	7.85	7

Source: Knox, 1976a.

respondent for that area of life' (Levy and Guttman, 1975, p. 364). The domain here is a question about life quality in a particular life area and the range is the possible answers to that question. Other domain-specific research on subjective social indicators includes the work of Wan and Liveratos (1978) on health, Seashore (1975) on employment and Fitzsimmons and Ferb (1977) on community.

Issues in quality-of-life studies

Aside from difficulties associated with social theory and value judgements, which are considered in succeeding chapters, there are obviously bound to be many problems associated with subjective social indicators. One is simply the sheer difficulty of establishing the *significance* of responses and findings. As Cullen (1978) notes, nothing is simpler than dreaming up evaluation scales and then finding a couple of hundred obliging persons willing to indulge in a pleasant box-ticking game. And yet the meaning and values which are represented by those responses may vary greatly. We have already seen how different people may respond differently to the same situation. Beyond that a number of researchers have noted a 'happiness barrier', or a tendency for people to respond in an overly positive manner at a general or global level (Campbell *et al.*, 1976; Allardt, 1977). At the same time, at specific domain levels, people are quite willing to be critical of their life situation and express considerable dissatisfaction about specific matters. This casts doubt on the efficacy of attempting to develop global measures, and it may be that domain-specific research has the best chance of capturing the rather elusive reality of well-being.

A related problem is separating out the effects of demographic and experimental variables on the subjective responses. These responses are influenced by such dimensions as the state of health, and basic biological make-up, as well as a person's unique value-set developed over a lifetime (Ward, 1980). The demographic variables are often used as a means of cross-classifying responses according to various population subgroups, as in the Knox study noted above. Experiential variables relate to the specific behaviour or experiences of individuals, for example, *activities* by which people come to terms with objective conditions (Kennedy *et al.*, 1978, p. 465). These activities are too often ignored in favour of subjective responses. Roos (1978), referring to the psychologist Leontjir, notes that activity is the means by which the objective and subjective in experience are related, and suggests that to ignore behavioural responses is to ignore the natural link between observed objective conditions and subjective feelings.

The study of these activities is the subject of a related field of interest concerned with time-budgets. These are logs or diaries of the sequence and duration of activities engaged in by an individual over a specified period, normally twenty-four hours (Converse, 1968, p. 42). The basic assumption of time-budget research is that time, like money, is in limited supply and so its allocation by an individual reflects his preferences and value-set, other things being equal. The actual allocation of time is determined by one of three methods: the diary, the 'what did you do yesterday?' interview and observation; or some combination of the three. The straightforward recording of the type and duration of activities suffers, of course, from a problem similar to that of ascertaining significance in subjective responses: the meaning of the activity to the individual may not be at all obvious. A repairman who 'moonlights' may want the extra money, enjoy the social aspects of visiting friends' homes, feel a sense of exhilaration at putting 'one over' on the boss and the taxman, or all three. An attempt to overcome this problem, and the limitations of the twenty-four-hour study, has been the development of the 'extended diary' which couples a log of activities with a recording of subjective responses to activities and events. These are later analysed in the hopes of linking objective experience to subjective response (Cullin, 1978). The two main problems with this are that it may be difficult to find people willing to participate, and secondly, discussions may still not tap the underlying perceptions and emotions of respondents. Nevertheless, time-budgeting does hold considerable promise for linking objective indicators and subjective responses.

A third difficulty with quality-of-life research is that individual correlations and ecological correlations may not correspond. In an individual correlation the variables are descriptive properties of individuals and not statistical constants such as rates and means; ecological correlations are about groups of people. The 'ecological fallacy' occurs in assuming greater homogeneity within a geographical area than is actually the case, and thus falsely ascribing the average characteristics of the area to individuals (Robinson, 1950). Kennedy *et al.* (1978) note that this problem is especially important in selecting a unit of analysis, for example, measurement of well-being at a city-wide level may be meaningless if most people identify more closely with neighbourhood characteristics. In addition they stress that researchers must always consider the cultural frame of reference in considering social indicator sets. The results of the Andrews and Inglehart (1979) study, noted earlier, bear this out.

Finally, we have mentioned the importance of the policy dimension in social indicator research, but there is little evidence of attention to this in subjective indicator research. The efforts at global measures of quality of life remain vague and general and it is difficult to imagine their value to policy beyond that of the average Gallup poll. Research cross-cut by specific demographic variables has much more potential policy usefulness. Knox (1976a), for example, identified strong regional variations in priority preferences – this has implications for the current debate on the devolution of power in Britain. Domain-specific research, on health, for example, also has policy potential – especially when disaggregated by demographic and experiential variables. Abrams (1978) notes the strong satisfactions associated with home-ownership as opposed to renting – this insight may have clear policy implications. In conclusion, quality-of-life research utilising subjective social indicators has clear policy potential, especially at a domain-specific level disaggregated by relevant variables. It does, however, face serious methodological difficulties which remain to be overcome.

Summary

This chapter opened by looking at the early attempts to define social indicators. These were ambiguous but the debate did suggest two important dimensions to social indicators. First, they might be descriptive or they might be normative. If the latter, then value-judgements played a key role in their development, and this role is explored in Chapter 5. Secondly, there was a commitment to indicators of the output of social processes rather than throughput or input. This commitment remains, although the development of useful, reliable output measures remains much more difficult than anticipated.

Two of the best definitions of social indicators suggested fives types of indicators could be identified by their policy use. These indicators were: informative, predictive, problem-oriented, programme evaluative, or target delineation indicators. Each would be operationalised in the context of an information system. A hierarchy of the statistical sophistication of social statistics and indicators was discussed and it was argued that overly narrow definitions served little purpose. The two most important elements of any social indicator effort were identified as methodological appropriateness and an understanding of the policy formation process. Discussion of other aspects of social indicators included the fact that they might be objective or subjective, *ex post* or *ex ante,* and aggregated or disaggregated. Different meaning of the terms social reporting and accounting were also discussed.

The last section considered subjective social indicators and quality-of-life studies, beginning with the pioneering work of Cantril and Maslow. The lack of correlation between objective and subjective measures was especially noted. Also important was the problem of gauging the significance of responses when individuals are likely to have differing perceptions of similar social situations, and give similar responses based on widely differing objective situations. Other issues including the problem of separating out the effects of demographic and experiential variables on subjective responses, and the usefulness of time-budgets for linking objective conditions to subjective responses were discussed.

3

Social Indicator Systems

> Social indicators, because they apparently manage to combine the somewhat conflicting attributes of relevance, objectivity, and convenience, have slotted comfortably into the paradigm of contemporary socio-economic planning in Europe, Australia, and North America. They have indeed become one of the central descriptive tools of normative policy analysis, and their use is now widespread at all levels of administration and control.
>
> (Knox, 1979)

During the past six years the direction of much social indicator research has been towards the development of organised groups, or systems of social indicators. The term 'indicator system' can generally be taken to mean a group of social indicators organised around component parts of the social system. The term is used in differing ways but usually implies consideration of a number of the diverse parts, or domains, that make up individual or societal well-being. Less than comprehensive groups of indicators can be termed social indicator sets.

The move away from attempts to develop just a few indicators towards groups or sets of indicators stemmed from research indicating a lack of correlation between various posited indicators at any given time. This implied that different variables were measuring different characteristics, and it could not be assumed that any one would act as a good surrogate for another. Also the difficult problems of aggregation ensured that attempts at highly composite indicators would fail to produce a reasonable measure. Research efforts tended therefore to avoid reliance on too few indicators and moved towards fairly disaggregated multidimensional indicator systems or sets.

With regard to the construction of these groups, or systems, of social indicators Zapf (1975) suggests four problem areas that must be dealt with to some degree in every case: the definition of some notion of welfare, the determination of system structure on theoretical or practical grounds, the selection and operationalisation of indicators, and the actual process of measurement. Each of these four criteria is not given equal attention in recent research; some research pays little attention to one or another of the problem areas. All social indicator sets and systems, however, have a determined structure, and it is this structure which suggests a classification for examining a variety of systems of social indicators.

This structuring of social indicator systems basically takes place in one of four ways:

(1) those organised programmatically;
(2) systems developed from social goal areas;
(3) systems developed around an individual's interactions and achievements over the course of a life-cycle;
(4) systems with a theoretical basis.

These categories are not mutually exclusive; the last especially will tend to combine with the others as research progresses. Perhaps a trend towards the disappearance of theoretically based systems as a separate category and the blurring of the distinctions among the other three will be a mark of future progress in social indicator development. At present, these categories are good reflections of the state of the art. In subsequent sections we examine in detail these various types of social indicator systems and examine recent research efforts in light of these structural categories, and in terms of the problem areas of indicator system development.

Programmatic development

Many social indicator sets are developed programmatically, that is, they are organised by means of the convenient breakdown provided by the institutional arrangements of society, such as housing, health services, religion, the law, transportation, education, and so on. Certainly it makes sense that social indicators would be called on to answer the information needs of various agencies, especially in government, and therefore be structured by organisational divisions among these agencies and by available data bases. It is common for indicator sets to be confined to a particular agency or programme type, for example, education, housing, or employment. More recently systems of indicators organised programmatically have been developed, most commonly by government. Social reports, for example, are often organised programmatically and generally make use of key statistical series, using the terms social statistics and social indicators variously. Although social reports are generally national in scope, other indicator systems may be national, regional, or local. A number of programmatic indicator sets are specifically local in character, and are often used to classify neighbourhoods. National social reports and the use of specifically urban social indicators are the subject of a more detailed examination in two later chapters.

Social Economic Accounts System

An extensive programmatic system of indicators, developed in the USA by Fitzsimmons and Lavey (1976), is the 'Social Economic Accounts System (SEAS)' which presents 477 community level indicators organised into fifteen programmatic categories. SEAS is designed to enable public officials, programme developers and social scientists to monitor the effects of various types of public investment upon a variety of indicators. These indicators are taken to reflect the quality of life of individuals in various domains, and the relative social position of groups of people in the community.

The indicators within each of the programmatic areas or sectors (e.g. education, health, welfare, etc.) are organised into *state* variables which describe people's lives at one point in time, *system* variables which describe the institutional arrangements affecting people's lives, and *relevant condition* variables which are state and system variables from other sectors affecting the sector under consideration. Within the state and system variables some are subjective social indicators, or attitudinal variables, obtained by resident survey. Table 3.1 shows some of the forty-four health sector variables in the SEAS system. Within the health sector, for example, a state variable is 'number of deaths per 1,000 live births', a system variable is 'number of full-time physicians per 100 population', a relevant condition variable is 'mean age of population', and within the state variables an attitudinal variable is personal satisfaction of residents with health services. Notice that the state variables tend to be output measures, while the system variables are measures of input and throughput. SEAS is within the recent North American emphasis on determining the social and environmental impact of public and private investment decisions.

In terms of Zapf's criteria SEAS contains no explicit notion of welfare. The indicators are comprehensively selected and operationalised, and considerable attention has been paid to measurement. The indicators are organised pragmatically, not theoretically, and SEAS can be described as a comprehensive scheme of statistics and social indicators. Although the lack of models of human behaviour is recognised as a problem with SEAS, the authors feel it is beyond the state of the art to expect a social indicator system designed for monitoring to present a complete causal model of change at this time. Because SEAS falls within a pragmatic sphere of social indicator research (i.e. investment decision evaluation), the emphasis on a comprehensive measuring system rather than a causal model is not surprising, and the indicators themselves are plausible and relevant to many community level resource decisions. The amount of implicit social theory embodied in such a comprehensive indicator system is large, however.

This problem with SEAS is recognised in later work of the authors of SEAS who take a step closer to the integration of their indicator system into a causal model (Fitzsimmons and Lavey, 1977). They developed a paradigm for the analysis of communities which conceptualises community as a systematic, interactive and dynamic entity. The purpose of this paradigm is to provide the theoretician or researcher with a common framework for using the community, with its subsystems, as a unit of analysis. An operational definition is proposed in which linkages are established between the fifteen programmatic indicator categories, five 'concept' categories (e.g. interaction, change, etc.) and eight potential research objectives (e.g. to identify types of interaction). In this manner it is suggested that a common framework is provided whereby various research activities relating to a specific community, or the concept of community, can be integrated to improve the theoretical and practical (investment decision) understanding of community.

CIPFA community indicators

Another programmatic indicator system is the Community Indicators Programme of the UK's Chartered Institute of Public Finance and Accountancy (CIPFA, 1979). Similar to SEAS, with an emphasis on *community* as a unit of analysis, it is less comprehensive, but further towards realisation as it actually publishes social indicator data for UK communities and attempts to aid decision-making by local authorities. The system is programmatic in part, in that it relies on extant data sources. Wherever possible indicators of individual 'need' are used in preference to input or throughput measures. The criteria for structuring the indicators are that they be readily comprehensible, disaggregated to the local authority level, and as up to date

Table 3.1 *Sample health sector variables from the Social Economic Accounts System (here SD is 'school district')*

HEALTH VARIABLES

Sector State Variables

1 Number of deaths per 1,000 live births in SD in 1970 by type (foetal, neonatal and maternal).
2 Number of deaths by age-group per 100 persons in that age-group in SD in 1970 (under 4 years, 5–14 years . . . 65–74 years).
3 Number of reported cases per 1,000 persons in SD in 1970 for selected morbidities (measles, diphtheria, whooping cough, and streptococcal sore throat and scarlet fever).

4 Median number of school loss days for illness per student in SD in 1970.
5 Average number of days of absences due to illness per worker at key employment establishments in SD in 1970.
6 Satisfaction rating: how satisfied are residents personally with the services or benefits they receive from the health sector?

System Variables

Human

7 Number of full-time equivalent physicians serving SD per 100 persons in SD in 1970.
8 Mean age of physicians serving SD in 1970.
9 Number of full-time equivalent dentists serving SD per 1,000 persons in SD in 1970.

Establishments

17 Number of hospitals serving SD in 1970.
18 Number of hospital beds serving SD in 1970 (short-term care, long-term care and mental health and special purpose).
19 Number of health care outpatient facilities serving SD in 1970.

Physical

21 Percentage of persons served by sanitary and safe drinking water in SD in 1970.
22 Median number of miles from population centres of SD in 1970 to closest (hospital and physician's office).

Services

25 Percentage of women giving birth who received pre-natal medical care in SD in 1970.
26 Percentage of births taking place in hospitals for women of SD in 1970.

Subjective

32 Importance rating: how important to residents is the health sector?
33 Influence rating: to what degree do residents participate in activities which influence decisions or operations in the health sector?
34 Equal opportunity rating: to what degree do residents of the community feel they have an equal opportunity to receive any benefits or services they desire in the health sector?

Relevant Condition Variables

35 Percentage of total dwelling units with all plumbing facilities in county in 1970.
36 Mean age of population of SD in 1970 (male, female).

Source: Fitzsimmons and Lavey, 1976.

as possible. The need indicators are further classified into normative need, that is target standards laid down by various authorities, and perceived need which is felt by individuals or expressed institutionally, for example, in the form of a waiting list for council (public) housing.

An interesting aspect of the CIPFA system not generally found in other social indicator systems is the identification of 'principal client-groups' for the range of services which the local government might offer. This makes the indicators themselves more readily policy-relevant. Client -groups are of three types: those directly identifiable (e.g. school pupils) who impose a mandatory obligation for service, those indirectly identifiable (e.g. the elderly) whose needs may or may not be met by local authorities, and the population generally, for such services as public transport. For example, a service need for the population group 'under 5' is 'nursery education' and indicators of service provision include 'places per 1,000 population' and 'pupils per nursery assistant'. For the client-group 'total population', one service is libraries and an indicator of service provision is book stock per 1,000 population. The CIPFA system also identifies or classifies the most similar local authorities to facilitate comparison of 'like' communities. Table 3.2 shows some of the indicators of service provision in the CIPFA scheme.

CIPFA proposes that its community indicator system is useful for three reasons. First, it is designed to facilitate the setting of priorities for resource allocation among various services in a local authority, both for policy and budget planning. Secondly, it assists in performance measurement – the study of efficiency or the ratio of inputs to outputs, and the study of effectiveness, which is the extent to which goals or objectives are met by service provision. Thirdly, the information produced by the CIPFA system provides ammunition for local governments in their negotiations with central government for various grants, like the rate support grant (Kemp, 1979).

In each case, it is suggested that the indicators can be used to examine (1) the comparative provision of a service between authorities, (2) trends in provision in relation to an indicator and (3) geographical variations in service provision within an authority. CIPFA may find that the system is more welcome for the second and third of these uses than the first, in so far as inter-authority comparisons may be unappealing to local officials. In any event, the CIPFA system proposes a notion of welfare based on normative and perceived need, the system is structured on practical rather than theoretical grounds, and many indicators are operationalised and measured based on available data sources, especially various census sources. CIPFA is especially noteworthy for its efforts to be relevant

Table 3.2 Indicators of service provision in the CIPFA system

Problem	Service	Indicator of Service Provision
Pensioners living alone	Home helps	Hours of service per pensioner living alone
Single-parent families with children	Social services	Expenditure per single-parent family or per large family
Large families with more than four children	Financial aid	
Married women working more than thirty hours with children under 5	Pre-school playgroups	Places per 1,000 children
Overcrowding	Housing	Number of households with more than 1 person per room per 1,000 households

Source: Chartered Institute of Public Finance and Accountancy, 1979.

to community level decisions and for disaggregating data for various client-groups.

Development by social goal area

A second method of structuring a social indicator system is to work from the general to the specific, that is, to identify social goals, refine them to generate subgoals or objectives, and eventually to arrive at some indicator, or indicators, of the achievement of that goal. The resultant indicator system may appear similar to a programmatically structured system but the important difference is the explicit internal logical consistency of the process of indicator development. This logical structure means that any particular indicator can be related back to some goal or objective specified by some member(s) of society. And although this process is no doubt implicit somewhere in many programmatic approaches the making of it explicit is valuable for two reasons. First, it facilitates the construction of causal models between goal or subgoal and any specified indicator. Secondly, and perhaps more important, it causes the value-judgements of the specific member(s) of society structuring the system to be exposed for critical examination. The disadvantage of this goal to indicator approach is that it can be difficult and time-consuming as in the example below. A further problem is that politicians and administrators may simply resist attempts to measure their achievement in specific areas. Conversely, the values reflected in the indicator system may be more than those of the researchers themselves and less than those of other segments of society. Researchers may subscribe to a narrow range of values associated with scientific enterprise (objectivity, verifiability, and so on) whereas different segments of society may subscribe to conflicting goals and priorities whereby they interpret the same data differently. A second example, based on law and public statement, seems to overcome some of these difficulties.

The OECD programme
This social goal area approach is the method chosen by the Organisation for Economic Co-operation and Development (OECD, 1973), 1976a, 1976b, 1977, 1979) in its programme to achieve standardised definitions of the social goal areas for which systematic indicators and assessments are most needed by their member governments. The OECD, which is comprised of twenty-four 'Western' governments, is developing central concepts which guide these member governments in the preparation of social indicators. The OECD working party decided early in its programme that it would concentrate on indicators of structural or institutional states or achievements. This distinction was made in recognition of the uncertainties in the

relationship between changes in structures and institutions and changes in individual well-being, in other words, the lack of causal theories of social behaviour. The programme avoided attempting to provide explanatory or predictive indicators even as it was recognised that policy evaluation and goal-setting endeavours are in great need of information bases which link cause with effect (Christian, 1974). The reasoning of the OECD is that social theory is far too unevolved to provide a conceptual framework for such indicators and that the political needs of the twenty-four member governments are best served by reaching consensus on a series of basic standards of individual well-being. As developments in theory take place, the system will be improved to take advances in partial or 'middle-range' social theory into account.

The diplomatic consensus process, a factor of prime importance to the OECD, required that agreement on the most general level of social goals take place first – these were labelled social concerns and are based solely on the judgement of political officers of the member nations. This method was chosen as the one most amenable to consensus. The OECD specifically rejected the derivation of indicators from existing statistics (i.e. programmatic development) because the impetus for their social indicator programme was related to deficiencies in existing data bases. A programmatic approach ran the risk of perpetuating these deficiencies by not generating new indicators, or by not causing existing statistical sources to be refined to the benefit of the member countries. A basic starting point of the effort was to differentiate between the identification of issues related to well-being and the evaluation of those issues. The former activity was seen as amenable to the consensus process in that the components of social well-being are similar across national boundaries and over time, even if the different evaluations leading to policy must be dissimilar to reflect geographic and temporal differences.

The determination of twenty-four fundamental social concerns grouped into eight goal areas was followed by the identification of a series of subconcerns, also by consensus. Table 3.3 shows some of the OECD's subconcerns and indicators. A social concern under the goal area 'health', for example, is 'the probability of a healthy life through all stages of the life-cycle' and two subconcerns under this area are 'length of life' and 'healthiness of life'. As a result of the continuation of this process, and the utilising of the appropriate technical expertise, provisional social indicators have emerged. Under the length-of-life subconcern, for example, there are indicators of life expectancy and peri-natal mortality. The indicators are ranked as to whether they correspond to all, or part of, a concern or subconcern, or whether they are the best available approximation of a direct measure. They are expected to reveal the level of well-being for each social concern, and changes in that level over time. Measurement will rely on existing data sources where available, and on extensions to data sources and innovation where necessary.

Table 3.3 *Concerns, subconcerns and indicators from the OECD social indicator system*

GOAL AREA 'A': HEALTH

1 Provisional working list of social concerns and indicators	*2* Concerns and sub-concerns	*3* Indicators
x2	A-1 *The probability of a healthy life through all stages of the life-cycle*	
	A-1-a Length of life	(1) Life expectancy at age 1 (20, 40, 60) (A)
		(2) Peri-natal mortality (A)
x1	A-1-b Healthfulness of life	(3) Proportion of predicted future life to be spent in a state of disability, on the part of those individuals not disabled as a result of a permanent impairment at ages 1, 20, 40, 60 (B)
		(4) Proportion of persons disabled as a result of a permanent impairment in selected age-brackets (B)
	A-2 *The impact of health impairments on individuals*	
	A-2-a The quality of health care in terms of reducing pain and restoring capabilities	(5) Maternal mortality (C)

| A-2-b The extent of universal distribution in the delivery of health care | (6) Physical accessibility: average delay between occurrence of an emergency event (e.g. accident, heart attack) and appropriate treatments (B) |
| | (7) Physical accessibility: average delay between awareness of functional disturbance of a non-emergency nature and appropriate treatment (B) |

xl

(8) Economic accessibility: Disposable income
– net expenditure on health insurance by households
– full cost of health services consumed by households

Disposable income
– net expenditure on health insurance by households
– net expenditure by households on health services (B)

Source: Organisation for Economic Co-operation and Development, 1979.

The OECD programme, in terms of Zapf's criteria, has a defined notion of welfare, namely, that of individual social well-being. The indicator system is structured by goal area determined by negotiation among nations. The programme recognises that it has two broad objectives: enlightening policy appraisal in the short run, and contributing to progress in modelling social interaction in the long run. It is dealing with the first objective immediately and will confront the second as it becomes politically and theoretically feasible. The indicators specified to date include key statistical series and synthetic representative series. At present the programme is focusing on areas of interest to member countries for the purpose of working out precise statistical definitions of indicators, examining different data collection mechanisms, and collecting actual data on a pilot basis. In addition, special reports are issued on relevant topics as they are needed (Jazairi, 1976; Johnston, 1976).

The SPES system

Another goal-to-indicator system, modelled in part on the OECD approach, is the Federal Republic of Germany's SPES (Sozialpolitisches Entscheidungs und Indikatorensystem) social indicator system (Zapf, 1977). This is similar to the OECD system except that rather than rely on a consensus process among negotiators, the SPES based its 'goal-dimensions' and 'goal-values' on extant German laws, regulations and programmatic statements of important groups in the society. In this sense SPES combined the explicitness of the social goal approach with some of the practical ease of the programmatic, which, as suggested, contains implicit social goals of at least some segments of society. This is perhaps easier in Germany where social intentions are specifically stated within the law, but might be more difficult in other countries. By system SPES means a systematic catalogue of goal-dimensions and indicators. Some of the goal-dimensions correspond to specific programmatic breakdowns, mostly bureaucratic agencies. Others, however, are specifically designed to cut across administrative structures. SPES was not designed as an alternative to national economic accounts. Rather income and productivity measures were incorporated into a broader system of welfare goals.

The first step in the development of SPES was the development of goal-dimensions by a detailed investigation of the law, the German Constitution, other regulations, and the most important programme-related statements of government bodies, major political parties, trade unions and employers' associations. This process took the place of the diplomatic consensus process of the OECD. The second step was the construction of goal subdimensions based on reviews of the professional literature related to that dimension. Under the goal-dimension 'income and income distribution', for example, subdimensions include level of income, equality in demand satisfaction, poverty in income, and income security and stability. The third and fourth step were the development of ideal social indicators of goal attainment and then working social indicators, which were the best possible given cost and data constraints. These social indicators were, wherever possible, output rather than input measures, and presented in time-series for at least two points in time. As a point of insight, each indicator definition was also seen as 'a theoretical hypothesis about the relationship of indicator and reality which on principle can be proved wrong or insufficient' (Zapf, 1977, p. 5). This process resulted in a system of 196 indicators of the goal subdimensions. Under the subdimension 'status of health', for example, there are nine indicators including life expectancy at birth, at 30, at 60, days of disability, days of hospital care, and a subjective health satisfaction index.

The fifth step in the SPES system was that of data collection, wherever possible in time-series given on a five-yearly basis from 1950 to 1975. The sixth step was also a point of insight in that it anticipated a problem of 'information overload' with 196 disaggregated time-series indicators which filled sixty-six pages. The solution was an additional abridged version which compressed the data into four pages with summary evaluations. The authors of SPES admitted that in compressing data they risked 'unsatisfactory compromises'; nevertheless they were right to offer a full version and an 'executive summary' as alternative packages, given that this disaggregated information overload dilemma is hardly amenable to clear-cut resolution. A last step for SPES, proposed as a future research topic, is to experiment with a variety of value-weighting schemes based on representative population samples, expert panels, or both. Finally, the authors of SPES offer a third point of insight in that they do not perceive of the indicator system as representing some consensus on the normative evaluation of indicators (i.e. are things getting better or worse?). Rather they propose the system be regarded 'as a contribution to political discourse' (Zapf, 1977, p. 5), which is of course what such systems should be.

Development by life-cycle

A third method of structuring indicator systems is to utilise the life-cycle, or stages from birth to death, of an individual as the basis for organisation. The indicators themselves arise from an individual's interactions with institutions during this life-cycle and his achievements in terms of societal norms and self-actualisation. These indicators cut across programmatic divisions.

System of Social and Demographic Statistics

The best-known of the life-cycle indicator systems is the System of Social and Demographic Statistics (SSDS) developed for the Statistical Office of the United Nations (1971, 1975). Much of the original concept and development of SSDS is the work of the British economist Richard Stone (1973). The SSDS system is based on the premiss that indicator sets structured programmatically cannot be indicator systems because insufficient provision is made for various kinds of connection between the different parts of the system. SSDS proposes that these linkages can be examined by taking, as a frame of reference, the life-cycle of the individual and examining the relationship of various phases (e.g. the learning phase) to other phases (e.g.

the earning phase or the retirement phase) and to the institutions involved (schools, employers, etc.). This is done by way of studying the 'stocks and flows' of individuals, or groups of individuals, where a stock is the state of an individual or group at one point in time, and a flow is changes in these states. In this way, it is seen to be feasible to portray clearly the manner in which changes in the structure and states of welfare of various cohorts in the population occur. These stocks and flows for varying 'life-sequences' can be displayed in matrix form and broken down into subsystems whose elements are more related to one another than to elements of other subsystems. These subsystems may well follow in the main broadly separate institutional lines, like health or education, but they do not arise from any particular institutional division.

Within these subsystems social indicators will be developed. A social indicator here is defined as a construct, based on observations and usually quantitative, that tells something about an aspect of social life of interest, or about changes taking place in that aspect of social life. This is a broad definition and social indicators are distinguished from other statistics only by relating to some area of social concern and satisfying purposes of curiosity, understanding, or action related to policy. Indicators are to be developed from factor analysis methods, index-numbered formulas referring to a base year, utility, or optimising functions, demographic life expectancy figures based on actuarial calculating, and subjective indicators arising from public opinion surveys.

The objective of SSDS is to develop a comprehensive social statistics accounting system for worldwide use. In this system demographic data based on life-cycle can be linked to institutional areas of government expenditure. A universal standardised form of data collection, classification and display is encouraged to assist in policy formulation at the international and national levels and to provide a firm basis for research needed to enlarge understanding of social processes. Additionally, some technical benefits in the data handling and processing fields are suggested. There will be a wide variety of indicators including comprehensive statistical series, composite indexes and synthetic representative series. In terms of Zapf's problem areas the SSDS system has no defined notion of welfare, and selection of indicators is incomplete as yet. It can be argued that SSDS indicators are being organised on theoretical grounds and Stone has put forward some model-building concepts, especially with regard to education. The framework for social data collection is of prime importance however, and it will be some time before any theoretical testing can take place as a result of SSDS. SSDS is at present a highly complex, comprehensive, organised system for collection and display of social data and demands correspondingly sophisticated data collection procedures, a situation which unfortunately does not hold in most countries of the world.

Development from a theoretical base

Some individual social indicators and indicator sets are being explored from a theoretical basis, that is, strictly in the context of causal social models which interrelate variables and thus explain some of them by others. This structuring by theory relates sequences of social events with data, and by quantitative methods, usually systems of equations, estimates relationships between the theoretically specified variables. Social indicators purporting to relate in some discernible fashion to social phenomena can be tested as to their ability to estimate and thus their selection over some other indicators may be justified. A very few social indicator systems are also beginning to be developed based on this explicit intention to advance the state of social theory.

One important source of this theoretical development is the work of the sociologist Kenneth Land and his various associates, who are modelling some of the interrelationships among aspects of society as represented in time-series social statistics, that is, repeated observations across equally spaced intervals of time (Land, 1975a; Land and Felson, 1977; Land and McMillen, 1980). These dynamic models are to be capable of accounting for changes in various social indicators, including trends and cyclic fluctuations, and they are to be useful for social forecasting. The models are dynamic in that they are concerned with relationships over time rather than with the comparison of cross-sectional samples. Land argues that systems of structural equations provide the most appropriate framework for the development of these models. One recent effort is, in Land's words, 'an integrated 21 equation model of how marriage, family, and population conditions, as indexed by macro social indicators, affect each other and are affected by other social, demographic, and economic forces' (Land and Felson, 1977, p. 328). In this case a *macro* model is one based on summary counts, averages, or rates defined on particular populations, as opposed to a *micro* model which is based on individual level data. Life-cycle effects in these models are organised in matrices similar to those used in the SSDS system.

This particular model of Land's is based on US annual national data for the years 1947–72. It was used to forecast values of some endogenous variables for 1973 and 1974, for example, marriage formation and dissolution. Comparisons between the actual rates and the rates predicted by the model then showed less than 2 per cent error in the predictions. A simplified flow diagram for this model is presented in Figure 3.1, where the arrows represent the twenty-one

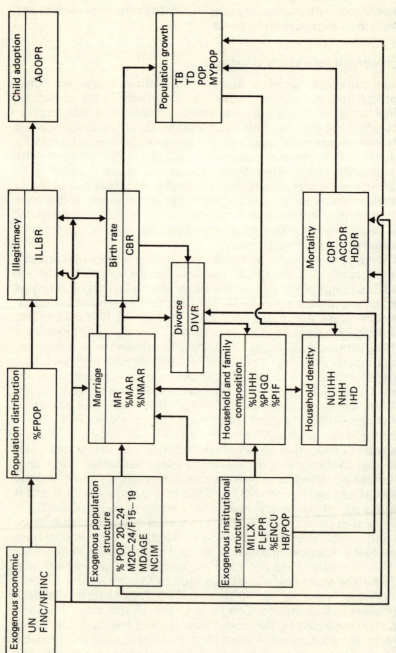

Figure 3.1 Summary flow diagram of a dynamic macro social indicator model of marriage, family and population in the USA.
Source: Land and Felson, 1977.

equations linking the variables. This 'path diagram' is a typical representation of a causal model in social indicators research, and such modelling is often called 'path analysis'. Land and Felson stress that even a complex model like this requires considerable simplification from reality and that some variables are taken as outside the model for convenience, for example, economic variables, but are obviously part of the socioeconomic system in general (1977, p. 352). These variables can be brought into the analysis by integrating this model with other social and econometric models and Land suggests that his model should be integrated into a larger societal model in order to estimate some of the effects of changes in demographic phenomena on other social conditions.

The most recent research by Land attempts to relate changes in American mortality rates to changes in various social, demographic, economic and health care conditions. Among many other findings, this latest model indicates that (1) changes in the age-structure of the American population have substantial impacts on changes in mortality rates for respiratory and circulatory diseases and (2) that the infective and parasitic diseases mortality rate is more closely related to per capita public health expenditures than to improvements in the general standard of living (Land and McMillen, 1980). Land's research provides not only a baseline of statistical evidence which can be further explored and refined, but in the case of (2) above, may well have ultimate policy implications.

Perhaps the most comprehensive attempt at a theoretically based system of social indicators to date is the work of Fox (1974), in collaboration with Van Moeseke. This research begins by noting that most activity in social indicator research has concentrated on the establishment of frameworks for data collection, and that theory has been for the most part implicit. Fox then recounts a number of concepts from various social sciences, especially sociology, psychology and economics, which might be integrated into a social indicator system model. The most important among these are Parsons's 'media of social interchange' and Barker's 'behaviour settings' concept. In very simple terms, Parsons suggests a series of 'things' which change hands between individuals, such as influence, money, power, value commitments, ideology, reputation, and so on; and Barker puts forward an elaborate classification system for identifying, describing and measuring the environments in which human behaviour takes place.

Fox integrates these and other concepts into a model of 'total income' which postulates that all of an individual's time can be organised as occurring in behaviour settings and that a person will allocate his time, his possible social roles and his 'media' among behaviour settings to maximise his total utility. All such allocations and rewards would be put into monetary values by way of determining opportunity costs of non-participation in the various behaviour settings. Fox puts this in the form of a mathematical programming model which includes various suggestions for converting media of interchange into monetary units. He further postulates that total income in this form is a more reliable measure of quality of life than economic income, and that an aggregation of total incomes could measure changes in life quality for families, communities, regions, and so on. Fox argues that the total income concept can provide a boundary within which the relationships of various social indicators to social subsystems can be tested, and it can be used as one of a number of criteria for choosing between alternative socioeconomic programmes. Fox also suggests that if total income is a valid concept it must be able continually to incorporate tested concepts and models from social sciences, psychiatry and social philosophy.

This total income model has a definite notion of welfare, is structured theoretically, and puts forward an accounting framework for selecting and operationalising indicators which relate to the social model of the concept. It might be argued that such a comprehensive attempt at social theory is premature and that attention is better directed towards establishing causal links between individual indicators and social phenomena. This model, however, provides a rigorous framework for that kind of more specific activity and has considerable value as a paradigm for relating social indicator research to the social sciences generally. It is, in short, a necessary innovation in social indicator research – a field generally given more to data measurement and organisation and much less to attempts at theoretical propositions.

Conclusion

There is little doubt that the development of systems of social indicators will continue, and methodological refinement, like improved social modelling, must be based on a more thorough understanding of the strengths and limitations of the systems approach. These social indicator systems, for example, may succumb to the numerous problems associated with aggregation, which are discussed in the next chapter. Also attention must be paid to policy-oriented value-judgements which may exist in any delineation of indicator sets which are selected to conform to perceptions and commitments of particular parties in the policy process. These value-judgements may hide behind a facade of statistical neutrality but social indicator researchers must demolish that facade, and replace it with a reasoned stance on the value and limitations of quantitative analysis.

The programmatic structuring of social indicator sets and systems will continue to be the favoured approach of many local, regional and national level governments. In spite of a number of theoretical limitations, this approach is relatively simple and cost-effective, and can generate data directly relevant to short-term social policy decisions. The chief danger is that the sometimes tenuous cause-and-effect relationships implicit in the indicators might go unnoticed by politicians and administrators who may overvalue the explanatory power of the indicators. Conversely, if theoretical problems are overemphasised, the indicators may be dismissed as useless and, worse, misleading, when in fact they do convey policy-relevant information. Sometimes indicator systems are presented in an overly complex manner, lengthy and replete with statistical jargon, so as to be unfathomable to all but a knowledgeable few. This situation must be avoided. It can be argued, however, that all decisions are based on imperfect data and providing the indicators are presented in a simple and meaningful fashion, the programmatic approach to indicators is a practical one for governments faced with day-to-day resource allocation decisions and limited resources.

Logically the social goal approach is almost an ideal worth aspiring to, because it directly and logically links social objectives to indicators which show the degree of attainment of those objectives. For non-governmental researchers, however, it remains an academic exercise to the extent that the selection of indicators reflects the researchers' own value-judgements on the components of well-being. The OECD approach, on the other hand, has evolved indicators in a political fashion in so far as each country's appointees to the OECD are representatives of the people of their country, an assumption which may not necessarily hold (for a critique of this effort see Radical Statistics Group, 1978). Further the process requires considerable resources if a consensus is to appear, and as it is difficult and complex it is unlikely to be undertaken in most pluralistic national contexts. It can be argued that some societal goals are implicit or explicit in laws, public statements and existing programmatic divisions and in this sense, the German SPES programme is perhaps a reasonable, practical compromise which combines the goal areas and programmatic approaches.

The life-cycle approach as embodied in SSDS has potential, not only as a systematic means of collecting and displaying social statistics, but also as a theoretical framework for relating elements and institutions in society to effects on individual well-being. At the present time, however, SSDS is very complex and the statistical requirements of the system are beyond the capabilities of most countries that produce social statistics or indicators, much less those that do not. For example, recent research in the USA indicates that even US data are inadequate for the SSDS system (SSRC, 1979). Until these information problems are overcome, differences observed between countries may reflect statistical and definitional problems, as well as differences in social development. Obviously the fruition of SSDS as a working system is many years off, if at all.

The continued development of causal models based on postulated social theory holds the key to the long-range future of social indicators. This is being increasingly recognised among researchers and those that make use of the indicators. Although work on complex social models of the scale of macroeconomic models may have some value, progress will mainly be made by concentration of attention on explanatory models which are at a low level of generalisation and thus close enough to reality to allow empirical testing to take place, for example, the work of Land in particular areas like health. In this way all types of social indicator research will move away from simple description to explanatory models useful for social prediction. Eventually the aggregation of these low level models may lead to more general social models and the social indicator movement will have fulfilled some of its earliest objectives. The results of these theoretical endeavours will enhance and change all other approaches to social indicator systems.

4

Social Theory and Models

In recent years, we have heard a great deal about how accounting and economics need to be enlarged to include 'social indicators' or 'social accounting'. But I don't think the need is for more numbers, at all. The need is for the basis of justifying the numbers – the model or world view which tells us what difference the numbers make.

(Churchman, 1975)

There are no facts without theories . . .

(de Neufville, 1975)

Several commentators on social indicators have argued that there is a need to locate social indicators within an explicit theoretical framework. Land (1971), for example, argued that a social indicator should be a component, that is, a parameter or a variable, in a sociological model of a social system or some segment of a social system. This was the first strong suggestion that social indicators needed to be more than some sort of statistical series. Lineberry *et al.* (1974), writing on the use of social indicators by municipalities, warned that the first conceptual limitation which should be identified when promoting indicator use must be the poor record of indicators in detecting causal relationships among various factors contributing to a specific social problem. They attribute this inability to the general lack of social theory. For example, indicators showing the incidence of juvenile crime in a city say nothing about the variety of psychological and environmental determinants of that crime – factors which have to be considered in allocating resources, say, between increased recreational facilities and more policing. Bunge points out that the very definition of social indicator of some life quality contains a causal notion relating that indicator to well-being. This would be acceptable if there were a science of well-being or at least some reasonable model. He goes on, 'since no such thing has been constructed so far, we are forced to use our treacherous commonsense to an extent that is uncommon in science. Which is a polite way of saying that, so far, the study of the quality of life has not been thoroughly scientific' (1975, p. 75).

This then is the problem: social indicators, virtually by definition, specify causal linkages or connections between observable aspects of social phenomena, which indicate, and other unobservable aspects or concepts, which are indicated. This can only be accomplished by postulating, *implicitly* or *explicitly*, some causal model or theory of social behaviour which serves to relate formally the variables under consideration. All social indicator research represents, therefore, some social theory or model, however simplistic. Much research to date laying claim to the term 'social indicator' research consists either of descriptive social statistics, which some people have argued are not social indicators at all, or of implicit postulations of causal linkages. It is argued here that the failure to make explicit an underlying theory or model impedes the development of social indicators.

It was noted in Chapter 1 that although high hopes were held out for social indicators as measures of social change, especially for the data requirements for policy-making and planning, the promise remains largely unfulfilled. The often obviously tenuous cause-and-effect relationships implicit in many sets of social indicators have caused them sometimes to be dismissed as useless and, worse, misleading by those who might find them most useful: politicians, administrators and others making resource allocation decisions. This lack of explicit theoretical statement or causal model has resulted in ambiguous definitions of the policy-relevant unobservable phenomena, for example, urban poverty, and the subsequent linkages to social indicators. Also these implicit theories or accumulations of time-series statistics have not permitted separation of exogenous and endogenous variables, that is, separation of the effects of public programmes from the impact of other social processes, for example, decreasing fertility rates or urban–rural migration. Only the explicit specification of the nature of the causal linkages within a model allows hypothesis-testing and thus the opportunity to establish the likelihood that some indicator indeed indicates that which it claims to indicate. It can also be argued that the making explicit of what is inherent in the research can help to expose the relevant value-judgements which the researchers bring with them to the task. This chapter relates social indicators to social theory and causal models and explores some of the difficulties associated with the development of theoretically based social indicators.

General aspects of social theory

A theory is generally argued to contain two elements: (1) abstract generalisations that move beyond simple descriptions of a particular incident or case and (2) an attempt to explain why or how something happened (Mullins, 1973). More specifically, a theory consists of a set of propositions that are interrelated, where a proposition is an established or proven relationship among variables and a variable is a changeable component of some phenomenon (Forcese and Richer, 1973). Put another way, sociological theory relates logically interconnected sets of propositions from which empirical uniformities can be derived (Merton, 1967). The most fundamental choice of a theory is its choice of a 'unit of analysis' which is a boundary within which the concepts of a theory have an invariant causal relation to each other (Stinchcombe and Wendt, 1975). Examples of such units of analysis are: the individual, a particular group of people, or an act; decision, or policy.

A useful distinction may be made between two types of sociological theory (Merton, 1967, pp. 39–51). The first type is unified social theory, or a total system theory, which attempts to explain all observations about every aspect of social behaviour, organisation and change. For example, the American sociologist Talcott Parsons attempted to establish a general theory which linked the psychological elements and socially determined elements in human behaviour. The second type of theory are theories of 'the middle range' which deal with limited conceptual ranges, limited aspects of social phenomena, and fall between minor working hypotheses and unified social theory. Middle-range theory is used principally to guide empirical inquiry, and is based in part on the feeling that expectations that unified social theory will evolve, or be discovered, in the near future are misguided. Unified theory is not always dismissed completely, however. Merton, for example, argues that sociological theory must proceed in two ways, first, by developing middle-range theories from which to derive hypotheses which can be empirically investigated, and secondly, by evolving more general theory that is adequate to consolidate middle-range theories. To concentrate on unified theory one runs the risk of an entirely wrong conception, yet to concentrate solely on middle-range theory is to risk emerging with specific hypotheses that account for limited aspects of social behaviour but remain mutually inconsistent.

Other authors argue that middle-range theories are indeed sub-units of larger conceptions, be they called unified theories, 'paradigms' (Kuhn, 1970) or 'scientific research programmes' (Lakatos, 1970), and that scientific progress occurs at a macro level, as entire paradigms are replaced by new ones. The implication of this argument is that the validated existence of middle-range theory is a function of the existence of its associated parent paradigm, rather than the empirical testing of deduced hypothesis at a micro level – this is termed the 'context of discovery' as opposed to the 'context of validation' (Wisman, 1978, p. 269). However, given that the social system is far too complex to be amenable to unified theory testing, it can be argued that the aggregation of micro level empirical hypothesis testing may well contribute to the reaching of some 'knowledge threshold' when a paradigm change may occur. Such an occurrence may also be related to wide socio-political changes – the issues surrounding the role of analytic rationality as embodied in social indicator research, and in policy-making, are taken up in the next chapter. Here I expand on the argument that incremental hypothesis testing at the micro level is essential to good social indicator research.

It is worth noting in passing that in advancing this argument one becomes aligned, *ipso facto*, with a group of social scientists who have been characterised as the 'new causalists' by Mullins (1973). These researchers, in the main sociologists, combine a strong methodological orientation for theory testing with an equal emphasis on the construction of substantive social theory. Their research techniques, such as path analysis borrowed from genetics, structural equation models from econometrics and error estimation from psychology, rely on large sample sizes (over 1,500), fairly accurate measurement and use of statistical correlation and regression procedures (Mullins, 1973, p. 214). Large sample sizes were, in turn, dependent on the development of computer technology, which facilitates intensive data manipulation and analysis.

A final definition of theory is worthwhile. Guttman (1979, p. 12) states, 'a theory is an hypothesis of a correspondence between a definitional system for a universe of observations and an aspect of the empirical structure of those observations, together with a rationale for such an hypothesis'. For social indicators the relationship to social theory is a two-step process. First, an hypothesis (an empirically testable proposition) is put forward that one variable (the indicator) is in a definable recurring relationship with one or more other variables (the indicated), that is, the postulated relationship is valid. If this is the case then secondly, the indicators can be used in further tests of the validity of postulated social theory. This usually involves the quantification of the theory, which is almost always essential to the assessment of causal hypothesis in that evidence used to assess the validity of the hypothesis is usually quantitative.

Both steps relating indicators to theory involve establishing the validity of an hypothesis. In the broadest sense this means establishing the extent to which the postulated indicator–indicated relationship agrees with behaviour manifest in a series of real-life observations (the sample). More specifically one must consider internal and external validity (Miles, 1975, pp. 20–2). Internal validity refers to the extent to which measurements in the particular test under consideration can be confidently accepted as reflecting reality. This means establishing, in terms of the above definition of theory, that the definitional system has been appropriately operationalised. It also requires consideration of the causal significance of the measurements – whether the same relationship might have occurred by chance or whether exogenous variables may have affected the relationship. External validity, on the other hand, refers to the confidence with which we can generalise from the particular research experiment and sample to wider populations and different conditions. The establishment of external validity for a social indicator means that it can be utilised in the second step of analysis, the validation of social theory. At this point, however, changes in any social indicator are subject to normative judgements, that is, it becomes a social policy issue whether a change in an indicator is 'good' or 'bad'. For example, we may establish that television ownership is one valid indicator of the propensity to use leisure-time. Whether, however, changes in such an indicator are good or bad is a social issue in so far as there are policies which may encourage or discourage television ownership and use, or subsidise educational programming. Where such interpretation is possible, it is important that the social indicator and the social theory be explicitly and formally related in a logical form which expresses all the important dimensions of that relationship. This logical form is usually called a model. At the first stage of analysis, indicator to indicated, this logical form can be termed a social indicator model, and at the second stage, indicators related to policy, it can be termed a social policy model (Land, 1975b, p. 20).

Theory and models

This term 'model' or 'social indicator model' is often mentioned in the literature. It is worth exploring briefly the relationship of models to theory. Most simply, a model is a likeness of something. A model is also an imitation or abstraction from reality that is intended to order and to simplify our view of that reality while still capturing its essential characteristics (Forcese and Richer, 1973, p. 38).

The word 'model', though, is used in a number of different ways. These four are common:

(1) as a prototype or exemplary type of something which should be aspired to (the 'Model Cities' programme);
(2) as a set of schematic plans showing what something is or how something should be developed (like a model of a machine or an architect's model);
(3) as a contentless general purposes data analysis procedure (like a linear programming model);
(4) as a mathematical model (like an econometric model, or Land's

21-equation demographic model discussed in the last chapter) (McFarland, 1975, pp. 361–2).

This last category can be defined as a series of statements in mathematical form involving abstract variables which may be equated for theoretical purposes with substantive variables in the field being examined (Leik and Meeker, 1975, p. 10). This mathematical approach is especially useful in the social indicator field where assumptions made about the relationships between social phenomena and indicators can be precisely expressed and, using mathematical reasoning, the relationships can be tested for causal effects, as in path analysis. Mathematical models are also useful for predicting trends in social change.

A further distinction can be made between descriptive and explanatory models (Forcese and Richer, 1973). Descriptive models contain only descriptive statements and the concepts in the model are not operationalised. An explanatory model contains explicit explanatory hypotheses and the important concepts are all operationalised. Further, a model in which all the concepts have been operationalised, and the relationships between them have been validated, is a theory. Thus, we have a continuum from descriptive model to tested theory.

The descriptive model may be useful for identifying characteristics of social phenomena, and is often termed a taxonomy, a conceptual framework or model, a typology, or a 'word model'. This latter term is the one used by Jeffers (1978) in his discussion of mathematical modelling. Such word models are seen as important for bounding and defining the research problem and as a logical prerequisite to later mathematical formulation of testable hypotheses. The process of relating a descriptive model to an explanatory model is sometimes called mapping, that is, stating in what manner theoretical constructs or observational variables and relationships are expressed in mathematical form. Levy and Guttman (1975) propose the use of mapping sentences for expressing this relationship. Table 4.1 is a mapping sentence for developing an explanatory model of well-being utilising subjective social indicators. A question, for example, about satisfaction with the way a particular respondent spends leisure time can be expressed $a_2\ b_1\ c_1\ d_2\ e_1\ f_1$ and from here mathematical formulation is a relatively easy step.

The explanatory model, then, specifies quantitative relationships among variables and identifies and tests causal linkages, and thus may become theory. Only type 4, 'the mathematical model' from the above list, could possibly fall into the explanatory category, although strictly mathematical models may not exhaust this category. However, we can rigorously define the explanatory category by insisting on (1) operationalisation and (2) specification of at least some causal relationships. Further, only explanatory models can become theory.

Table 4.1   *The mapping sentence*

The Mapping Sentence

A

The $\begin{pmatrix} a_1 & \text{cognitive} \\ a_2 & \text{affective} \end{pmatrix}$ assessment by respondent (x) of the

B

$\begin{pmatrix} b_1 & \text{state of} \\ b_2 & \text{government's treatment for} \end{pmatrix}$ the wellbeing of his social (reference)

C   *D*

group $\left\{ \begin{array}{ll} c_1 & \text{self} \\ c_2 & \text{government} \\ c_3 & \text{State} \\ c_4 & \text{institution} \\ c_5 & \text{new immigrants} \\ c_6 & \text{poor} \\ c_7 & \text{other individuals} \\ c_8 & \text{on the whole} \end{array} \right\}$ with respect to its $\left\{ \begin{array}{ll} d_1 & \text{primary internal} \\ d_2 & \text{primary social} \\ d_3 & \text{primary resource} \\ d_4 & \text{neighbourhood} \\ d_5 & \text{town} \\ d_6 & \text{State} \\ d_7 & \text{World} \end{array} \right\}$ secondary

E

environment, concerning a $\left\{ \begin{array}{ll} e_1 & \text{general} \\ e_2 & \text{specific} \end{array} \right\}$ aspect of life area

F

$\left\{ \begin{array}{ll} f_1 & \text{recreation} \\ f_2 & \text{family} \\ f_3 & \text{on the whole} \\ f_4 & \text{security} \\ f_5 & \text{health} \\ f_6 & \text{economic} \\ f_7 & \text{education} \\ f_8 & \text{religion} \\ f_9 & \text{society} \\ f_{10} & \text{immigration} \\ f_{11} & \text{work} \\ f_{12} & \text{information} \\ f_{13} & \text{communication} \end{array} \right\}$ according to his normative criterion for that life area

$\rightarrow \left(\begin{array}{l} \text{very satisfactory} \\ \text{to} \\ \text{very unsatisfactory} \end{array} \right)$ in the sense of the element from facet *B*.

Source: Levy and Guttman, 1975.

A tested explanatory model is a theory that has 'epistemic' and 'constitutive' significance (Dumont and Wilson, 1967). Epistemic significance is the operationalisation of concepts such that words or conceptual abstractions are linked by explicit rules of correspondence to observable features of the empirical world. Mapping is the process by which this occurs and as epistemic significance increases so obviously does internal validity. Constitutive significance means that the constructs comprising the theory are interlinked so that they serve to predict and explain the empirically discernible behaviour (the data). Precise hypothesis formulation and testing in a model therefore leads to epistemic and constitutive significance and social theory. Although a causal model might be used to simply 'represent' some theory (as a schematic plan), in social indicator research it is mostly the case that models are constructed as part of the process that leads to the development of social theory. This is the case by Warren *et al.* (1980), for example, who argue that the assessment of fit between social data and model can be viewed as a strategy for learning more about the relationships among variables, and thus assisting the development of social theory.

There are two additional points to be made. First, a model may be 'a sometimes true theory' in that it only holds for one environment rather than all environments, where an environment is the area within the boundary where promulgated cause-and-effect relationships hold (Stinchcombe and Wendt, 1975). For example, a model of the UK economy holds for that one environment and no other. A model becomes a theory in two ways: (1) by specification of which environments the model applies to and which it does not, or (2) by building the model up by attaching auxiliary models to it until it becomes applicable to many environments, at the limit to all environments. It has been suggested, for example, that social indicator theory can be advanced by gradually expanding the environments of various economic models into socioeconomic fields. The second point is that the model is not to be confused with the data itself or the underlying theory – the model serves logically to relate postulated theory to observed behaviour.

In summary it can be stated that a continuum of theoretical development exists from (1) descriptive models through (2) explanatory models and (3) tested middle-range theory to (possibly) (4) unified theory or general paradigms.

Theoretically based social indicators

For a decade now the study of the quality of life has occurred without there emerging any agreement on social indicators which can reliably claim to measure it. Moreover, traditional economic measures such as GNP or rate of inflation still command much more interest than any potential social indicator. This is directly related to the lack of development of social indicator theory and the associated lack of operationalisation and specification of causal linkages. For just as economic indicators are interrelated components of some economic model based on theory, so social indicators must fit into social or socioeconomic models based on theory. This theoretical approach is essential if one is to postulate and measure the strength and direction of causal linkages between indicators and indicated social phenomena, and between indicators and policy. Further, only the testing of a theoretical proposition can lead to a justification for the selection of one social indicator rather than another.

Most authors who consider the necessity for models or theory argue a similar case. This is that social indicator, and social policy, models are necessary, and from explanatory models will flow middle-range theory, and unified theory, or paradigm shifts, might conceivably come from this process. Moser (1973) suggests that social indicator theory will develop much as economic theory did, that is, theories and indicators in parallel development with concentration on middle-range theories in specific fields such as education, mental health, and so on, leading to more general theory. De Neufville (1978–9) also argues for attention to middle-range theory so that progress towards reliability will take place through interactive model-building research. She argues as well for attention to the overall paradigm which structures problem formulation, defines research priorities, and serves to relate data to model to theory. Fox (1974) argues the same case for parallel development using simple models for two or three variables applied to existing data. Land (1975a) suggests that 'sociometric' sociological models are required by social indicator researchers, and hopes that increasing interest in time-series statistics will stimulate researchers to make their theories explicit enough for dynamic quantitative modelling to take place. Brand (1975) does not think a 'model of society' (unified theory) will ever be constructed but that every effort should be directed towards explanatory models for specific fields such as the housing market, or the educational system. Fanchette (1974) suggests that economic models be made socioeconomic models by the gradual inclusion of social variables. This would ease the problem of developing full-scale social indicator models. This last suggestion is of considerable interest, although it does carry with it the danger that economic models might be termed socioeconomic without the necessary empirical testing of the included social variables.

In summary, the theme is common, even though differences exist in approach and in ultimate limit. The problem in the social indicators field is to integrate indicator and policy models based on theory, and data, by various quantitative methods. These models will postulate that certain measurements lead to an understanding of some series of social events and quantitative method will estimate the strength and direction of relationships between postulated variables. In spite of a number of exhortations to this end what has tended to happen is that the difficulty of constructing social models and relating empirical data to theory has limited the attempts to develop explanatory models. Rather, researchers have concentrated on (1) descriptive social indicators – the description of social states and changing trends – and (2) the prescriptive function of indicators for policy-making and planning, that is, making normative judgements and/or recommendations based on measurements by some selected indicators. These latter have often reflected implicit and tenuous cause-and-effect relationships. Given that many authors have argued the case of the advancement of theoretically based indicators, it is worthwhile to explore some of the reasons why, with a few notable exceptions, this is not generally taking place.

Difficulties associated with social indicator modelling

Certainly one of the reasons for this general lack of development of explanatory social indicator models is simply the difficulty associated with their construction and empirical testing. Often the term 'experimental' in the social research field does not refer to systematic experimentation but rather to innovatory programmes. Systematic experimentation only occurs when the conditions of an experimental approach are realised as nearly as possible, that is, operationalisation and specification of causal linkages (Rivlin, 1971). Attempts at realisation of these conditions suggest that a number of problems will be associated with the empirical testing of social indicator models.

First, selection of a proper social indicator or set of indicators can be difficult. There may be a wide variety of output associated with a particular dependent variable. Even when a significant positive relationship is shown between an input and an output, it is often weak, and multiplying the number of indicators to have one check another is no real guarantee that each and every one is not a poor indicator (Bunge, 1975, p. 67). Social phenomena are complex and multidimensional and often a comprehensive range of indicators is necessary to reflect the quality of life in some subject area, or domain. All too often the necessary demographic data are simply unavailable – various government departments may not have the resources or the inclination to collect the kind of time-series data necessary for social indicator modelling. Departmental or institutional bias may distort data which may reflect quite different administrative needs, and the reinterpretation of data collected for one purpose is often not satisfactory when needed for different purposes, for example, administrative data for research purposes (Brewer, 1978–9, p. 165). At the extreme some argue that it is tautological for any institution's own data to be used in the construction of social indicators designed to evaluate that institution's performance (Hayden, 1977). This view ignores some of the realities of resource and data availability but does suggest the problem of value orientations which will be examined in the next chapter. Additionally, data may not be available at the proper geographical level of analysis – data on what is essentially a neighbourhood level social problem (e.g. vandalism) may only be available on a citywide basis.

The need for comprehensiveness and multidimensionality, and the often poor correlation between objective social indicators and individuals' perceived life quality, sometimes leads to the presentation of an unwieldy array of objective and subjective indicators within a simple model. In the abstract this approach is understandable but may lead to models so complex, and with so many assumptions, as to be untestable. The most practical approach is to define a manageable number of variables either from the onset or selected from the larger social indicator set. If one is mainly interested in prediction, factor analysing a somewhat larger set of indicators and using the resultant factor variables in a regression analysis is a useful technique (Van Meter and Asher, 1973). But if one is specifically interested in making causal statements, simple sets of indicators, while having lower predictive power, are conceptually clearer and more amenable to testing.

A second related difficulty is that the operationalisation condition of a scientific experimental approach requires quantitative measurement. But, as Brand (1975) has pointed out, it is illogical to believe that unquantifiable information is of less importance than that which can be quantified. For example, the value of a human life, the value of an ancient church, the value of 'peace and quiet', or the value of undisturbed countryside are notoriously difficult to measure, yet were important issues in debates over the location of the third London airport. Yet, the tendency will almost always be to rely on quantified data, indeed it is difficult to imagine not doing so, and especially where empirical testing of causation is the objective. In addition to being continually aware of the limitations of any quantitative approach, the solution to this problem lies in the increasing introduction of indirectly measurable subjective variables to quantitative data analysis. Blalock (1975, pp. 359–79), for example, argues that although this introduces additional unknowns into a causal system, those unknowns have always been implicitly present in any event. He suggests that careful conceptualisation of the causal relationships in a model before data collection commences is a necessary step in incorporating these subjective aspects. The policy-making importance of the quantitative/qualitative dichotomy is examined in Chapter 5.

A third problem is that hypothesis testing requires replication. This depends on stable operationalisation of the important variables – a situation which does not always hold in the social policy field where definitions and problem parameters may change rapidly. Also there will almost always be uncontrolled factors which will affect results, and ideally an experiment must be repeated a sufficient number of times to average out the effects of these uncontrolled elements. Isolation of programme variables from other external social effects may be difficult, however, and the broader the effects of the programme the more likely that external factors influence dependent variables. If the research is connected with the implementation of specific programmes it may be found that different administrators implement in different ways. The need to innovate or change social programmes to obtain better results while they are ongoing can make experiments unreliable. If administrators are convinced of the worth of a programme they may try to influence the research accordingly, or if otherwise, to hide the results. Proposals for experiments might be a means of achieving delay in instituting real policy action, and reports on unsuccessful projects may well be suppressed.

Further, to contribute to middle-range theory a social indicator model will have to define its boundaries so that it will be known to apply in specified environments and not in others. This boundary definition requires replication. Often, however, resource limitations, or a more policy-oriented role on the part of researchers (in local government departments, for example), does not permit replication of studies using social indicators and replication is therefore confined to the academic or research institute milieu. This understandable situation can be greatly improved, nevertheless, by increasing the opportunity for replication in each study by explicit conceptualisa-tion and mathematical formulation where possible, even if testing of the model is not likely to take place. This enhances the chances that critical examination of policy-oriented social indicator research will occur in those suitable academic environments by making it that much easier to grasp the intent and the assumptions that might be tested. This precise conceptualisation also facilitates the making of connections among diverse pieces of work. The interaction between the practical policy-oriented sector and the theoretical-academic one is a necessary development in social indicator research.

Fourthly, there are time-horizon problems – an area especially important for social indicators in that the most valuable definitions call for indicators to demonstrate a historical pattern of timing and co-variation with social change (Land, 1975a). There may be conflict, however, between the desire for valid, reliable results which require long periods of research, and the equally urgent need to obtain results quickly and at a low cost for administrators. The interesting effects of various inputs into social programmes may show up only after a number of years or even decades. For example, inputs to education or family assistance programmes may have long-lasting effects that are only wholly apparent in later stages of an individual's life-cycle. Problems arise because many research efforts are short-term, often due to funding restrictions. Further, government policy-making, especially for innovative programmes, usually requires a fairly quick feed-back of results in an evaluative mode. Social problems like poor schools, or deprivation of inner city residents, demand that politicians evaluate proposed solutions and active programmes over a short period and with an eye towards their political acceptability. This situation does not lend itself to the stability most advantageous to social indicator research. It is, however, the reality of the situation and again part of the resolution to the dilemma lies in the type of explicit conceptualisation mentioned above.

Further improvements may be achieved when data collection techniques are geared to the needs of predictive and causal research using time-series data. Recently governments are recognising that their traditional role of collecting time-series economic and demographic data should be expanded into other 'social' areas. The task is for the researchers to ensure that the measurement system for social variables is constant and rigorous enough to be of use in the co-variation analysis and predictive time-series analysis necessary to validate social indicators and make them useful for developing social policy models. These problems of indicator selection, quantification, replication and time-horizon are not insurmountable. But they do make movement along the continuum from explanatory model to middle-range social theory difficult, and no doubt account for some of the lack of activity in this area. These problems must be addressed in attempts to construct and test models relating indicators to phenomena.

Difficulties associated with aggregation

Social indicators are sometimes differentiated from other social statistics by the fact that they involve some combination of two or more simple indicators within a model. It is argued that this type of composite index is more useful than a host of individual indicators. This might be the case, for example, where one wished to measure housing quality and so combined measures of dilapidation with measures of overcrowding. A composite index requires that unlike measures can be transformed into a common scale so they can be added together. This procedure is sometimes followed by a 'value-weighting' of indicators in an attempt to express the differential contribution of each indicator within the composite indicator either to general quality of life or to a specific domain of life quality, like housing.

There are difficulties associated with aggregation of indicators and with the choice of a weighting scheme. If no differential weighting scheme is used, that is, each indicator is equally weighted, the prior choice of indicators becomes all-important and this, in effect, simply transfers the value-weighting to the choice of indicators (Craig and Driver, 1972). For example, Little and Mabey (1972) in their attempt to designate Educational Priority Areas in the UK found that the weighting schemes they tried were inadequate and opted instead for equal unweighted indicators. If some arithmetical scheme is developed for weighting it will have to presuppose a model of social behaviour which assumes that its components are additive. This might be the case in the housing quality example above, but not the case, for example, for measures of health status and social mobility which if simply combined might result in a meaningless index. Nor would it necessarily be the case for many combinations of social effects. Approaches such as principal component analysis, summing rank scores, or transformation to normal standard form face difficulties because the weights implicit in these methods do not necessarily have any relationship to the weights which individuals would ascribe to them (Holterman, 1975, p. 34). Those relationships can only come from a presupposed social model. Other weighting schemes are based on administrative or expert opinion, perhaps gathered by methods akin to the Delphi technique. This again involves some presupposed model, if only implicitly on the part of the 'experts'.

In the preceding section we noted that the empirical testing of the relationship of a single indicator to some social phenomena presents a number of difficulties. Even leaving the problem of value-orientation aside for a moment, the introduction of composite indicators or weighting schemes complicates the situation further. Figure 4.1 outlines this. A model of the relationship between phenomenon a_1 and a single indicator x_1 can be put forward for testing and will face the problems of indicator selection, quantification, replication and time-horizon. A more complicated model of the relationship between phenomena a_1, a_2 and some composite indicator y_1 (the sum of normalised x_1, x_2) can also be put forward and will face all the same problems as the first model plus the further difficulty that it must be proven that summing x_1 and x_2 provides a meaningful measure, that is, that the relationship between a_1, a_2 and y_1 is the sum of unweighted x_1 plus x_2 and not something else. Further complexity is introduced when some weighting formulas are put into the model to be applied to indicator x_1, x_2 to give a weighted composite indicator y_2. These weighted formulas, in fact, constitute an additional model in themselves which sets out some relationship between indicators x_1, x_2 and weighted indicators wx_1, wx_2. This model presupposes or has established that the weighting formulas hold true. Thus the aggregation and weighting of social indicators is also an aggregation of causal models and the level of difficulty rises accordingly.

Phenomenon	Single indicator	Weighted indicator
a_1	x_1	wx_1
a_2	$\dfrac{x_2}{\Sigma = y_1}$	$\dfrac{wx_2}{\Sigma = y_2}$
	Composite non-weighted indicator	Composite weighted indicator

Figure 4.1   *Possibilities for aggregation of social indicators.*

These methodological problems associated with aggregation are underpinned by the difficult question of whose values are input into the value-weighting scheme. Although research utilising social indicators, especially in conjunction with high-powered statistical techniques, often has the appearance of value-free objectivity, this is obviously not the case and there is considerable contention over these issues. The impact of value-influence is best handled by recognition that the process of indicator selection and development of weighting schemes is a political action to be examined publicly, and by ensuring that a diversity of value-orientations is represented in the process. Explicit research formulation in a causal manner will aid in identifying the values associated with indicator selection. Weighting schemes can be based on the preferences of individuals and institutions concerned with the particular area of life quality under consideration, perhaps by way of sample survey. This would probably be the most acceptable means of developing a weighting scheme in that it could provide empirical data with which to begin testing the presupposed weighting model. The policy issues surrounding aggregation and value-weighting are taken up in Chapter 5.

The problems associated with aggregation of indicators are numerous. This is not, however, to argue against aggregation or value-weighting in principle. Rather, it is to suggest that unless one is aware of the values and the complexity inherent in the process one risks making naive assumptions about the validity of the resultant composite indicators. Further, if it is accepted that the avenue to social indicator development is the incremental building-up of tested simple models, then we must rigorously and clearly formulate those models.

A conceptual framework for social indicator research

Just as one can view social indicators in terms of the increasing level of aggregation, so another useful perception is in terms of dimensionality – that is, the number of discrete variables representing dimensions of human life considered in the research. Figure 4.2 summarises this situation where each vertical line represents a new level of dimensionality and each horizontal line represents a postulated cause-and-effect relationship between indicated phenomenon and indicator. Each horizontal line therefore implies a vertical one which in turn means the usual three elements of research necessary for hypothesis testing and validation: social theorising, modelling, and data collection and manipulation.

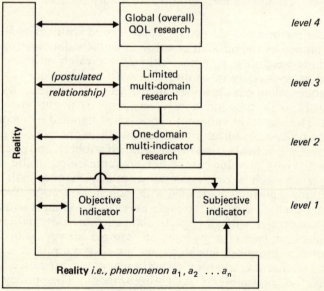

Figure 4.2　Simple conceptual framework of the levels in social indicator research.

At the first level we find research efforts directed towards refining those few single indicators which are deemed important by the policy process and which have a considerable perceived or apparent effect on the quality of life. These are usually simple demographic indices like the rate of unemployment, the divorce rate, the crime rate. These research efforts are directed towards first, understanding and refining the data collection and data manipulation procedures which these variables are based on, and secondly, attempting to isolate the endogenous variables from the effects of other social changes. For the crime rate, for example, it is often pointed out that changes in the rate can as easily be due to changed public attitudes to reporting crimes as to any real increase in crime. If police response to petty crimes is poor or uninterested, as it may be if they are short of resources, people may give up reporting those minor crimes. The quotation about Waco, Texas, which opened Chapter 1 is an extreme case, but the opposite effect is quite common: an improved crime-reporting system results in a rise in the crime rate. That rate, of course, reflects *reported* crimes, and not necessarily the true level of crime. Considerable ongoing research is necessary if the true meaning of the crime rate indicator is to be made clear to policy-makers.

There are virtually no subjective social indicators which are isolated in a similar fashion to the crime rate or unemployment rate unless one includes Gallup poll type questions usually commissioned by newspapers. With the exception therefore of a few important single indicators, most objective and subjective social phenomena are too complex to be summarised with a single indicator, and multiple indicator sets are required.

At the second level of dimensionality one finds important research in a single domain, utilising groups, or sets, of social indicators which attempt to reflect the multidimensionality of the domain. This type of research makes use of objective or subjective indicators, or both, and the domain may reflect an environmental context (e.g. housing), a social role (e.g. employment), or a personal characteristic (e.g. educational attainment) (Rodgers, 1977). The most common domain for study is health – examples include Culyer *et al*'s (1971) attempt to develop health status indices, Anderson's (1973) structural equation model of a health care delivery system and Evans and Chen's (1978) indicator set for comparing medical manpower and facility resources in different regions. Housing is the other common domain for this level of research – a good example is Dennis's (1978) examination of the use of certain housing indicators to define geographical areas suitable for a programme of house renovation grants and neighbourhood improvement. Single domain research generally tries to assess the worth of an indicator or set of indicators as a measure of social reality in the particular domain.

The third level of hypothesis testing and dimensionality consists of multi-indicator research across a limited number of domains. This may take the form of attempts to explain a variable in one domain in terms of changes in variables in other domains. An example of this type is Vigderhous and Fishman's (1978) research into social indicators of marital instability which set up a model to try to explain changes in divorce rates in terms of changes in certain demographic variables, unemployment and marriage rates. A different type of research at this level attempts to develop groups of social indicators which either allow social change to be monitored over time, or target indicators which help to delineate geographical areas or population subgroups for special policy intervention. An example of the former is 'socioeconomic accounts system' (SEAS) developed to provide community level information for planners, and described in the previous chapter. An example of a multi-domain target indicators set is Webber's (1977) system for classifying residential neighbourhoods in the UK, which is examined in Chapter 7.

Another type of multi-domain research at the third level is more aggregated and attempts to measure limited aspects of quality of life, usually for particular social groups. Ward (1980), for example, reviews a number of efforts to establish quality-of-life measures for elderly people in residential institutions. A last type of this level of research examines the relationship between objective and subjective measures of the same phenomenon – we have described a number of examples previously. This third level of research is proving to be a most promising one. Attempts at a lower level often suffer from cross-domain influences and interactions which are difficult to ignore, and attempts at the highest level prove either unwieldy if highly disaggregated or oversimplistic if aggregated.

The highest level of dimensionality in social indicator research, therefore, is the attempt to measure global (i.e. overall) quality of life across all the domains or life-concerns having important significant impact on human beings. A number of these research efforts concentrate solely on individual perceptions using subjective social indicators. These were described in Chapter 2 and their main value has been in determining important perceptions within domains, and relative intensity of feeling among domains, rather than actually measuring overall QOL. Others have limited their variables to objective indicators and again very little progress has been made towards any overall measure. On the contrary, the results of highly aggregated objective indicator QOL research have tended towards the ludicrous. We have noted the problems with Forrester's QOL index; later we will examine in some detail the problems with an attempt to measure overall QOL in American cities. Certainly at the present time this level of aggregation is proving virtually impossible to come to grips with – a not unsurprising situation given the relatively simple state of our abilities to do social modelling.

Summary and conclusion

The theoretical or formal approach to the development of social indicators advocated in this chapter can be described in the following steps:
(1) development of a problem statement or descriptive model;
(2) formulation of an explicit causal (explanatory) model in words and/or some type of diagram, for example, a path diagram;
(3) operationalisation, that is, the statement in measurable terms of the postulated relationships between social indicators and empirically derived variables, for example, in a system of equations;
(4) testing, and perhaps retesting, of the model.

This type of approach is the only one which will allow for the continued development and refinement of social indicators in aid of social theory. There are two additional benefits. First, this type of formulation provides greater power and precision than less rigorous forms of discourse and makes it easier to scrutinise for errors of reasoning. Secondly, this approach, by abstracting and simplifying basic concepts, provides a means of making connections between diverse pieces of research. This is important in the relatively new social indicator field where there is a plethora of overlapping definitions and imprecise terminology which makes it very difficult to relate research at one conceptual level (e.g. single-domain studies) to that at another (e.g. multi-domain quality-of-life models). If resource allocators and researchers are to benefit from one another's experiences only this type of formal approach can help search out the common lessons from problem situations which, at face value, appear unique but are perhaps much less so.

This formal causal approach should not be seen as a prescription but rather as a philosophy of approach. This is especially important in governmental departments and other research programmes which have immediate resource allocation implications, and are faced with time and budget constraints. In these cases there is no doubt that steps (3) and (4) above often will be difficult if not impossible. The precise statement of the problem and the formulation of a model are still of great value. The former will describe directly the resource allocation problem at hand and the latter, however simplistic, has value in its explicitness which allows others to grasp the nature of the important variables. In such situations thinking causally about a problem, and perhaps constructing a path diagram that reflects causal processes, will facilitate clearer, more rigorous statements and may generate additional insights into the problem. It also promotes the critical examination of policy-oriented social indicator studies in the academic environment. This can only be to the long-run benefit of policy-making and we will see in a later chapter how this interaction is occurring in the field of urban deprivation studies.

In summary, development of a social indicator science requires that concentration be on explanatory models of social subsystems and attendant indicators. These models should have operationalised concepts and causal relationships expressed in propositions which will be empirically tested to establish whether linkages exist between indicators and other unobservable variables. Although direct work on unified theory may have some value, progress will mainly be made by concentrating much attention on explanatory models which are at a low level of generalisation and thus close enough to reality to allow empirical testing to take place. In this way social indicator research will move by way of social experimentation incrementally away from simple time-series statistical description to explanatory models useful for analysing social causation and for predicting social change.

5

Social Indicators and the Policy-making Process

> The technical expert, in selecting the mix of variables for inclusion in the composite index, is usurping a political decision. Even if his decision is politically legitimated, the political choice later appears as a technical necessity and obtains a spurious objectivity.
>
> (Webber, 1975)

> There are no facts without theories and the only way a statistician can keep out of politics is to collect only irrelevant data.
>
> (de Neufville, 1975)

In the social indicator field the verifiable identification of causation and the development of reliable predictive capacity, although important, ultimately serve only a further step: the enlightenment of the policy-making process. The rise of the social indicator movement itself was to a great extent predicated on the belief that social science research could shed new light on previously shaded aspects of government social policy. The provision of such information was to result in better, more balanced decisions, closer in tune to an elusive social reality, and based more on fact and less on fancy, intuition, or hidden subjective judgements. In short, social measurement and especially social indicator research is at least partially based on a positivist orientation to decision-making which argues that policy-relevant information is always superior to poor information, or none. The word 'partially' needs to be stressed here, however, because such a positivist approach is at best a limited and incomplete reflection of the complexity of the policy-making process. Social indicators, if relevant to decisions, become by nature part of this policy-making process and this raises a host of political and bureaucratic problems at least as knotty as those of causality and prediction.

Who will use them?

A recurring theme in any discussion of the political usefulness of social measurements is the potential opposition to, or non-utilisation of, the research by politicians and bureaucrats alike. Sometimes resistance is based on the alienating effect of incomprehensible statistical jargon or on the sheer expense of providing sophisticated information and monitoring. These difficulties are relatively straightforward and the answers are fairly obvious. Many times though the situation is more complex. For elected representatives social indicator research may stir up waters better left calm and may provide uncomfortable material useful to opponents at the ever-near next election. Administrators are reasonably concerned with such things as keeping their jobs, getting promoted, increasing agency size, power and budget, and minimising organisational conflict, and may not see social indicators as serving any of these ends. And if social indicators are to be useful, they may have to be disaggregated and linked causally to specific programmes or administrative units within government. This move may well be resisted.

It is equally likely that there may be a direct relationship between agency performance and willingness to assist in data gathering, that is, the poorer the performance the more the resistance to measurement. And if inter-jurisdictional comparisons are intended, for example, among district councils in the UK, the fear is generated that the purpose of social indicators may simply be to provide a league table for the general public or for central government to monitor the spending of individual local governments (Capps, 1977). Even segments of the public themselves may resist social measurement. Little (1975) notes the resistance of the Italian community in the USA to demographic data on organised crime (i.e. the Mafia). In the UK the issue of whether to include questions on race in the 1981 Census generated considerable argument on both sides. Especially vociferous were those who argued that such questions were 'racist', and might be used by the government in a 'witch-hunt' against black immigrants.

Equally, social measurements of one sort or another are often used by opposing sides in vehement arguments about the future racial make-up of the population of Britain. This is an example of a warning Biderman (1966) gave, as far back as the Bauer-edited volume which more or less coined the term 'social indicators', that indicators could be used as 'vindicators' to prove preconceived notions of social health or malaise. In another example in the UK, the Thatcher government's new (1979) wages and prices index, called the 'standard of living index', is seen as a vindicator by the trade unions. This index takes into account recent cuts in direct taxation and thus will show a markedly lower inflation rate than the old retail price index, which only reflected indirect taxation. The Trades Union Congress argues, however, that these direct tax cuts are associated with public spending cutbacks resulting in reduced levels of public services which are not reflected in the new index, but do result in a real lowering of living standards, and thus the new measure is contrived to disguise the true picture. To further complicate the issue the trade unions feel that the development of the new index casts doubt on the non-political reputation of the Central Statistical Office which prepares it, thus confirming de Neufville's dictum that the only way a statistician can keep out of politics is to collect irrelevant data.

Brand (1975, p. 86) gives us a scenario of another kind of vindication which he describes as the fig leaf strategy of government:

> The procedure is simple and well known. When you are threatened by some unpleasant development, do a statistical appraisal of the situation. Unless you are extremely unlucky you will be able to get some figures which will justify you in doing what you were going to do anyway – often nothing. Even better, get someone in a university or research agency to do the study for you. You have a fair chance of knowing what he is going to say anyway so you can hand pick your chap and when he finally presents his report (usually two years late anyway, which is all to the good) it vindicates you.

Related to this is Henriot's (1970) important point about being careful that concentration on one set of problems, say, those of American blacks in inner city slums, should not obscure what may be other equally pressing social problems, for example, those of poor whites in Appalachia or native people in the western states. Henriot also warns that the social indicators movement tends to assume that contemporary social problems reflect a lack of information rather than diverging and conflicting values in society. Even more ominously, Miles (1978) warns that social statistics and indicators may hide the machinations of powerful interests and bureaucracies in society, possibly furthering their own ends at the expense of the less knowledgeable.

Accusations of quantificationism

Social indicator research is about operationalising social phenomena and many people equate such analysis with quantification. The policy issues and problems associated with quantified techniques are very contentious and there are numerous critiques of their use in government decision-making. Rittel and Webber (1973) suggest that the limitations of quantified analysis are due to the fact that policy problems are 'wicked' problems, which cannot be clearly defined and which exist in pluralistic societies which lack objective definitions of welfare and equity. For Strauch (1975) the difficulty with policy problems is that they are 'squishy', meaning that they are less amenable to quantitative-analytic technique than some analysts would like us to believe. Some authors suggest that advocates of increasing use of quantitative methodology are more concerned about the technical competence of their methodology than about the fit of the postulated model to the policy problem. This 'quantificationism' occurs in spite of the illogicality of allowing 'hard' quantitative data to drive out 'soft' qualitative data. The obvious cause of these events is that the measurement of quantities and changes in quantities is easy compared with measurement of qualities and changes in qualities and this difficulty is common to many analytic techniques which might make use of social indicators. For example, in cost-benefit analysis there is the problem of evaluating and pricing extra-market factors which are likely to be subordinated to those factors to which some market value can be ascribed. In environmental impact assessment it is the problem of the non-measurable value of amenities. And in social indicators itself it gives rise to the distinction between objective and subjective social indicators.

Even with those factors which are amenable to quantification there are numerous difficulties. First, many indicators are poor proxies for the phenomena they purport to reflect. Secondly, the phenomena they reflect often have unknown social determinants and consequences. Thirdly, if social indicators are to be aggregated in any way this requires that the diverse indicators be normalised, or related to some common denominators, so they can be compared and contrasted. One common method of doing this is to use monetary values, as in cost-benefit analysis, but of course there are many important factors which cannot be expressed in monetary terms, and indeed this is part of the reason for the rise of social indicators. Otherwise indicators must be value-weighted, explicitly or implicitly. If quantitative information is left unaggregated in its generic form, for example, traffic noise in a housing quality survey, then it is difficult to assess the meaning of a particular change in the indicator for the people involved. In locating a new highway, for example, how does one trade off two decibels of increased noise for x units of increased accessibility, especially when these impacts may accrue to different individuals? One could argue that such indicators are best left in a disaggregated format and there is a considerable case for doing so, but one must equally be aware of decision-makers' limited resources of time and their natural and quite understandable aversion to large digests of statistical information, that is, information overload.

Value-judgements and social indicators

There are two general types of value-judgement important in social indicator research. The first are value-judgements contained within, or integral to, the research itself and the second are those purposefully input to the research. Both are *de facto* value-weighting although only the latter is usually termed so. All value-weighting is potentially a 'political' activity.

One of the most common and telling criticisms of social indicators is that they posture under a guise of neutrality when in fact the value-sets and assumptions of the researchers tacitly guide both problem definition and analysis. This is often the result of dichotomisation of means and ends in policy-making – the making separate of the question 'what to do' from that of 'how to do it' and the resultant separation of the role of decision-maker from that of analyst. At the extreme this results in the case where the analyst is given the decision-maker-determined objectives and the 'facts' and expected to deliver the data which will decide the solution – black box optimality. Even in less extreme cases the value-laden aspects of the concepts and procedures of social indicators can be unpurposefully concealed and this helps foster the myth of value neutrality. This has caused some people to suggest that the notion of neutrality 'serves primarily as a cover-up to protect the social scientist from moral self-scrutiny and moral questioning by others' (Ladd, 1975, p. 180).

In fact in many cases social indicator research is imbued with cultural value assumptions, indeed whenever a social indicator is normative, that is, indicates some positive or negative change in a social phenomenon related to well-being, it is impossible that it be value-free. The difficulties of value-orientation have been identified, for example, in the use of social indicators in local urban deprivation studies in the UK and urban quality-of-life studies in the USA, and we will examine these in more detail in later chapters.

Even in the choice of the policy problem and the subsequent definition of that problem internal value-judgements can play a commanding role. In the choice of the policy problem it is almost always politicians or vocal or influential interests whose values prevail but in problem definition the social researcher may play an important role. For example, in the case of urban deprivation those who define the problem as substandard facilities have quite different value-sets from those who define it as one of inequality in society. These differing perspectives are often described as a 'cycle of poverty' orientation versus one of structural inequality, and association with one or the other often amounts to a virtual ideology. It is the case that politicians and researchers who share similar value-sets, or ideologies, will generally gravitate towards similar problem definitions and ultimately similar social policy arguments.

Finally, the very choice of one particular approach to social indicators over another is also value-laden, often implicitly. This can be for one or more of a number of reasons. First, the delineation of the particular policy options on which data is collected often reflects the combined value-sets of politician and researcher, as in the example of urban deprivation. Secondly, social measurement expends resources like time and money, and the very fact that measurement takes place implies that some importance has been attached to the measure. Often the selection of the particular indicators which serve to give dimension to the problem reflects a value-choice, often the researchers', as to which dimensions are important and which are not. In the urban deprivation example some researchers may therefore emphasise indicators of substandardness in housing, health service provision and recreational facilities, while others would emphasise indicators of income and inequality and unemployment. In research examining various systems of indicators for measuring urban quality of life, which is often attempted in the USA, Gehrmann (1978) notes that the result of the choice of a *particular* social indicator system can be wildly differing rankings of cities – as much as forty-five ranks out of sixty! This not only points up the necessity of being aware of how important indicator selection may be to the resultant policy analysis, but also suggests the futility of aggregation at the overall QOL level. Thirdly, if measurement levels in indicators are used as criteria for selection among alternative policy options this may also be value-laden. Nash *et al.* (1975, p. 84) argue that any selection criteria 'must reflect some value set . . . which determines what things are to count as benefits and costs and how they are traded off against each other'.

Value-judgement or ideology in social indicators is therefore inevitable and value neutrality impossible. This does not negate the value or necessity of social indicators but it does mean that it is essential that value-judgements be expected and made as explicit as possible in the analysis. The pretence (or the myth) of value-neutral objectivity must be actively discarded and the people best able to do this are social researchers themselves.

Social indicators and value-weighting schemes

Following the usual quantification of data in social indicator research comes the choice of whether to aggregate (or sum) the resultant data into simpler composite indicators or to leave it in an unaggregated form. The aggregation usually requires that unlike measures be transformed into a common scale so they can be added together, for example, in studies of housing quality which sum measures of dilapidation and overcrowding into a common indicator. This is sometimes followed by the development of a value-weighting scheme which attempts to express the differential contribution of each piece of data to some specific decision criteria or to the general quality of life of various groups of society. There is considerable divergency, however, among researcher and decision-makers as to the relative advantages and disadvantages of aggregation and value-weighting.

Some people are generally opposed to aggregation and their main argument is that it hides or loses information important to the decision process and may serve to obscure the strengths and weaknesses of various policy alternatives. Further, they argue that value-weighting all too often does not reflect the values of those persons who are most affected by the decisions. Knox (1978), for example, warns of the pitfalls of 'cultural imperialism' where the value-weighting represents an operational definition of some welfare concept reflecting the researcher's values rather than the values of those whose welfare is under consideration. Although this is a danger in most social science research, it becomes a critical issue where social indicators are used in resource allocation. This school of thought, tends to argue that value-weighting is best done, *post* analysis, by the politicians who, when presented with data important to a decision, make mental trade-offs among alternatives which reflect some sum of the value-judgements of their constituents.

Other researchers propose that aggregation without value-weighting avoids problems, that is, simply adding up the quantified measures converted to some common scale (money, units, etc.) without regard to value-judgements. In fact, as we have seen, this simply transfers the value-weighting to the choice of indicators and so the choice becomes all-important. Also such a scheme presupposes a model of social behaviour which says its components are additive. That might be the case in the housing quality example above, but not for other measures from development domains which if combined might give a meaningless indicator. Nor would it necessarily be the case for many combinations of social effects and so, in a number of cases, some form of value-weighting must accompany the aggregation. Those who support value-weighting argue, on the other hand, that a disaggregated analysis usually results in 'information overload' in the form of a welter of statistics and mountains of indigestible documentation. Further, since value-weighting is at least implicit in every policy analysis, they argue there is positive value in making the process explicit and thus exposing it to scrutiny and debate (Birch and Schmid, 1980). The key question in developing any such value-weighting scheme is of course 'whose values?'. Three answers are generally put forward: the politicians', the experts', or the public's.

Politicians' preferences

Value-weighting based on politicians' preferences take two forms. The first is to study past government decisions and, if consistent, to use the implicit revealed preferences in those decisions to impute value-weights. This has recently been done, for example, in a study of the closure of branch railroad lines by British Rail (Brent, 1979). The revealed preference approach argues that the appropriate source of the expression of such value-weights is within the political system and that such studies avoid all the problems associated with trying to get politicians to express preferences directly. This is seen as a useful means for the politician to come to grips with the weightings implicit in past decisions, to use them in all or part if thought satisfactory, or to change them in duration or magnitude in the future if they were wrong. The proponents of the revealed preference approach are quite ready to point out its main limitations: that it is a sufficient, but not necessary, explanation of past behaviour unless one assumes rationality and full information for decision-makers – a situation which patently does not exist. This causes value-weighting models based on revealed preferences to diverge from reality. However, all models diverge from reality and the approach gives a valid, but partial, perspective on policy problems, especially if similar situations are to occur in the future and the preferences revealed demonstrate a consistent pattern in decision-making. British Rail, for example, may intend more branch line closures in the 1980s and this study may well help reveal underlying and more specific criteria for decisions than are normally available for public consumption.

A second way of dealing with the politicians' preferences is, of course, to ask them, and then to operate on the assumption that their preferences reflect some democratic mix of their constituents' values. For example, one recent proposal suggested that various combinations of programme outputs could be ranked by asking politicians to put their selected units of output in rank order (Schmid, 1975). The methodology of 'asking' is much the same for politicians as it is for experts and involves either more or less rigorous straight-forward interviews or the establishment of some panel of value-judgers. For example, one proposal for assessing environmental impact suggested the formation of a weighting panel which would include representatives of government, industry, public interest groups, community organisations and other parties potentially affected by the outcome of the assessment (Sondheim, 1978).

Sometimes social indicators are value-weighted by using the Delphi technique, which is basically iterative polling of politicians or experts, with feedback. This involves a group of anonymous persons who are interviewed in two or more rounds, and in each round are presented with the cumulative results of the previous round and asked if they would alter their projections accordingly. Anonymity is used to avoid psychological and personality problems of group interaction which may hinder face-to-face dynamics, for example, domination of a value-weighting scheme by a strong personality or a leading reputation. As the rounds progress the panel's membership, which may number seven to a hundred or more, are expected to consider the degree their weights differ from group consensus and to revise the estimates they choose. In this way, a consensus of opinion arises.

Studies of the usefulness and validity of Delphi-generated weights are conflicting. Some suggest that Delphi does produce reasonable weightings which stand up to *de post facto* analysis, and that different panels produce similar results (Ament, 1970). Others decry Delphi's lack of a theoretical base or criticise it on political grounds. Bisset (1978, p. 53), for example, says, 'averaging the implicit weightings of a group of experts is not satisfactory unless it can be demonstrated that such value judgements meet with popular approval'. Sackman (1976), in a study for the Rand Corporation where Delphi was first developed, finds that Delphi is not empirically linked to objective and independently verifiable external validation criteria. He suggests Delphi be replaced by rigorous questionnaire techniques. Probably the biggest limitation to Delphi is the fact that the consensus of opinion is reached not by a comparison of arguments of substance but due to whatever personality factors cause one sort of individual to hold his ground and another to compromise (Fowles, 1976). Both Delphi and rigorously designed questionnaires, however, probably do offer another valid, if partial, approach to structuring value-weighting schemes, as long as their underlying assumptions and methodological limitations are made explicit.

Expert opinion

Although asking politicians to value-weight social indicators seems reasonable as they do so implicitly in any event, reliance on so-called 'expert' opinion is easily and probably fashionably dismissed as undemocratic. Nevertheless, there are issues in which value-weightings based on estimation by professionals, administrators and others with experience in a given area are useful. These issues are of fairly specific scale and involve those policy problems in which value-judgements, attitudes and social relations play a minimal role. For example, the detailed and fairly routine planning problems pursuant to more general policies, like minimum standards for public provision of correctional facilities or physical infrastructure in a new town design, can often be weighted by professional opinion without any great danger to democratic principle. This is not true of more strategic level policy problems where value-judgements constitute one of the main criteria for choice. For example, a decision about whether to build a resource-based new town or expand an existing town is hardly a technical decision. Expert opinion is also not very useful whenever there is likely to be a strong divergence of opinion over a social issue. Research in the UK, for example, shows that criteria used by 'experts' to delineate areas for special housing programmes in urban areas were arbitrary and inadequate from the residents' point of view. The question of what constitutes housing dilapidation is obviously contentious, especially in the face of the threat of wholesale 'urban renewal' (Dennis, 1978).

Public preferences
In a recent essay, Tribe (1976) takes the view that the *process* of policy-making is at least as important as the result itself. In other words, not only must justice be done, it must be seen to be done. Sometimes useful value-weights for social indicators come from politicians and experts. There are many cases when this is insufficient, however, and the preferences of the public, or some segment of it, must be surveyed as part of the analysis. In recent years there has been a growing trend towards developing public participation in governmental decision-making and one has to look at the interest in road-building schemes, or applications for new power stations, dams, coalmines, or other environmental changes to see this demonstrated. Such value-weighting based on the surveyed preferences of some sample of the public finds favour in a variety of disciplines concerned with policy-making. Dissenting voices tend to be those who are critical of any weighting scheme and who feel that complete disaggregation is the only honest approach to indicator presentation. However, even highly disaggregated survey data may be of considerable value to policy-makers, and such surveys can provide a reasonable base of empirical data with which to begin testing the presupposed value-weighting model.

Survey approaches to value-weighting often form part of a public participation exercise which includes publicising and interaction among analysts, administrators and the public. The information collected as a result of a public participation exercise can be used to value-weight in two ways. First, some analysts argue that such data, sometimes used in conjunction with expert opinion, can directly structure an explicit mathematical weighting scheme which in turn is applied to objective data (Gordon and Niedercorn, 1978). Although such an approach runs the risk of making unsupportable causal assumptions and assuming a monolithic public instead of one made up of diverse and competing groups, it cannot be dismissed out of hand. For although it is no doubt wise to be wary of those who would quantify the unquantifiable, it is unwise to avoid quantifying the quantifiable. Rank-ordering is certainly possible and, as in the technique of planning balance sheet analysis, weights can be associated with different sectors of the public (Lichfield *et al.*, 1975). This is best done in the framework of a *sensitivity analysis* which establishes upper and lower boundaries for the value-weights and then demonstrates the 'robustness' of different policy options to changes in the weighting scheme. If small changes in value-weights result in an altered ranking of options then it is wise to be very cautious in the application of the weighting scheme.

Another approach to using survey data is to provide it as a complement to the social indicators in the analysis and allow the two kinds of information to be synthesised by the decision-maker. This indirect approach avoids many theoretical problems but does carry with it the danger that the decision-maker will ignore the information or do the synthesis badly. That, however, is the stuff of political debate and if this seems the best approach the researcher can only exhort that all the relevant opinions be considered.

In either case measuring public preferences may prove difficult, but the importance of doing so cannot be underrated and the methodology is steadily improving. The simple surveys of straight-forward questions, which suffer from problems such as respondents' strategic behaviour, are now superseded by survey formats using the Likert scale of measuring respondents' satisfactions–dissatisfactions on a five or seven point continuum. This gives a relative intensity of preferences if not interval scales. Other techniques are being developed which may yield interval data, distinguish between personal judgements and judgements about a wider community, and force the respondent to consider costs and benefits at the same time –a problem for simpler surveys. Techniques such as 'budget pies' for assessing citizen preferences in US urban expenditure (Clark, 1974) or the use of priority evaluation games in the UK for evaluating preferences in environmental and transport planning may well be expanded to other social indicator fields (Hoinville and Courtenay, 1979). These techniques give each respondent a limited amount of 'resources' which can be 'spent' on a variety of alternative service mixes. A priority evaluation scheme was recently used by London Transport as part of its planning for the rejuvenation of underground stations (Woudhuyson and Law, 1979).

Where active public participation is not feasible, subjective social indicator data may provide important policy information. This may serve to alert policy-makers to attitudinal changes which presage actual social change (for example, dissatisfaction with public transport provision leading to increased auto usage) and to make civil servants more accountable by citizen evaluation of services.

Although citizen perceptions of poor services may not correspond with the actual service level, such information may serve as a useful 'litmus' or warning sign of something amiss between citizen and government. And a well-designed survey of subjective indicators can reveal the diversity of opinion about a policy issue, rather than simply the opinion of the articulate in society.

Where public participation may be useful for value-weighting it must be actively promoted by those administrators and policy-analysts who hope to realise its value, and such promotion includes providing reasonable access to information at a *useful* time in the policy process. The value of public participation is that it provides information essential for the clarification of most policy problems, and increases the incentives for the public to co-operate with, and appreciate, the policy process. The quality of the information collected, and the level of appreciation of the policy process by citizens, will be proportional to the amount of publicising and inter-action which occurs. That is, participation is based on sharing information, which in turn really means sharing power. Unfortunate-ly, some governmental bodies may well resist public participation for this reason. The links between publicising and education, and the quality of information collected, are nevertheless quite clear (Vauzelles-Barbier, 1978).

Value-weighting and distributional equity

One of the most contentious issues in policy analysis may be the role of distributional equity – whether 'who gets what' should structure the value-weighting scheme and thus explicitly influence the analysts' recommendations as to which policy option is preferable. The issue, like many, first arose in relation to the use of cost-benefit analysis (CBA) and the arguments, although less well defined, are generally mirrored in the other areas of policy analysis.

Social researchers generally fall into three schools on the issue. The first argues that analysts should remain silent with regard to the distribution of wealth in society. The argument is not that questions of distributional equity are unimportant, but that all distributional value-weighting should be done *post* analysis by politicians. And since value-weighting requires interpersonal comparisons of utility which can only be highly inaccurate, to engage in such an activity is to confuse clients of policy advice or to lend spurious scientific authority to personal prejudices. Other perceived dangers of explicit value-weighting are (1) the risk that numerical value-weights are determined by non-representative bodies, for example, bureaucrats masquerading as responsible policy-makers, and (2) that such value-weights can and would vary not only from region to region but from time to time according to changing power structure and political fashion (Mishan, 1974).

An increasing number of researchers, and many in the social indicators field, now argue, however, that redistributive effects are an important policy consideration. Little and Mirrlees (1974, p. 53), for example, say:

> The argument that the project evaluator, if he be a civil servant, should take the existing distribution of income or wealth as ideal (implying that he need not 'weight' the consumption of different income groups differently), on the grounds that the government has the power to make it what it likes through other measures, principally taxation, does not hold water.

Analysts of this school recognise that the weighting of indicators according to some judgement about justice or equity is implicit or explicit in any policy decision, and the analyst can aid the decision-maker by considering the social welfare implications of a variety of distribution weights.

Finally, a last small school take an overtly value-laden stance to distributional equity. Among these are analysts who accept the existing distribution of income and the concept that the market alone can determine value through prices. Others reject this possibility in its entirety in that their value-judgements on distributional equity are quite different from, for example, those who have a Marxist perspective on economics. Also in this school are those analysts who argue for a particular distributional arrangement. Their recommendations are often based on research organised to sustain their particular political viewpoint.

Of these schools of thought on value-weighting and equity the second is most practical, but any attempt to value-weight by distributional equity criteria, however laudatory, does face problems. Firstly, any redistribution may involve administrative and information costs which have to be considered in the analysis. Secondly, identifying exactly who benefits and who bears the costs of government decisions may be difficult, especially for the costs. And it is quite possible for any one person to benefit and bear costs from the same project, for example, a person who flies a lot and lives near a noisy airport. Thirdly, interpersonal comparisons are fraught with difficulty – a new motorway can be a benefit to a commuter and a cost to his home-working next-door neighbour. Fourthly, what economists term the marginal level of utility may vary according to income level, that is, a pound to a poor man is worth more than a pound to a rich man. Fifthly, substantial external effects, like pollution, may make it difficult to identify distributional effects.

Lastly, any incorporation of distributional weights by researchers might be viewed as an attempt to usurp decision-makers' political power.

The elements of policy-making

So the political problems and dangers associated with social indicators will exceed the already complex ones relating to causality and prediction. The latter are amenable to the development of social indicator models, but the former require that social indicators be incorporated into models of the policy-making process. The failure of social indicators quickly to meet the level of the expectations raised in the 1960s and early 1970s was due both to an underestimation of the methodological difficulties to be faced and to an over-simplification of the reality of the policy process. This policy process has been discussed in detail by this author elsewhere (Carley, 1980), but it is useful to summarise that conception in terms of social indicators because it deals with important aspects integral to any policy-making mode. The policy-making process can be viewed as consisting of three major elements: value conflict and resolution or 'politics', bureaucratic maintenance and promotion, and analytic rationality; and three activities: policy analysis, decision-making, and implementation. A look at each element in turn throws light on the nature of policy-making and the relationship of social indicators to that process.

The value-conflictive element in policy-making involves the promotion of values related to a multiplicity of goals and objectives. This value promotion is the natural human result of a diversity of value-judgements in society on the means to, and the ends of, 'a better life'. The tools of this process are activities like negotiation, bargaining and partisan mutual adjustment, and it is manifested in many ways such as debates in Parliament or Congress, pronouncements by politicians, in-fighting in Cabinet, public hearings, and a host of other activities which are the tangible aspects of politics as perceived by many people. This societal process has as its goal the allocation of resources according to some form of resolution of conflict which may take the form of satisfactorily completed bargaining or power-wielding. The topics of the conflicts themselves are usually more concerned with matters of distributional equity rather than allocative efficiency, that is, deciding 'who gets what' in society, rather than how most efficiently to provide the 'what'. This value conflict is a dominant element in policy-making and I will return to it shortly.

The second important element of policy-making is the administrative or bureaucratic. This includes routinised activities, which are those employed for the purpose of simplifying the decision environment and avoiding conflict in the policy process by means of a series of standardised procedures and criteria for dealing with policy questions (Fry and Tompkins, 1978). This process is not necessarily purposive in nature – actions and small decisions may accumulate to result in resource allocation by the workings of the bureaucratic process. The development and utilisation of social indicators by this bureaucracy may be suppressed at the one extreme, and manipulated or perverted at the other, to serve any of the agency's own multi-functional objectives and tasks like co-ordination of organisational sub-units, maintenance or acquisition of new resources or power, career promotion, or adaptation in some way to the external environment. Caplan and Barton (1978, p. 446) describe this situation in terms of an organisation's 'information policy' taking precedence over the substantive content or significance of the information.

It is also within the bounds of the bureaucratic element that implementation of programmes and decisions takes place. Policy-making is not a linear process leading from problem formulation to decision to solution, although some simplifying models may conceptualise it in that manner. Rather it is an iterative process in which tentative solutions based on particular value-sets cause reformulation of the original problem definition and the data needs for meeting that problem. An understanding of these iterative workings of the bureaucracy is important to a grasp of the role of social indicators in decision-making and implementation.

The third distinctive element of policy-making is the application of analytic rationality, or social scientific method, to resource allocation decisions. This is reflected in the emerging field of policy analysis and in the development of a number of rational techniques ranging from cost-benefit analysis to evaluation research – all of which can and do make use of social indicators. All rational analyses, as an idea or a model of behaviour, have in common a process which involves some statement of goals or objectives relative to a policy problem in idealised or conceptual terms, followed by a restating of these in operationally measured terms. This operationalisation is of course at the heart of social indicator models. In analytic rationality consideration may then be given to mixes of various alternatives which fulfil the objectives or 'solve' the problem. This in turn may be followed by the development of some value-weighting scheme which reflects judgements about the comparative importance of progress towards objectives. This process is based on the 'rational man' model of welfare economics and systems analysis and probably arose in reaction to government in which decisions were perceived as overly dependent on political and bureaucratic factors in the face of increasingly complex policy problems. Whatever the reason, we have seen that value-weighting involves the interjection of politically formed value-judgements into the analysis, for example, in the selection of some social indicators over others. It is at this point that the distinction between the value-conflictive and the rational elements of policy-making begins to blur because the application of value-weighting schemes is a political activity, although some would treat it as only a technical activity.

Unlike the political element of policy-making, analytic methods have been basically concerned with allocative efficiency rather than distributional equity. They first tended towards optimisation, that is, they treated resource allocations as problems with a single solution. When this stance proved impossible to maintain, the orientation moved towards what Simon (1957) called 'satisficing', that is, not searching for a single optimal policy alternative, but attempting to identify an acceptable, sub-optimal solution, for example, in measuring performance in the delivery of urban services. The most recent analytic techniques are those which are more concerned with problem clarification than either optimising or satisficing. Social impact assessments, which make use of many social indicators, are an example of this approach. To an extent these 'problem clarification' techniques have arisen as a reaction against overemphasis on allocative efficiency at the expense of distributional equity.

Most policy decisions are formed from some mix of the value-conflictive, bureaucratic and analytic elements of the policy-making process and the mix varies according to the nature and scale of the policy problem at hand. A worthwhile perspective on the role of social indicators in policy-making requires an understanding of the importance of integrating their inherently rational approach with the overriding value-judgemental aspects of any policy problem – overriding because social indicators only take on policy meaning when weighted values are ascribed to them. This perspective also requires that due regard be given to the scale of the policy problem because the ability of analytic rationality to approximate or model social reality tends to decrease as problem scale increases.

Academic research and policy analysis

Social indicator research tends to be either academic, that is, take place in universities, or policy-analytic, that is, be done in or at the bequest of government departments. Academic research, or discipline research, is an endeavour pursued by an independent investigator who is free to choose the set of values which will be applicable in the research and who is usually divorced from the decision-making process (Reynolds, 1975). The academic researcher is often concerned with research quality and the pursuit of knowledge for its own sake. The policy analyst, on the other hand, is usually working directly or indirectly for government or private institutions interested in enlightening or influencing decision-making, and he must be very careful and explicit about what value and whose values are injected into the analytic process. Other characteristics of policy analysis as identified by Coleman (1972) are (1) an audience of political actors, (2) short-term satisfaction of information needs and (3) an ultimate product which is designed to influence policy rather than contribute to existing knowledge. These 'action-oriented' principles clearly distinguish policy analysis from its academically oriented kin, which usually has more general or indirect effects on decision-making and implementation. Policy analysis, on the other hand, is intended directly to affect decision-making, and it is the means by which the element of analytic rationality is conveyed into policy decisions. But the elements of value conflict and bureaucratic maintenance have equally direct effects on decision-making and cannot be ignored. Now it is in the nature of policy analysis to tend towards the orderly, the systematic and the quantitative, especially when faced with an exceedingly complex modern reality. But policy analysis which oversubscribes to rationality or undervalues the value-conflictive and bureaucratic elements in policy-making will be poor policy analysis because it will be based on a model which will be overly divergent from social reality.

Also, the activity of policy implementation has been ignored for the sake of simplifying the argument here, but in fact its importance is not to be underestimated. On the contrary, it is not unusual to see top level political initiative, coupled with the most rational of forward plans based on extensive analysis, grind to a dead halt by failure to come to terms with the bureaucratic aspects of a particular policy. Study of this administrative aspect of policy-making, especially implementation research, is a vital subject in its own right and much work needs to be done to understand the concept of a bureaucratic information policy and the relationship of social indicators to that policy.

Finally, academic research and policy analysis exist in a symbiotic relationship – good policy analysis is predicted on a theoretical base provided by academic researchers, which in turn justifies itself by its relevance to policy analysis and ultimately the process of government. This is readily apparent in the social indicator field. In the UK, for example, the use of somewhat arbitrary collections of social indicators to locate specific geographical areas of poverty or deprivation for special resource allocation has been examined and found wanting by a number of academic researchers (Dennis, 1978; Brindley and Raine, 1979). This research not only contributed to our knowledge about the spatial orientation (or lack of it) of poverty but had far-reaching policy implications, in that a number of such programmes (examined in Chapter 7) were reconsidered. Similarly, in the USA the incautious acceptance of subjective social indicators as direct measures of urban service quality is questioned by Stipak (1979a) who points out that higher levels of perceived performance do not necessarily imply higher levels of service delivery. Clearly, then, useful policy analysis is related to good discipline research, even if the parameters which define them differ.

Overcoming political dilemmas

Aside from promoting interaction between academic researchers and policy analysts, what are the other possibilities for overcoming some of these political dilemmas? For the policy analyst, one of the main responses to the general problems of quantification and value-weighting has been the development of subjective social indicators used in various forms of indifference analysis. Such an approach supposes that individuals can differentiate, or preference-rank, between combinations of alternatives that yield greater or lesser satisfaction to them, and that it is unnecessary that they be able to measure this exact difference. In this way subjective rankings can substitute for objective measures where they are impossible to obtain. These preference-rankings are usually based on the preferences of politicians, experts, or some sample of the public at large and, although these rankings cannot be aggregated with any other data, they do illuminate aspects of the policy problem which might otherwise go unexamined, and offer some guidance as to the nature of the trade-offs that might be made. Some authors, for example, have argued that the most important use for social indicators is determining the subjective alterations in people's perception of quality-of-life changes due to government activity (Moffat and Reid, 1976). This is a worthwhile goal for some research and there is no doubt that objective-only data can mask serious deficiencies in programmes. For example, the number of amenities in child care homes may be of no great interest if the young residents are highly dissatisfied with staff attitudes. It seems that a number of subjective indicator research efforts might be more relevant if they were more directly linked with policy issues.

At the same time it pays to be wary of an overcommitment to satisfaction measures. Brand (1975) notes that a satisfied society is not necessarily a worthwhile goal for government and suggests that Germans in 1938 would probably have been more satisfied with their society than in 1932, but that this meant virtually nothing. Research by Buttel et al. (1977) has demonstrated that satisfaction levels measured by the common Likert-type scales may reflect respondents' pre-existing ideological orientation and the level of their ideological integration into society more than anything else. Perceived well-being, therefore, may be dependent on ideological stance which may or may not in turn reflect personal or local dissatisfaction. While such research does not prove that direct measures of well-being are inadequate it does suggest that considerations of political and/or class structure may be important to assessments of the policy relevance of subjective social indicators.

Aside from these subjective indicators, another way of structuring social indicators may be to use sensitivity analysis to establish upper and lower, and best and worst, bounds for hard-to-quantify impacts and then to demonstrate the effects of various courses of action on the alternative policy outcomes. For example, people being questioned about some preferred residential density/neighbourhood amenity trade-off would be unlikely to specify some optimum mix but might quite easily specify a range of acceptable mixes which in turn could help generate alternative planning options. Such use of sensitivity analysis might serve to bring more qualitative impacts into an analytic framework, although there has been little research to date on this in the social indicator field.

Finally, the myth of value neutrality can be laid to rest by, first, promoting communication between researchers and decision-makers to break down as much as possible the means/end dichotomy and encourage understanding of the values *and* limitations of quantitative analysis. This requires that social indicator researchers be explicit about the applicability of quantifiable data to particular policy problems, some of which may be quite amenable to quantitative analysis while others are not at all. This explicitness is crucial in cases where unmeasurable data is of paramount importance because it will mean the researcher will have to be content with weak inferences and suggestions rather than any determinant propositions. In other words, when the amount of uncertainty which unmeasurable aspects introduce into the analytic model means that no clear statement about a policy problem can be made from a quantitative perspective, it is the researcher's responsibility to state this explicitly.

Secondly, a kind of intellectual pluralism needs to be institutionalised alongside any quantitative research (Kramer, 1975). This entails formalised debate among different researchers and between researcher and those with other, differing, limited perspectives on the problem at hand. This debate would be fruitful in promoting synthesis among policy actors to a decision, for example, in a particular government department.

Thirdly, institutional or 'task responsibility' must be

complemented by a moral responsibility on the part of the researchers (and those who would make use of their services) to make explicit the value-judgements within the research (Ladd, 1975). This moral responsibility cannot be abrogated by someone else's responsibility: one cannot say, 'it is the politicians' job to point out the value-judgements in social indicators, not mine'. On the other side of the coin the role of the researcher should not be limited to that of technician, but should also be that of an interested party involved in other aspects of the decision-making process so as to become as sensitive as possible to the nature of that process. Meltsner (1976, p. 269), for example, argues that:

> analysts should be encouraged to consider implementation concerns when defining the problem and presenting their recommendations. It is not enough to determine . . . what to do, analysts should also get into the business of how to do it. I realise that our current dearth of knowledge about implementation makes this rather empty advice, but at least it pushes us in an appropriate direction.

In this vein it is important that the analyst attend crucial meetings related to the proposed policy change, make recommendations at a hierarchical level appropriate to the level at which implementation will take place, and foster co-operation among the various interested administrators.

A call for more policy-modelling

The necessary model-building which must complement policy analysis takes two forms. First, social indicator models promote identification of causality and improve predictive capacity. This is obvious and there are a number of good examples in the literature, for example, Goodman (1978) on housing quality, and Land and Felson (1977) on the relationship between marriage, family and population change. The second type of model, the social policy model, considers value conflict and/or bureaucratic elements in its conception. These are uncommon. Miller (1979), for example, berates social scientists for their apparent inability or unwillingness to do policy-relevant research which includes formulation of the social problem in such a manner that relational statements can be controverted by evidence. He goes on to propose a conceptual scheme for policy-oriented research which distinguishes policy-manipulable variables from non-manipulable structural variables, and relates them in a specified model which is in turn related causally to a target variable. This echoes earlier arguments by Shonfield (1972), who pointed out that the reason economics has a policy advantage over other social sciences is that it works with *manageable* aggregates of social data, where 'manageable' means information which a practical man can use to influence some segment of the social system.

Davies and Knapp (1980) take this further in their proposal for a 'production of welfare' approach to social service modelling which relates indicators of need, objectives and varying levels of inputs to outputs in the provision of services. The inputs include both (1) resource (e.g. staff numbers) and (2) non-resource factors (e.g. staff attitudes). The outputs are reflective of both (1) psychological well-being and (2) costed welfare consequences. Causal linkages in this model may run both ways, true output rather than intermediate output indicators are used where possible, and special attention is given to the complex relationships which may exist between dependent variables and the external policy environment. Like Miller, Davies and Knapp stress a focus on resource inputs which are controllable by decision-makers, and they argue that theoretical models which do not have such an emphasis are less practically useful to policy decisions. The level of aggregation of resource inputs which social indicator researchers seek to generalise about should also correspond to practical alternatives for management. Non-resource inputs are not ignored, however, as the effects of variations in resource inputs on outputs may be correlated to simultaneous variations in non-resource inputs. For example, a minimum level of resource input may be a prerequisite for a strong effect on output by some non-resource inputs. Davies and Knapp apply their theoretical approach to the study of the outputs of residential homes for the elderly.

With a few exceptions, however, there has been a lack of policy-modelling in the social indicator field. This has hindered its development and its acceptance by those who might be expected to make the most use of social indicators – politicians and especially administrators. One reason for this lack of acceptance, identified empirically by Caplan and Barton (1978), is insufficient power – a problem of unstudied causation and poor predictive capacity. Another, however, is the general failure to relate social indicator research to the determinants of information policy in decision-making structures.

Given that organisations which might use social indicators are multi-functional units with tasks other than goal attainment (e.g. maintenance, growth and conflict resolution), a fruitful approach may be for researchers to integrate the measurement model of much social indicator research with one that identifies the dynamics within the organisation which contribute to task co-operation and goal attainment, and may foster willingness to develop reliable indicators.

Such a behavioural model concentrates on observable patterns of organisational interaction, the motives of participants and the collective purpose of the programme as manifested through organisational activity (Goldstein *et al.,* 1978). This is the emphasis of the proponents of implementation research who argue that 'how things get done' should be studied in a framework that takes as the basic unit of analysis individuals and groups working in an organisational context, where problems of the real world have to be matched to relatively fixed channels of action and information (Lewis and Flynn, 1979). The tools of such research include participant observation, interviewing, issue analysis and the use of such techniques as the repertory grid for studying the values, perceptions and beliefs of actors in government. Such an approach, however, does require additional resource expenditure and a considerable knowledge about the purposes, operating routines and personality interactions of the organisation.

A good example of the potential for structuring such an approach, although not directly concerned with information needs, is Coleman's (1973) proposal for a conceptual system for studying purposive action in bureaucracies or, as he puts it, the mathematics of social action. Such a study goes beyond a straightforward cause-and-effect relationship to consider the consequence for actors (say, administrators) of the effects of policy decisions or 'event outcomes'. In Coleman's system such political and bureaucratic activities as negotiation, obligation and trading are organised within a simple set of concepts: actors, events, control of actors over events, interest of actors in events. These in turn are operationalised in such quantities as: power of an actor in the system, interest of actor in event, final control over the event, and so on. Coleman goes on to suggest a mathematical framework for such a study of collective decision-making in a bureaucracy. We can note the similarity between Coleman's conception and that of Fox (1974) who proposes the study of a series of 'things' such as money, power and influence which are traded among actors. Where Coleman suggests the bureaucracy as the unit of analysis, Fox suggests community. In fact, given that social indicator research seems most useful to policy-makers in a format disaggregated to the programme level, it might be most beneficial if such models were constructed in single domains, like housing or health.

Although the difficulty of such modelling may be daunting, the concepts are of utmost interest. If research into such aspects of policy-making as implementation or knowledge utilisation is to move beyond the anecdotal, it is important that such attempts be made, even if only at a fairly specific or elementary level. As de Neufville noted in 1975 (p. 68), 'the "scientific" analysis of many social questions is still in its infancy, but that is no reason to proceed without models – we must make do with the best we can'. This is still true. The combination of the more rational, causal, goals-achievement models with such behavioural models may eventually help us understand and resolve some of the many political and bureaucratic dilemmas in social measurement. This will move the social indicator field towards a more complete perspective on the role of information in policy-making systems.

Conclusion

If social indicators are to have a policy usefulness above and beyond that of social statistics it is important they be of sufficient power to be of use, that is, they do *indicate* a relationship between *a* and *b,* and that relationship is of interest to decision-makers. This clarification of causal path and direction is of course not sufficient to guarantee policy usefulness, and the development of social indicators of interest to policy-makers involves a related condition – that of institutionalisation. Caplan and Barton (1978), for example, call for substantial efforts to institutionalise the importance of social indicators into government operations in conjunction with policy planning and goal setting. The term itself reflects de Neufville's (1978) central argument for making indicators policy-useful. She defines institutionalisation as the setting-up of procedures and practices which promote the existence of an indicator, legitimise its methods and concepts, and develop a tacit consensus on the acceptability of the measures, concepts and methods of the indicator.

Institutionalisation helps mitigate against problems of misuse of indicators as propaganda (vindicators) and against non-utilisation. In the first case this is by insulating the indicators from the immediate vagaries of day-to-day politics so that misuse is difficult. In the latter case indicators must have sufficient power and exposure so that they cannot be ignored for purposes of political whim, and must be integrated into the policy-making process. This integration requires reworked institutional arrangements in government so as to provide a context for considering not only rational information needs but the political and bureaucratic factors influencing those needs. There are a number of criteria for gauging the degree of institutionalisation, including: the extent of long-term financing for regular production of the measure, the existence of active interest groups who use and support the continuance of the data series, media and public consciousness about the importance of the indicator, direct links between the indicator and the conduct of public policy, and the fact that the agency producing the indicator is respected, and not subject to immediate political control (de Neufville, 1975). The unemployment rate is probably the classic highly institutionalised indicator – it cannot be ignored, everybody is aware of its importance, it is directly related to public policy, and any attempt to alter its method (say, misguided seasonal adjustment) is usually subject to a storm of debate. At the other extreme might be some attempts at general quality-of-life studies which are often ignored, unrelated to any particular policy and too general to satisfy anyone's particular information needs.

Any institutionalised indicator with sufficient power is not overly broad in scope – it reflects the level of the policy problem or area to which it is addressed. Housing indicators, for example, dealing with broad problems of overall housing stock supply will be quite different from those addressing the housing and related problems of certain immigrants. This may seem obvious but many social indicator reports contain pages of data irrelevant to policy which is decidely off-putting to administrators. Misguided attempts at comprehensiveness which result in 'information overload' must be dealt with by attention to synthesis and communication. Researchers seldom wish to camouflage critical issues but sometimes do just that by refusing judiciously to select and highlight data critical to the policy issue. If any criticism can be put to social indicator studies from a policy point of view it must be that many have been too broad and vague and have not concentrated on policy-manipulable variables.

Finally, there may be a problem in institutionalising indicators in so far as the process requires some kind of commitment to a medium- to long-term perspective on information needs, and such a perspective might be lacking where government is more interested in short-term survival. This problem, however, is hardly unique to social indicators and is best viewed as part of the ongoing, and hopefully creative, tension between the rational and political-bureaucratic factors in policy-making. As such the solution lies in the promotion of well-informed decision-making with various social indicators as one component of the process of 'informing'.

What, then, does a good set of policy-related social indicators look like? First of all it might well consist of specific objective indicators collected by a variety of means. These indicators would in the main be disaggregated, but not to the extent that they became too complex to be of use. Where moderate aggregation took place the disaggregated back-up data would always be available. Where possible some attempt at a sensitivity analysis would reveal how changes in policy-manipulable variables would affect the outcomes. The objective indicators would in most cases be complemented by subjective attitudinal indicators and preference-rankings gathered by the promotion of a public participation exercise, and expert opinion where suitable. Both components of the analysis would be carried out and presented in such a manner as to aid in public debate, often at the expense of pointing to any determinate policy solution. And to further that debate, the results of the analysis would be presented so as to be understandable to all concerned, with a hierarchical structure of information leading from a general synopsis to detailed data and methodology, and overtly technical jargon confined to detailed appendices. Included in the general synopsis would be a discussion of the limitations of the analysis and the likely internal value-judgements to be expected in such an analysis, such as indicators excluded or unmeasurable. The detailed sections of the report would include a discussion of the methodological limitations of the social indicators being used.

Summary

This chapter identifies a variety of political and bureaucratic constraints on the use of social indicators in policy-making, including those associated with non-use, misuse, quantification, and value-judgements and value-weighting. The last is often attempted by the development of weighting schemes which are seen as a means of systematically attaching social values to quantitative data in policy analysis. These schemes usually involve the revealed or expressed preferences of politicians, experts, or some segment of the public. There are different schools of thought on the benefit of such schemes, however, with some analysts embracing them wholeheartedly, and others arguing they are best ignored. The chapter has explored some of the contentious issues in value-weighting, especially with regard to distributional equity.

The basic elements in the policy-making process were identified as value conflict, bureaucratic maintenance and analytic rationality. The relationship between academic research and policy analysis was examined. Means for overcoming the political dilemmas and constraints on the value of social indicators were discussed, including: the use of sensitivity analysis, improved communication, a commitment to intellectual pluralism and moral responsibility, and especially improved policy-modelling and institutionalisation of indicators.

6

National Social Reporting

I would contend that the interested reader has as much to learn from *Social Indicators 1976* or *Perspective Canada II* as from *The Joy of Sex.*

(Brusegard, 1978)

Recognising that data do not speak for themselves, *Social Indicators 1976* nevertheless proposes to maintain a discreet silence on their behalf.

(Seidman, 1978)

From the beginning a major element in the social indicators movement has been attempts to supplement data on the national economy with more socially oriented information, in what are often called national social reports. These reports are generally compendia of social indicators and contain a wide variety of basic objective data divided into categories reflecting either programmatic divisions in government administration or some mix of social concerns. This information is presented in table, chart, or graph form, and may also include attitudinal data and written commentary on the statistics. In the last decade such social reports have been issued, many on a regular basis, in no fewer than thirty countries. At least ten of these reports are directly entitled 'social indicators'; others use such terms as social report, perspective, panorama, and so on. Zapf (1976) notes, for example, that 'the social indicators movement is undergoing a remarkable transformation. What began essentially as an academic crusade is becoming a routinised reporting procedure by governmental agencies.'

The antecedents of these efforts at social reporting go back a few centuries to the development of the concept of statistics. We noted this was a word with the same root as that of 'state', and which originally meant the collection of quantitative facts about the state. And as governments have assumed an increasing responsibility for the provision of services over time, so has a long-term need arisen for data with which to evaluate the value-for-money of that provision. This need is represented in a continuing increase in the number of social statistical reports issued by government in the nineteenth and twentieth centuries (Encel *et al.*, 1975). More recently the work of Ogburn, the US Commission on National Goals and NASA's 'space-race' generated interest in social quantification, and all form part of the foundation of social reporting. These efforts culminated in the brief *Towards a Social Report,* whose author, Mancur Olson (1969, p. 86), noted 'for all of their virtues, the national income statistics don't tell us what we need to know about the conditions of American society. They leave out most ot the things that make life worth living.' Part of the solution is of course a social report, first appearing in the USA in the form of a chartbook. The Central Statistical Office in the UK, however, was first off the mark as its fairly successful annual *Social Trends* first appeared in 1970.

Although the social reports of various countries are obviously somewhat different, they in fact have more in common than not. Most generally they tend to be descriptive reference sources, designed to tell what is happening to social conditions and trends, rather than to make normative statements about what should be done about a given social situation. Social reports provide background information about recent social changes and trends, perhaps disaggregated by various common demographic and geographical variables. And although each statistic or indicator is implicitly selected so as to have at least some general policy relevance, social reports are not usually directly useful for analysing particular policies, except as they provide a background perspective.

Most social reports are divided into general programmatic or goal areas such as health, employment, income, recreation and leisure, public safety and justice, environmental quality and others. Some have special sections dealing with important topics such as the family, poverty and income distribution, ageing, urbanisation, equality, housing, and so on. Brusegard (1977, p. 29) classifies the types of information in most social reports according to what is being described:

(1) a contextually definite state of affairs or condition, for example, number of educational facilities;
(2) a change in some state of affairs, or condition, for example, a changing educational attainment level in a population;
(3) a characteristic of some state of affairs or condition, for example, the distribution of educational attainment across a region;
(4) a characteristic of some contextually definite group, for example, the educational attainment level of a particular age-cohort in the population.

Not all social reports, however, are as wide-ranging as those described above – some focus on particular sectional topic areas such as housing or health.

Finally, in terms of Zapf's criteria for evaluating social indicator systems discussed in Chapter 3, social reports generally have no explicit notion of welfare; the system structure is practical rather than theoretical, with complete operationalisation of the indicators selected. Both the quality of measurement and the amount of detail presented generally reflect what is available in the governmental statistical service itself.

Two international frameworks potentially, if not yet practically, useful for organising social reports were described in a previous chapter: the UN's SSDS and the OECD's development programme on social indicators. As might be expected, the lack of an international framework has not at all deterred the issuance of the thirty or so national social reports, or series of social reports, mentioned above, and indeed the search for an internationally comparable framework is currently more the offspring than the progenitor of active social reporting. Here we look at two English-language social reports in some detail, and a few others more superficially.

Social reporting in the United Kingdom

It befits the first of the modern social reports, *Social Trends,* to be considered in that order. This publication, now in its tenth volume, is described by its current editor (Thompson, 1978b, p. 653) as designed to 'bring together statistics which would facilitate judgements about social change' in a descriptive, rather than prescriptive, manner. The latest volume follows the basic format of its predecessors, although some new data appear and some disappear from the roster each year. (Those which disappear from print are usually still available from the data archives, however.) The chapters, or programmatic divisions and social concerns, are:

(1)   Population
(2)   Households and families
(3)   Social groups
(4)   Education
(5)   Employment
(6)   Income and wealth
(7)   Resource and expenditure
(8)   Health and public safety
(9)   Housing
(10) Environment and transport communications
(11) Leisure

(12) Participation
(13) Law enforcement

Social Trends always begins with two to five articles on varying topics – such as measurements of urban deprivation (Allnut and Gelardi, 1980); the trends in housing tenure (Holmans, 1979); subjective social indicators (Hall, 1976); time-budgets (Hedges, 1974); and health indicators (Culyer *et al.,* 1971). This is followed by the social report which consists of charts and tables with interspersed commentary. The social report for 1980 consists of 312 charts and tables with commentary on 212 pages, followed by a calendar of important governmental legislation and activity for the previous year plus an appendix of definitions of important terms. Under the chapter 'Health and public safety', for example, there are fifteen charts and twenty-six tables with commentary. Figure 6.1 shows a sample page in the chapter on health with charts and commentary giving us a snapshot of smoking and drinking habits in the UK during the 1970s.

The origins of *Social Trends* are related to the fact that the government statistical service in the UK is not centralised, and each executive department has its own statistical staff. In addition, however, the Central Statistical Office (CSO) in the Cabinet Office links these departmental activities and formulates interdepartmental statistical initiatives (Thompson, 1978b, p. 653). In 1967 the CSO began considering whether a new publication was needed to draw together social statistical information scattered amongst departments. The formation of a social statistics section in 1968 gave rise to *Social Trends,* and the first editor saw one of the publication's main tasks as pulling together, for the first time, social data from a multitude of sources and reassembling that information in a new and interesting way (Nissel, 1979). The general approach would be to pose the questions 'what is happening to people in the UK and what are the trends?' rather than concentrate on government or institutions. Where possible, attention was to be on output or throughput indicators rather than input indicators. To reinforce this approach the section on public expenditure which occupied the first chapter in Volume 1 was moved to the end of Volume 2 where it has remained, now relabelled 'resources'. And unlike many of the social reports of other countries, *Social Trends* was to be an annual. Originally conceived as a complement to the monthly *Economic Trends* from the same department, *Social Trends* came to reflect the fact that most UK social statistics, such as those relating to health, housing, criminal justice and the General Household Survey, were issued annually.

Aside from consolidating existing social statistics from different

HEALTH AND PUBLIC SAFETY

Admissions of patients with primary diagnosis of alcoholism or alcoholic psychosis to mental illness hospitals and units in England and Wales are shown in Chart 8.18. During the period 1970 to 1977 the largest increases in admissions occurred in the under 25 age group (men: 139 per cent;

women: 375 per cent). The increase in all-ages admissions for women was nearly twice that for men. Findings of guilt for drunkenness among women under 21 rose by more than 150 per cent from 1970 to 1977 in England and Wales, and by more than 60 per cent for men under 21.

Chart 8.18   Alcoholism – admissions[1] to mental illness hospitals and units: by age and sex

England and Wales

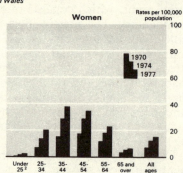

[1] Admissions with a primary diagnosis of alcoholism or alcoholic psychosis.

[2] The rate for 1970 was 0·4 per cent.

Source: Department of Health and Social Security; Welsh Office

The 1978 *General Household Survey* figures on cigarette tobacco smoking are given, by age and sex, in Chart 8.19. The decline in the prevalence of cigarette smoking which was evident in the mid-1970s became less marked. In 1972 the prevalence

among men was some 52 per cent, dropping to 51 per cent in 1974, to 46 per cent in 1976, and to 45 per cent in 1978. The percentages of women who smoked were: 41, 41, 38, and 37 respectively.

Chart 8.19   Cigarette smoking habits: by age and sex, 1978

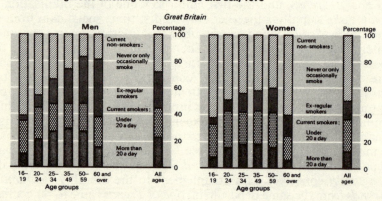

Source: General Household Survey, 1978

Figure 6.1   *The layout of* Social Trends, 1980.
Source: Thompson, 1979.

sources, a second major purpose of *Social Trends* was to identify gaps in the social statistical framework. And although many social statistical series were by-products of administrative needs and procedures and new surveys were not feasible, much data could be reworked and retabulated to good effect (Nissel, 1970). For example, in the health field, such new tabulations as death – by cause – by age highlight the very different problems of infant, child and young adult mortality. In the population section such tabulations as individuals per household, and families per household, give a different perspective on household formation.

The main concepts of *Social Trends* continue through its latest edition. It continues to fill a valuable role as a general guide to social statistics across administrative boundaries, and with combined charts, tables and running commentary. Weaknesses are noted too, however. Bulmer (1979) notes a decline in the quality and relevance of the accompanying articles, lack of attention to non-governmental data sources, and perhaps a lack of growth and insufficient attention to developing the concept of social indicators. Nissel (1979) notes something similar: perhaps a lack of purpose and an inattention to the nature of the audience. A number of these points are taken up later in this chapter.

The CSO also issues a number of more specific social reports. *Regional Statistics,* for example, gives social information plus data on production, distribution, investment, agriculture and energy, for eight regions in Great Britain. The *Statistics of Education* series issues a variety of volumes each year specifically dealing with aspects of the educational system, like teachers, school leavers, universities, and so on. Similar publications are issued annually by the CSO in conjunction with government departments, for example, *Health and Social Services Statistics for England.*

Social reporting in the United States

It took five years after the issuance of *Towards a Social Report* for the USA's first effort to appear. *Social Indicators 1973* was followed in turn by *Social Indicators 1976,* the second of what looks to be a triennial publication. This has been described by its chief editor as 'a comprehensive graphic collection of statistical data selected and organised to describe current social conditions and trends in the United States' (US Department of Commerce, 1977, p. xxiii). Like the UK volume, this one stresses that the statistics and social indicators it contains are strictly descriptive and that it is not attempting to provide any explanations of why or how the conditions described came about.

Social Indicators 1976 is a large volume, with about 375 charts and an equal number of tables on 647 pages, including a lengthy introduction and eleven chapters. The chapters, or programmatic divisions, include:

(1) Population
(2) The family
(3) Housing
(4) Social security and welfare
(5) Health and nutrition
(6) Public safety
(7) Education and training
(8) Work
(9) Income, health, and expenditure
(10) Culture, leisure, and use of time
(11) Social mobility and participation

Each chapter has the same layout: a brief text, the charts, statistical tables, technical notes and references to further reading. The main emphasis in *Social Indicators 1976* is on the multi-coloured charts. A typical chapter is 'Health and nutrition'. The written commentary takes up less than two pages, then seventy coloured charts on forty-three pages are followed by twenty-three pages of back-up tables and three pages of technical notes which consider briefly the quality of the data and definitions of terms used. Figure 6.2 shows us three of these charts giving us a time-series display of life expectancies in the USA in this century.

A purposeful lack of a written commentary distinguishes *Social Indicators 1976* from *Social Trends* and no doubt prompted the comment about its 'discreet silence' (Seidman, 1978). This lack was remedied, at least in part, by the separate publication of a special January 1978 issue of *The Annals of the American Academy of Political and Social Science* in which sixteen articles develop the implications of the data and social trends in *Social Indicators 1976* and criticise the editors for a variety of omissions and transgressions. Similar analytical treatment of the volume followed in the journal *Contemporary Sociology* of November 1978. *Social Indicators Research* of April 1979 also considered the American and Canadian social reports in some detail. Some reviewers find such academic debate on social reporting woefully lacking in the UK, and Bulmer (1979) suggested that this lack of analysis limits the quality of *Social Trends* and its potential to generate interest in the theoretical issues in social indicators. *Social Trends,* however, already contains written commentary *and* articles – Bulmer's call is for more 'analytic backbone' to the articles. And as American lay readers of *Social Indicators 1976* are unlikely to come across *The Annals,* the idea of a written commentary plus charts and tables has much to be said for it, and perhaps the US publication is rightly taken to task for its 'discreet silence'.

Life Expectancy at Ages 20, 40, and 60, by Sex and Race: 1901-1970

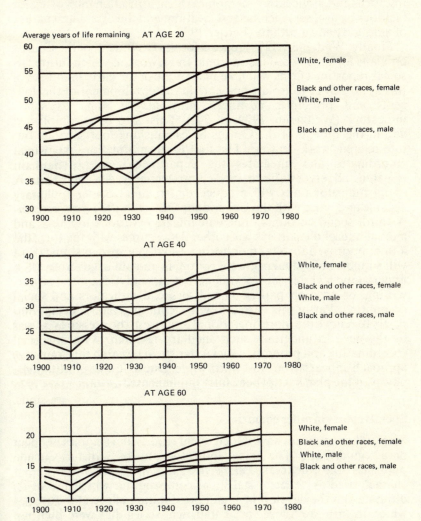

Figure 6.2   *Graphs,* Social Indicators, 1976.
Source: US Department of Commerce, 1977.

A number of sectorial social reports have also been issued in the USA. Among the most prominent is the biennial *Science Indicators* which uses charts and tables to give time-series data on the resources, activities and products of American science (McGinnis, 1979). Another, in the health field, is *Health: United States.* This is an annual publication which details health care costs and finances; resources and services by geographical area; utilisation rates of health facilities by age, sex, income and location; and the extent and nature of morbidity and mortality (Lerner, 1979).

Finally, Weitzman (1979) reports for the US Bureau of the Census on plans for the revised institutional framework in which future US social-reporting efforts will take place. One of the basic premises of this approach is 'to isolate and extend the development of the concepts and principles advanced previously relating to social indicators' (Weitzman, 1979, p. 241). This is to be accomplished within the Bureau of the Census by establishing four separate but interrelated 'work centres'. The first is an information unit which co-ordinates and integrates the department's social statistical research and serves its library and computer needs. A second unit, the social indicator unit, will produce the triennial *Social Indicators* volume and liaise with the UN and the OECD in their programmes. A third, social accounts, unit will integrate various monthly and annual household surveys with other data sources with the eventual aim of improved societal monitoring. Finally, a special studies unit will support individual researchers from in and out of government in undertaking a variety of research activities, analytic studies, report-writing, or position papers related to social indicators and social accounting. Partly this is to allow in-depth analysis to occur, and partly to relieve the more operational units from the pressures caused by the need to undertake such ancillary research. As a means of co-ordinating and promoting social statistical research this four-unit approach appears to be most worthwhile. Due to funding limitations, however, the plan has not been fully implemented as yet.

Social reports in other countries

Many other countries have issued social reports and a number appear on a regular basis. The Social Indicator Unit of Statistics Canada publishes the biennial *Perspective Canada,* which has been characterised as 'a social statistical compendium which has as its ultimate aim the development and presentation of social indicators' which in turn are 'those social statistical series that were high use social data series or those that were called social indicators by the planning establishment' (Brusegard, 1979, p. 262). The obvious problems inherent in such a definition are recognised by the editor of

Perspective Canada and we return to them shortly. The Canadian volume naturally includes data on many of the same topics as the US or UK volumes, but some categories are unique; for example, allocations of time, cultural diversity, bilingualism and native peoples. The last two especially reflect areas of major social issue in Canada.

The same is true of the Australian Bureau of Statistics biennial *Social Indicators,* first published in 1976, which includes a data section on 'aboriginals'. The French Institut Nationale de la Statistique et des Etudes Economiques (INSEE) has published the annual *Donnés sociales* since 1973. The 1978 edition includes a substantial section on the demography and activities of women and the family, including data on the working mother. The charts and tables in the French volume serve to illustrate very extensive written commentary.

An interesting data division in the Dutch *Social and Cultural Report* is the section on 'problem groups: concentrations of deprivations and shortcomings'. The Finnish sectorial social report *Cultural Statistics* (1978) of their Central Statistical Office includes time-series information on the arts, communication (radio, TV), leisure, and sports and youth activities, over the period 1930–77. Many other countries issue social reports, but with the exception of some sectorial reports, and some data divisions unique to particular countries, most of these social reports are basically similar in approach and subject matter and therefore appeal (or do not) to similar audiences. A list of social-reporting efforts from around the world can be found in the US volume.

The audience for social reports

The editor of *Social Indicators 1976* describes the essential task of social reporting as the effective communication of social data and interpretations to as wide an audience as possible with the aim of fostering informed public consideration of important social issues (Johnston, 1978b). The evidence on whether this communication is taking place is scanty, but worth consideration. Brusegard (1978, p. 269), editor of *Perspective Canada,* suggests that the original intention of many social reports was 'to provide a decision-making tool for high-level policymakers. The audience for social reports were the policymakers themselves and the planning establishments who served the usually elected policymakers.' Other possible audiences include a general audience of interested citizens and interest groups, a business audience, and an education audience in secondary schools and universities.

There is little evidence that social reports are used to any great extent by decision-makers, except perhaps as general background data. The only detailed research on social report usage, by Caplan and Barton (1978), involved questioning 204 high-level American federal government officials before and after the publication of *Social Indicators 1973*. Before publication 94 per cent indicated that social indicator data would be valuable in policy-making and monitoring. One and a half years after publication 202 of the original sample and 68 other officials were re-contacted. Many were completely unfamiliar with *Social Indicators 1973* and only 115 were willing to be re-interviewed. Of these only 4 per cent reported that they actually used the publication and another 16 per cent were familiar with its contents. Of the remainder of the second sample 78 per cent were totally unaware of the existence of the publication, although 37 per cent reported using some sort of social indicators regularly. Those who used the publication itself, or were familiar with it, had a history of using social science data.

While Caplan and Barton's finding cannot be generalised beyond the particular social report they studied, it is interesting to look at some of the reasons given for non-use. The most frequent was that other sources of similar information were more relevant and accessible. Most of these sources were from the same Bureau of the Census that issued *Social Indicators 1973*. The second most common reason for non-use was that the data were too general and too aggregated. One respondent referred to it as 'wall-to-wall macro-data' (Caplan and Barton, 1978, p. 442). This bears out Seidman's (1978) contention that social reports are not detailed enough to be applicable to the great majority of policy issues, and at best serve as a reference to other data resources. A number of critics tackled the American volume for its lack of integration and interpretation. This latter point may apply more specifically to the American social report and may not be true of, say, the UK's *Social Trends* or France's *Donnés sociales,* with their extensive written commentary. What further mitigates against generalising beyond this particular case is the fact that so many of the original sample were totally unaware of the existence of *Social Indicators 1973*. This is not necessarily a problem of social reports *per se,* but perhaps of publicity. This volume was the first effort of the Bureau of the Census in the way of a social report, and so a considerable amount of unfamiliarity is not unexpected.

The editors of *Social Trends* never seem to have felt that their publication would really be useful for specific decision-making and always emphasised its role as giving background information. Nissel (1974, p. 3), for example, saw *Social Trends* as giving 'statistics for enlightenment' which were needed not only by 'administrators and policy-makers at all levels but also by the general public, particularly in its role as final arbiter of the success or failure of government policies'. The current editor says that when considering an audience for *Social Trends* the most important point is 'the belief that democracy requires an informed public opinion' (Thompson, 1978b, p. 654). He aims *Social Trends* at the well-informed, reasonably numerate, journalist, or worker for a pressure group.

Although no readership analysis for *Social Trends* has been undertaken, some distribution figures are available. These show that of a press run of 6,325 for Number 7 some 1,225 were issued directly to government departments, about 3,000 were sold over the counter in the government's bookshops and 1,500 distributed by subscription. Of these subscribers 33 per cent went to public and university libraries, 16 per cent to commercial bookshops for resale, 13 per cent to local governments, 13 per cent to individual academics, 10 per cent to businesses and 6 per cent to overseas governments (Thompson, 1978b, p. 658). If one were to make the not unreasonable assumption that the over-the-counter sales were distributed in roughly the same manner this would substantiate the 'four-audience' classification for social reports and point to a strong emphasis on the general, interested citizen audience and the educational audience, a smaller but notable researcher/government audience and a relatively small business audience. The policy-makers themselves are probably reached most effectively, then, as part of the general or government audience for these background data, and indirectly through the research function. On the latter point, for example, an informal survey of this author's some thirty fellow workers at a major UK social research institute showed a majority made use of *Social Trends* at one point or another, most commonly to provide a 'background picture' to more specific types of policy analysis. *Social Trends* seems especially useful for providing background data in one field for researchers in a different field, and helps bridge the gap between social science and government statistics. In terms of reaching the general and educational audiences, such information in *Social Trends* as that on distribution of net wealth in UK society, or on the workings of the poverty trap, or on working mothers, obviously relates to important issues for the politically aware reader.

The social reports prepared in the 1980s are likely to be more closely oriented towards the needs of their real audiences, comprising interested citizens and the educational and research sectors, rather than policy-makers *per se*. Brusegard (1978, p. 276) of *Perspective Canada* argues that 'the planning elite will unearth the information they require with or without *Social Indicators, 1976* or *Perspective Canada II*, but the people who pay their salaries need all the help they can get'. One good offshoot of such a perspective is that Statistics Canada is now supplementing its social report with a booklet and teacher's guide on delineating social issues and social problems with social statistics. Other countries could profitably follow suit. In addition, further research on who uses social reports, and for what purposes, could clearly enhance the quality and usefulness of the volumes and aid the essential task of social reporting as effective communication.

Major issues in social reporting

Do social reports contain social indicators?
Such broad attempts at national social reports are open to criticism from every side. In spite of the fact that social reports from no fewer than ten countries contain the words 'social indicator' in the title, the question of whether they actually contain social indicators remains a contentious issue. This argument is partly one of definition. The US volume reflects the all-inclusive definition which considers anything non-economic as a social indicator, to the extent that even the most basic demographic information on gross population changes is considered to be 'social indicators of a special kind'. At the other extreme are many social scientists, beginning (as we noted) with Land in 1971, who argue that by very definition social *indicators* must be concerned with cause-and-effect relationships and model-building. Bulmer (1979), for example, argues that while *Social Trends* is an intelligent synthesis of available social statistics, it does not really contain any social indicators, a contention which the editor of that volume would probably not choose to dispute.

The resolution of the semantic aspects of this issue may lie in a definition which differentiates levels of social indicators. Horn (1978) proposed a number of dimensions which tend to distinguish social statistics from social indicators. First, statistics tend to be value-free while indicators are normative and related towards a stated or implied goal. Secondly, statistics are oriented towards inputs represented by measures of objective conditions, whereas indicators are oriented to outputs or results and may also reflect demands and their satisfaction. Thirdly, statistics can be collected empirically without a definite conceptual framework intended to derive an *ex post* analysis of some social condition. Social indicator research generally begins with such a framework.

Social reports to date, then, are really collections of useful statistics and do not contain explanatory measures which represent inferences drawn from the analysis of relationships among specified variables. The use of such models of the process of social change, and of hypothesis testing in developing social indicators, is essential in the long term. It is too much, however, to expect that these current efforts at social reporting be based on such models, given that such a modelling process is only in its infancy in the social sciences generally. Nor can such published social reports be expected to contain time-series data extensive enough for any manipulation like a regression analysis, and there is no reason they should. They merely summarise trends for individual consideration.

Finally, and in spite of the number of volume titles to the contrary, social reporting and social indicators are not the same thing. Social reporting is 'the issuance of statistical and textual material descriptive of social conditions and processes present and occurring in the country in a way that attempts to make obvious possible contributing factors to, and consequences of, conditions and trends' (Brusegard, 1979, p. 263). Social indicators exist within that definite conceptual framework described above. Social reports profitably contain indicators but may not necessarily do so. The proportion of social indicators in social reports will rise in relation to the number of valid, policy-relevant indicators which social scientists are able to develop.

Values, categories and aggregation in social reporting

These definitional arguments are not entirely semantic, however. They also stem in part from deeper questions about the relationship of fact to values. The editors of social reports may feel they are presenting 'facts' for others to interpret, but such factors as the selection of some data to the exclusion of other data, the choice of disaggregations and the method of arranging the subject matter by chapter are all normative acts based on some implicit theory as to the nature and the important components or domains of human welfare. Attention focused on one set of indicators will certainly remove attention from a different set ignored in the social report. There is also the problem of 'vindication' raised in Chapter 5. Obviously the data selection in the social report should be subject to the same scrutiny as any other value-judgements in the policy-analysis process, and to this end there is considerable value in the kinds of debate which surrounded *Social Indicators 1976*.

A very basic issue raised with regard to many countries' social reports is whether these efforts should relate in some way to specific national objectives or priorities or pressing social problems, in a manner more direct than rather vague references to quality of life or social well-being. One reason this question arises is that government statistical agencies are duty-bound to remain politically neutral, and for good reason. Thompson (1978b, p. 654) of the UK's Central Statistical Office says, for example, '*Social Trends* cannot succeed unless supporters of all political parties can accept it as a source of statistics which are selected fairly and are presented impartially'. The problem with trying to be 'fair and impartial' is that one can be accused of an 'offend no one' attitude which results in vague, unfocused social reports which are of little value to anyone (Shostack, 1978). Also government statistical agencies are conservative by nature and present information more or less in accord with government policies. Horn says, for example, that in Australia it was up to reformers and academics to press the government to gather statistics on the disadvantages suffered by aboriginals, migrants, or women at work. He notes wryly that the Australian Bureau of Statistics is not 'imbued with spontaneous zest for social change' (Horn, 1978, p. 366). The same is no doubt true in most countries and obviously a balance must be struck somewhere.

As we noted in discussion of the OECD social indicator system, the derivation of social indicators on the basis of prior consensus on explicit social goals and objectives is expensive, time-consuming and of limited value where it is possible at all. Also, social reporting is not intended for, and cannot serve the function of, analysing performance of particular agencies or programmes. Rather, national social reports help broaden the perspectives of non-experts who wish to get a general feel for the statistics of a social problem area, possibly as a preliminary step to more detailed consideration. As such they make an important contribution to public debate.

A related problem is that of determining some means of organising the social statistics. The solution usually reflects some mix of grouped subject matter according to institutional divisions and salient social concerns. Whatever the decision, criticism can be expected. Those sections of social reports organised along institutional divisions are criticised for failing to promote a greater understanding of social processes and the relationships among various social factors. Seidman (1978, p. 718) on *Social Indicators 1976* notes that 'the categories are those a government finds comfortable and familiar, and as the federal government is often criticised for a lack of coordination across agencies, so there is a lack of coordination across chapters'. Those organised according to salient social concerns, on the other hand, run the risk of faddism, and overconcentration on social factors of passing interest at the expense of those not currently subject to influence and debate.

However, as with many aspects of social indicators, to criticise is easy and to construct very difficult. As Johnston (1978a) of the US report argues in rebuttal, a programmatic structure based on institutional divisions is familiar and convenient to users and encourages a ready approach to the statistics. Further, government agencies must be cost-effective which means that social statistics are bound to reflect the organisation of those agencies responsible for the collection of the data. This is especially true as most of the data will have been collected for other purposes, with inclusion in the social report as an additional benefit. The practicalities of government statistical collection tend to dictate an institutional approach, even while the most important defect in official social statistics may be the divergence between administrative and scientific concepts – a divergence lessened by data organisation according to social concerns (Halsey, 1972). Obviously there is no particular solution to these dilemmas, much less any means of pleasing the variety of social report users. The editor of *Social Trends,* to emphasise concern with people rather than policies, argues for a bias against chapters corresponding too closely with the concerns of particular government departments (Thompson, 1978b). This is a useful approach, especially from the social scientist's point of view, and reflects the fact that the organisation of social reports must be based on some judicious and flexible mix of data organised by institutional framework and social concerns.

A third contentious issue in social reporting concerns the extent to which disaggregation shall be presented, and by what variables. Because social reports are national in coverage and very wide in scope, much of the data is highly aggregated, if for no other reason than that otherwise the reports could and do become unwieldy in size. The dangers of over-aggregation in QOL indexes have been discussed and the same case holds for social reporting. As Hope (1978, p. 244) puts it, 'in the case of a social indicator, ambiguity is simply achieved by a process of averaging, thus washing out the specific contributions to the average of its elements or components, in particular eliminating those components which are of differential salience to differing groups in society'.

Disaggregation can help increase understanding of the social conditions under study and is therefore a worthwhile objective of social reports. But the disaggregating variables chosen or not chosen are also a matter of value-judgement. The US social report disaggregates typically by age, sex and race and only occasionally by income or education and for this it is taken to task (Parke and Seidman, 1978). The danger in this is that neither age, sex, nor race is amenable to policy intervention, whereas disaggregation by variables reflecting socioeconomic status might be much more enlightening and relevant to policy considerations. In a review of the first US social report Ramsy (1974) noted that European reports more commonly disaggregated by indicators of socioeconomic status, and this helped relate the statistics to structural elements in society which might be possible targets for intervention. In this matter the UK's *Social Trends* fares better and one finds not only the usual age, sex and colour disaggregation but also those by occupational type and household type. In the latter case, for example, interesting comparisons can be made on income, wealth and family expenditure pattern differences among pensioner families, one-parent families, two-parent families without children, and so on. These kinds of disaggregations relate in turn to such policy-manipulable factors as the setting of pension levels and welfare benefit levels.

Finally, Parke and Seidman (1978, p. 14) raise the important point that the inclusion of such disaggregated data in social reports may not simply be a matter of the editor's determination to do so, especially as such reports rely on data generated for other primary uses. Such disaggregation may not be available and the statistical system itself may have to be pressed towards the collection of socioeconomically disaggregated statistics.

Conclusion

In spite of the number of criticisms which have been directed at specific social reports it seems they can, and probably do, serve useful functions of general enlightenment, education and contribution to broad public debate for an audience of interested layman, policymakers, students and researchers. The suggestion that these social reports are statistically unsophisticated is true, but there is no argument for waiting for the field of social indicator modelling to catch up to the evident social information needs of the audiences of the reports. In 1975 de Neufville warned that the development of social indicators was to be a lengthy and complex process and this situation still holds. Distinguishing social statistics from social indicator models helps relieve social reports from some of the burden of unsophistication. More important, perhaps, is the need to reinforce everyone's understanding of the value-judgements associated with choosing different data sets, different categories and disaggregating variables.

One problem with social reports will always be what is included and what is left out. Things left out mean criticisms of ignoring or hiding data. Too much included and the reports become unwieldy. In every case the hand of a judicious editor is important, and both the US and UK volumes do well in clearly identifying their editors and thus emphasising the inevitable personal touch in statistical compendia. Beyond this there is an argument for increasing the variety of sectional social reports in such fields as health, science, housing and income distribution (Dever, 1979). These sectional reports could include more highly disaggregated data, a more complex presentation, and be directed at the statistically sophisticated reader, such as the social scientist. The sectional reports would not, however, be used at the expense of the more general compendia, which serve a different audience and a different and important role.

On the matter of amount of textual material or statistical displays there is no evidence that written commentary *or* graphics conveys more information to people. What does seem to be the case is that a mixture of both is essential to a good understanding of the data across a variety of audiences. This may account to some extent for the relatively good acceptance of *Social Trends* and the somewhat vehement criticism directed at *Social Indicators 1976*. The addition of social commentary and articles from sources external to the report's issuing agency is also suggested from experience in the US and Canada (Brusegard, 1979) and the UK (Bulmer, 1979).

Finally, for all the criticism directed at social-reporting efforts it is not likely that the need for social data relevant to government activity will diminish in the least, and an important continuing role for social reporting is easily forecast. This role will most profitably relate to the development of social indicator models, but it should not be confused with the development of such models.

7

Social Indicators at the Urban Level

In any planning exercise hard facts are needed on which to
base forecasts of available resources, demand for services,
usage of and the level of service likely to be achieved.
(Dorman, 1979)

The application of precise and detailed statistical
techniques to such an ambiguous area [as urban
deprivation] is about as meaningful as using a micrometer
to measure a marshmallow.
(Edwards, 1975)

Social indicators have found some of their most extensive practical
(and impractical) applications in the field of urban analysis – the
study of the nature and the workings of cities. This chapter looks at
three very different uses of social indicators for urban analysis and
gives examples of these applications. The first involves *intra-urban*
indicators – the examination of geographical divisions and population subgroups within a city. Examples are taken from the extensive
use of such indicators in the UK. The second approach involves the
development of *inter-urban* indicators, sometimes used for
comparing and contrasting different cities with one another,
especially in the USA. The third approach concerns the development
of indicators of *performance* in the delivery of urban services.
Examples of this recent emphasis on performance measurement are
drawn from both North American and UK experience.

Intra-urban social indicators

One of the most common uses of urban level social indicators is for
the identification and description of particular geographical areas of
cities for planning and policy purposes. This type of activity is common both in the UK and in North America. Flax (1978) for example,
identified fifty-seven such studies in the USA with such names as
QOL studies, needs assessments, community profiles and neighbourhood surveys. In the UK there are virtually as many, and this is
obviously an important use of policy-related social indicators. This
type of social indicator data is used across a spectrum of activity, from
simple area classification schemes to normative resource allocations.

At one end of this spectrum are the classification schemes which seek to identify and separate areas in the city according to how like and unlike they are in terms of some social characteristics. In the middle of the spectrum are social indicator data sets used to compare and contrast previously classified areas according to their performance on one or more dimensions of life quality, for example, on health or housing. At the other end of the spectrum are schemes which use social indicators, in combination with some set of normative judgement criteria, selectively to allocate resources to particular areas, sometimes called priority areas, or to population subgroups. These latter schemes are often described by the terms 'positive discrimination' in the UK and 'affirmative action' in the USA.

The origins of intra-urban analysis
Like much activity which now falls within the field of social indicators, these types of urban analysis have their roots in research begun long before the term social indicators was coined. In this case the use of statistics to identify and describe urban areas has its origins in the 1920s in the work of the journalist-turned-sociologist Robert Park, and what came to be known as the Chicago school of sociologists. In furthering their theory of human ecology (that social development could be understood by analogy to biological processes in space), Park and his associates examined in detail the overall pattern of Chicago neighbourhoods and the social characteristics of individual areas (Brindley and Raine, 1979). These areas were described according to their population structure, mobility, ethnic make-up, employment situation and housing characteristics, and recorded in a series of Local Community Facts Books. Although the human ecology theory is now largely discredited, the value of the Chicago school's contribution to the systematic study of urban areas remains untouched.

An important extension of Park's work was the Chicago Community Inventory initiated in 1946 by Ernest W. Burgess and Louis Wirth, Park's colleagues at the University of Chicago. This was to be an inventory of data on the Chicago metropolitan area, maintained on a current basis, and useful for both policy and administrative purposes, and as a data base for sociological research. This programme, still in existence, continues to provide a variety of services, including (1) analysis of census and other data for city departments, such as planning, education, and health, and for private agencies, including welfare, housing, religious and business groups; (2) the preparation of population estimates and projections; (3) the collection of new data; (4) serving as a liaison between local agencies and the national Bureau of the Census; and (5) conducting basic sociological research into urban problems (Hauser, 1968, p. 863).

Around the same time as the Chicago Community Inventory was being set up an interesting development in the use of census data was under way in California. There Shevky and Bell (1955) attempted to develop multivariate statistical techniques for analysing census data. The purpose of the exercise was to attempt to verify their theory of 'social areas' which postulated that urban social structure and development, in terms of increasing urban scale, could be explained by reference to three constructs. The first was social rank, which was indicated by such measures as years of schooling, employment and occupational status, cost of housing and possession of various household facilities. The second and most important construct was variously called urbanisation or family status and was measured by indicators of the population's age/sex-structure, type of housing tenancy, fertility rates, female employment rates and number of single-family dwellings. The third construct was ethnic status which was measured by the relative concentration of specified ethnic minorities (Timms, 1971).

This attempt to explain the underlying factors in increasing urban scale became known as the Shevky–Bell model, and was used in many studies to differentiate residential areas by developing a typology of 'social areas'. A variety of Social Area Analyses based on these three constructs was undertaken, with some support for the Shevky–Bell model from analysis of US cities, but very little from analysis undertaken in other parts of the world. By the mid-1960s much of Shevky's general theory of urban structure was dismissed as a rationalisation of empirically derived factors, rather than the results of theoretical reasoning (Brindley and Raine, 1979, p. 275).

Like Park's theory of social ecology the lasting importance of Social Areas Analysis was not in its theoretical propositions but in its contribution to the systematic empirical study of urban areas. This contribution was the impetus for the continuing use of principal component analysis and cluster analysis in the examination of census data. Both techniques are attempts to discover and describe structure in a previously unstructured array of data, in the hope of simplifying the understanding of a complex data set. The principal components method, a form of factor analysis, is used to group variables in a correlation matrix into a smaller number of representative units according to their contribution to the variation in the matrix. Cluster analysis attempts to group data according to the similarity of observations. The most common clustering method is called stepwise, hierarchical clustering, illustrated graphically in Figure 7.1. This process begins with N observations (in the figure numbered 1 to 10) which are subsequently combined with the most similar other observation at each stage. The process continues until all N observations are combined in a single group, but of most interest are intermediate steps, for example, at *a, b,* or *c,* where the observations are grouped into a moderate number of clusters, here 6 at *a,* 3 at *b* and 2 at *c.* The point at which one 'takes a cut' of the clusters for interpretation depends, of course, on the objectives of the analysis. Shortly we will examine the practical application of this technique to a grouping of residential neighbourhood types.

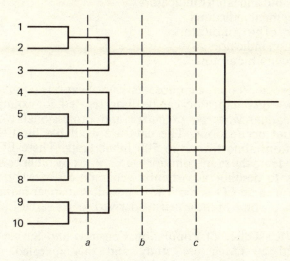

Figure 7.1   *Cluster analysis diagram.*

These and similar research programmes presaged many modern urban social indicator efforts. From Park's work we find a commitment to systematic intra-urban analysis. The Chicago Community Inventory put the stress on organised, time-series data from the census, and from Social Area Analysis we inherit the application of statistical techniques useful for simplifying and combining complex data sets. All these elements are present in the social indicator programmes of the 1970s discussed in the following sections.

Census-based social indicators
In the 1970s in the UK there was a great expansion in the number of projects which made use of 1971 Census of Population data for various types of urban analysis. Much of this expansion was prompted or facilitated by the widely increased availability of Small Area Statistics (SAS) from the census. These were first made available on a very limited basis in 1951 but in 1971 the amount of social data was greatly expanded and this made the SAS especially useful for

deriving social indicators applicable to small sections of cities, called enumeration districts (EDs).

The SAS are divided into seven topics:

Demographic and fertility indicators
Housing indicators
Household and family indicators
Employment indicators
Country of birth indicators
Migration indicators
Socioeconomic groups

The last, socioeconomic groups, consists of various population sub-groups by which indicators can be disaggregated, for example, semi-skilled manual workers, executive and professional workers, or agricultural occupations. The data are available for EDs, which contain from almost none to 700 inhabitants. These EDs can be aggregated into the more common wards, into any other combination necessary to describe a particular geographical area, or when the population in an ED is too low to permit statistical manipulation. Examples of some of these census-derived social variables are given in Table 7.1.

The UK's Office of Population Censuses and Surveys (OPCS) conducted a census use study and this revealed numerous applications of SAS-derived indicators to urban analysis (Hakim, 1978a, 1978b). Included in these were the use of such indicators by local government departments to develop descriptive area profiles, by community workers in housing and minority relations, and by health and community-medicine planners. The census indicators enter into the formula which allocates revenue from central to local governments. They have also been used for such diverse purposes as locating BBC transmitters, routing natural gas lines and producing local atlases. Social scientists made use of SAS indicators in urban social geography and in studying voting patterns. Finally such indicators have been used to produce area classifications or typologies which have a range of planning and research applications, and it is to one of these that we now turn.*

The classification of residential neighbourhoods
One of the most complete area classification techniques is that of the Planning Research Applications Group (PRAG) at the UK's Centre for Environmental Studies. The PRAG technique is a strategy for

---

*For a discussion of similar neighbourhood classification activities in the USA see Stegman, 1979, and Kolodny, 1978.

census data analysis which aims to help decision-makers and planners understand complex, heterogeneous, metropolitan areas where any one individual cannot be expected to have first-hand knowledge of conditions, and where raw census data result in 'information overload'. For example, the SAS has 1,600 data cells for each census enumeration district, and these have an average population of 450. This gives a typical city or London borough an available data set of over 1 million items. What the PRAG technique attempts to offer is a strategy which will pick out patterns from the details, without losing too much original information, and which allows detailed examination of parts of the pattern as particular issues demand (Webber, 1978b, p. 275). The basis of the PRAG scheme is the summarisation, as precisely as possible, of a diversity of residential environments found within cities. This is done by developing a typology of residential neighbourhoods which are as homogeneous as possible in terms of their scores on a variety of social indicators. This classification provides three basic sets of information: first, a conceptual definition of different area types, secondly, a location in physical space for classified neighbourhoods and thirdly, a means of comparing such areas across a variety of variables.

The PRAG scheme has made use of forty indicators derived from the census Small Area Statistics to develop a typology of neighbourhood types. Table 7.2 is a list of those forty indicators. The indicators themselves were chosen to provide a balance among housing, demographic structure, and social and economic conditions. Within these topics the indicators were chosen according to the effectiveness with which they had been able to discriminate among residential environments in pilot studies in three urban areas (Webber, 1977). A computerised cluster analysis was used to aggregate residential types on the basis of their similarity measured by reference to the forty indicators. The process was continued until thirty-six neighbourhood types were identified as the least number of types which adequately differentiated among neighbourhoods. These thirty-six, although sufficiently different for the purposes of analysis, were seen as still too many for ready comprehension, for example, in a coloured map. Yet if fewer were chosen, the homogeneity of the types would diffuse. The solution for PRAG was to continue the clustering until eight types were identified, and then to offer a dual level of analysis, at thirty-six or eight types, depending on the problem. Table 7.3 lists the eight social area types identified by the PRAG analysis.

By using either the eight or thirty-six neighbourhood type classification, different areas can be examined by reference to a variety of social indicators. For example, for each area

Table 7.1 *Census-derived social variables.*

Demographic indicators	Housing indicators	Employment indicators
Percentage of females aged 20–29 who are married	Total number of private households	Percentage of economically active males who are sick
Married persons per 1,000 total population aged 15–24	Percentage of households which are owner-occupied	Percentage of population in private households who are students aged 15 and over
Married persons per 1,000 total population aged 35–44	Percentage of households rented from local authority	Percentage of total population with secondary education (i.e. total population with A level or ONC)
Percentage of males aged 35–39 in households who are married	Percentage of households which are private, rented unfurnished accommodation	Percentage of all in employment with secondary education (number of persons in employment with ONC or A level as a percentage of all persons in employment)
Fertility ratio of married women	Percentage of households which are private, rented furnished accommodation	
	Percentage of households which are rented privately	

Ratio of children aged 0–4 years to married women aged 15–44 years

Children born per 100 married women aged 16–29 years in households

Children born per 100 married women aged 30–44 years in households

Percentage of persons living in private rented furnished accommodation

Percentage of persons living in private rented unfurnished accommodation

Percentage of dwellings which are vacant

Percentage of occupied dwellings which are shared

Percentage of professional and managerial (SEGs 1, 2, 3, 4 and 13) with A level or ONC

Percentage of unskilled workers with A level or ONC

Percentage of total population with higher education (degree or HNC)

Source: Hakim, 1978a.

Table 7.2 Forty variables used to classify UK urban areas

Variable	Definition
Age-structure	
1 0–4 years	
2 5–14 years	
3 15–24 years	proportion of population within each age-group
4 25–44 years	
5 45–64 years	
6 65 years and over	
Household composition	
7 Household size	persons per household present
8 Married adults	proportion of population aged 15 and over who are married
9 Fertility	children ever born per married female aged 16–19
10 Single non-pensioner	proportion of households { with one person not a pensioner
11 5 years migrant	changing address within previous 5 years
12 NCW descent	proportion of residents with both parents born in the New Commonwealth
Housing	
13 Owner-occupiers	who are owner-occupiers
14 Council tenants	renting from local authority
15 Unfurnished	renting privately unfurnished
16 Furnished	renting privately furnished
17 No inside WC	lacking the use of { an inside WC
18 No bath	a bath
19 Shared dwellings	in shared dwellings
20 Overcrowding	living at { over 1 person per room
21 Serious overcrowding	over 1·5 persons per room
22 1/2 rooms	occupying { 1 or 2 rooms
23 Large dwellings	7 or more rooms

proportion of households

24 Dwelling size   occupied rooms $\begin{cases} \text{per household} \\ \text{per person} \end{cases}$
25 Rooms/person

Transport
26 Car-ownership   cars per 100 households
27 2-car households   proportion of households with 2 or more cars
28 Walk to work   proportion of workers $\begin{cases} \text{walking to work} \\ \text{travelling to work by bus/train} \end{cases}$
29 Bus/train to work

Socioeconomic status
30 Professional/managerial $\left.\begin{array}{l} \\ \\ \\ \\ \\ \end{array}\right\}$ proportion of heads of households in each category
31 Non-manual
32 Skilled manual
33 Semi-skilled manual
34 Unskilled

Employment
35 Married women's activity rate   proportion of married women who are economically active
36 Agriculture   proportion of economically active engaged in $\begin{cases} \text{agriculture} \\ \text{manufacturing/mining} \\ \text{services/government} \end{cases}$
37 Manufacturing/mining
38 Services
39 Unemployment   proportion of economically active males seeking work
40 Students   students aged 15 or over as a proportion of persons present in private households

Source: Webber, 1979.

Table 7.3   *Social area types defined in the PRAG analysis*

1	Rural areas and areas of mixed character
2	Areas of established high status and elderly population
3	New owner-occupied estates of high status and young age-structure
4	Areas of older terraced housing and elderly population
5	Areas of extensive public housing
6	Areas of extensive public housing and acute social stress
7	Areas of low-status multi-occupied housing with serious social stress
8	Areas of high-status rented housing, students and other single people

Source: Webber, 1979.

socioeconomic groupings, employment categories, travel to work modes, or household types can be associated with types of housing tenure and patterns of household amenities and occupancy rates.

Aside from furthering the understanding of complex urban areas, the PRAG scheme is seen as having four potential policy applications (Webber, 1977). The first is as a sampling frame for other surveys, and the second is as a framework for organising non-census data, for example, subjective social indicator data. The third application would be to assist in choosing the relevant social indicators which could be used in defining areas for special policy attention. The fourth and related application would be to select priority areas either in terms of particular localities, or for particular types of areas (say older medium-density housing) to which urban policies might be directed. In addition, the effect of shifting policies and resources towards particular types of residential neighbourhoods can be better gauged in a PRAG type framework. In these last two options the PRAG scheme moves towards normative application of social indicator data which is examined in more detail in the next section.

Are there limitations to descriptive classification techniques like this one? The authors are the first to admit so. The most basic is the direct link between the PRAG technique and the now somewhat discredited Shevky–Bell theory of Social Area Analysis which leaves the classification techniques without a reputable theoretical basis. Webber, the author of PRAG, recognises this and argues that be that as it may, PRAG stands on its practical effectiveness for understanding urban structure, and as a policy tool (Webber, 1978a). The first criterion for policy usefulness is of course whether the system actually serves as a good vehicle for classifying Britain's residential neighbourhoods, that is, are the groupings realistic for different cities and regions? The early evidence is contradictory and more research needs to be done to validate the scheme.

Other limitations are those shared by most attempts at social indicator systems. First, the choice of input variables is ultimately a political choice, as stressed in Chapter 5. Webber recognises this and argues that the use of PRAG techniques needs to be clearly linked to political priorities in the jurisdiction where classification is being carried out. Secondly, the indicators obviously involve some causal statement and one needs to tread cautiously about any universal interpretation of particular indicators. For example, in one locale a high rate of shared housing amenities (e.g. shared bath) may be indicative of slum conditions while in another locale the same indicator will reflect well-educated young single people living close to city centres.

A related problem concerns the classification used in a normative manner, as a guide to allocating resources to alleviate social stress, say, in housing. If this is done by ranking districts based on a composite indicator, analysis of the differences in the scores of individual families on different possible measures of housing deficiency reveals that the ranking is highly sensitive to the indicators chosen (Webber, 1978b, p. 277). The selection of a weighting scheme is clearly a political decision, a situation not always reflected in the normative use of area classifications.

Allocating resources to 'deprived' urban neighbourhoods
A variety of programmatic indicator systems and sets has been developed during the last decade out of a concern for identifying or remedying multiple deprivation or social malaise in older inner city neighbourhoods, and among the disadvantaged. These positive discrimination schemes seek to go beyond an informative classification of neighbourhood types to make normative, or prescriptive, judgements as to the geographical location of urban deprivation, or particular population subgroups suffering socioeconomic deprivation. To these, additional resources would be allocated. These efforts, sometimes termed priority area policies, are based on the assumption that the multiply deprived can be identified as suffering from a complex condition, greater than the sum of its parts, which would benefit from extra resources over and above those normally provided. Positive discrimination programmes must necessarily make use of social indicators to identify where or to whom additional resources should be allocated (Edwards, 1975).

During the past ten years the British government has introduced a number of such schemes, especially in the policy areas of education and housing. Most of these have been 'area based', that is, based on the assumption that there are discrete, geographically identifiable neighbourhoods within cities, suffering from deprivation, which would benefit from special treatment. These programmes involved the designation of certain areas in which all individuals, or all those who fell below a certain level of welfare, would qualify for aid. In some cases environmental improvements, presumably benefiting the area's population generally, were also undertaken.

Canada has also had some experience of such programmes, especially housing and neighbourhood renewal schemes such as the Neighbourhood Improvement Programme. In the USA, positive discrimination was first embodied in area-based schemes such as those under the short-lived Model Cities programme, or the Head Start programme which attempted to provide additional educational facilities for young children in deprived areas. Soon, however, the emphasis shifted to affirmative action schemes in education, employment practice and manpower development aimed at subgroups in the population. The basic assumption of these programmes has been that disadvantaged people needed more assistance or expenditure in order to be able to perform at the same levels as advantaged groups, or in order to improve their situation rapidly (Miller, 1974). Such additional assistance, for example, included incentives and quotas for black or female employees in proportion to their place in society. The following discussion takes the UK by way of example, but many of the conclusions and reservations about the use of social indicators for such purposes are equally applicable to areal or subgroup schemes.

One of the earliest (1967) and best known of the UK schemes was a compensatory educational programme called Educational Priority Areas (EPAs), inspired in part by Head Start. The EPA programme involved allocating additional resources to schools in specific areas. These resources took the form of higher teachers' pay, more teachers' aides, increased capital expenditure and wider provision for nursery education (Lawless, 1979). The EPAs were identified by local authorities using social indicators of apparent multiple deprivation and poor physical environment. Such indicators included: occupation, size of families, supplements in cash or in kind from the state, overcrowding and sharing of houses, poor school attendance and truancy, numbers of retarded or handicapped pupils, children with linguistic difficulties, children receiving free school meals, high pupil turnover and high teacher turnover (Little and Mabey, 1972). During the 1970s the EPA programme was very active. EPA teachers, for example, received up to £300 ($600) additional salary. Nursery education was greatly expanded. An Educational Disadvantage Unit was set up to act as a focal point for comparative research into alternative educational programmes. By 1980 a number of EPA programmes had lapsed, although the teachers' pay supplement was still in operation.

A second important policy area subject to positive discrimination has been housing. The programmes themselves include Housing Action Areas (HAAs), Priority Neighbourhoods and General Improvement Areas – all designated by sets of social indicators. HAAs, for example, involved some 3 to 4 per cent of the worst housing in Britain, not destined for demolition. They gave the designating local authority the power to offer preferential house renovation grants and to force improvements to be undertaken, at the extreme by compulsory purchase. An HAA is expected to run for five years. The social indicators for defining HAAs are both physical and housing indicators, and demographic indicators. An HAA represents not just poor housing stock, but housing *stress* involving the interaction of physical and social conditions.

The housing stock indicators used for designating an HAA include lack of amenities such as a fixed bath or shower, hot and cold water, or an inside WC; poor conditions of dwellings; and bad external layout such as lack of backyard. The indicators of social conditions in potential HAAs include room density of over 1·5 persons per room; shared cooking, bathing, or toilet facilities; and the concentration in an area of households, such as old age pensioners and single-parent families, likely to suffer deprivation. In addition a variety of other criteria were suggested, including short periods of residence, large families, families without cars, little or no house renovation and numbers of children in care (Dennis, 1978). The actual designation of an HAA involved combining such indicators as the local government considered relevant and then drawing boundaries accordingly.

There were a variety of other positive discrimination programmes in the UK, such as the Community Development Projects, the Urban Aid Project, and the Inner Area Studies. All depended on social indicators to delineate areas or population subgroups suitably in need of positive discrimination. Each programme in particular, and the concept in general, has generated considerable debate and criticism as to its efficacy and the nature of its flaws. The debate reflects a number of the more general issues related to social indicators, discussed in Chapters 4 and 5.

Issues in allocating urban resources with social indicators
A common issue is the question of data availability, as there are few ready sources of urban social indicator data. Researchers often undertake their own surveys but this can be expensive and time-consuming. This has resulted in a strong emphasis on census data and its refinements, like Small Area Statistics. While such data can be comprehensive and quite useful, they will not always enlighten us as to unique characteristics, such as local problems of environmental quality or traffic. Nor does the census cover the variety of social

variables which might be needed for particular studies. The boundaries of census tracts, or enumeration districts, will not necessarily correspond to the areas under study, nor will other administrative boundaries used as a framework for collecting social statistics. There is also no reason to assume that social areas delineated by statistical procedures will conform in any way with social and geographical 'neighbourhoods' as identified by social networks, activity patterns, or mental maps. It is better to treat such areas as statistical phenomena rather than social reality (Brindley and Raine, 1979, p. 279).

Another problem is that the census is only taken infrequently, at five- or ten-year intervals, and data may be two to twelve years out of date. Some socioeconomic trends, such as the decentralisation of population and employment from older city centres, may well shift more rapidly than census data would indicate, and yet be of paramount importance in positive discrimination programmes.

Perhaps more complex are the theoretical problems all too common in social indicator research. Lack of theoretical development and implied causation haunt urban social indicators, and the more closely they are allied to resource allocation decisions the more this is the case. Where resources are to be allocated, indicators must be normative along a continuum of good to bad, high to low, and so on, or conclusions about alternative allocations cannot be made. Often, however, indicators are employed which have an ambiguous relationship to the general concept of poverty or deprivation, for example, car-ownership, large family size, or low economic activity rate. The last can indicate the presence of students or the early retired, as well as unemployment or underemployment. Car-ownership may be high in deprived rural areas with little public transport as well as in prosperous suburbs (Knox, 1978). Again it may be low among city centre dwellers with ready access to public transport.

Many studies confuse input measures of the provision of urban services with output measures of quality of life, or the lack of it, in the form of deprivation. The level of social service provision, for example, is no measure whatever of the need for services, although it is useful when the efficiency of service delivery, or performance, is the issue. Such problems of specifying appropriate indicators relate in turn to the theoretical conceptualisation, that is, the formulation of a testable working definition of urban 'deprivation' which is an unobservable phenomenon which can only be measured by surrogates. Such conceptualisation has often been either fuzzy, or formulated on preconceived political value-judgements, rather than on empirical research. Edwards (1975) notes, for example, that the selection of the indicators, based on such value-judgements, has in turn implicitly defined urban deprivation, rather than the other way around.

A related problem is one of attributing more significance to an *area-based* analysis than is warranted. Statistical techniques such as principal components and cluster analysis may overemphasise the differences between urban areas, given that it is their task to differentiate (Brindley and Raine, 1979). For example, one area may be distinguished from another because it contains 5 per cent more single-parent families – a difference which may not have any particular significance in reality. On the other side of the coin is the danger of committing the ecological fallacy which is the assumption that the characteristics of individuals in a delineated area are the same as the average attributes of the area.

These issues are of critical importance for geographically based social indicators and especially in positive discrimination programmes which assume that discrete and identifiable areas of deprivation exist to be 'treated' by increased resource expenditure. Unfortunately for the proponents of such area-based schemes, research suggests that the degree of spatial concentration of deprived persons is relatively low.

Holterman (1975), for example, studied the concentration of housing stress as measured by Small Area Statistics. She took the worst 5 per cent and worst 15 per cent of urban enumeration districts in the UK on a variety of measures and determined a series of 'concentration ratios'. These ratios represented the number of persons (or households) in those 'worst' EDs with a particular form of deprivation as a percentage of persons (or households) in all urban EDs. The results are given in Table 7.4. For example, for the households 'lacking exclusive use of all basic amenities', only 18 per cent of those would be in priority areas if the worst 5 per cent of EDs were so designated, or conversely, 82 per cent of households deprived on that measure would be outside the priority areas. In addition Holterman found that *within* 'worst 5 per cent' EDs it was often the case that a majority of the population were not deprived, even if two or three deprivation indices were 'overlapped' to approximate a kind of multiple deprivation. Similar results were found in the education field by Barnes (1975) who reported that educationally deprived children were not especially concentrated, and that variations within schools were often more marked than variations between schools or districts. For example, for every two disadvantaged inner London children in Educational Priority Areas there were five outside those areas.

The evidence for *multiple* deprivation, that is, scoring high on more than one indicator of deprivation, is also weak. For example, a study of the worst 10 per cent of EDs for overcrowding and worst 10 per cent for lacking a fixed bath could find only about 15 per cent of EDs in the worst category for both indicators. Lawless (1979, p. 142) suggests that 'it is more realistic to think of . . . deprived areas as being of different types containing different combinations of deprivation' rather than as discrete areas of multiple deprivation of all types. A similar argument is put forward by Webber (1975), who suggests that the housing indicators of overcrowding, sharing of amenities and lack of a fixed bath have very different distributions.

Table 7.4   *Spatial concentration of urban deprivation: percentage of all individuals with characteristic of indicator in the EDs exceeding the 5 per cent cut-off value of the indicator*

Indicator	Concentration ratio	
	5% cut-off level	15% cut-off level
Share or lack hot water	23	53
Lacking bath	30	64
Lacking inside WC	28	61
Households overcrowded ($>1\cdot5$ p.p.r)	33	61
Shared dwelling	51	83
Lack exclusive use of all basic amenities	18	47
Males unemployed but seeking work or sick	16	36
Females unemployed but seeking work or sick	12	31
Households without car	7	21
Socioeconomic group 11	18	45
Children 0–14	11	27
Pensioner households	9	25
New Commonwealth ethnic origin	51	81

Source: Holterman, 1975.

Such studies raise questions of both *equity* and *efficiency*. For within a priority area there is a great likelihood that the majority will not be deprived and resources may be misdirected, thus fostering inefficiency. And is it more efficient to direct limited resources to the worst 1 per cent of EDs, or spread them thinly over the worst 15 per cent? On the equity side, however one uses indicators to define socially deprived areas, unless half of Britain is so designated, more poor will be outside the areas than in them and any special treatment may be inequitable. Another problem of equity is whether the citizens in the designated areas agree with the statistical assessment, and whether they desire special treatment. On the former issue, the delineation of the boundaries of priority areas could be supplemented by subjective social indicators, but measures of satisfaction as resource allocation measures would be fraught with obvious difficulties. On the latter point there is always the danger of an area becoming stigmatised by designation as a 'deprived' area. Research by Dennis (1978) into the designation of Housing Action Areas in the UK shows that such designations do not always meet with the residents' approval, nor do these residents necessarily agree with the choice of criteria for defining deprivation. Stegman's (1979) research in New York City points to a similar problem: that neighbourhood classification schemes which generalise variations in physical and socioeconomic conditions across entire neighbourhoods stigmatise certain streets or blocks which have, in fact, more than adequate housing and social conditions. On both points it is important that citizens be involved in the neighbourhood assessment process whenever resource allocation is the intention, and that the units being classified be kept small and checked carefully 'on the ground' for realism.

The problem of value-weighting discussed in Chapter 5 also rears its head here. Any combination of indicators used to assess multiple deprivation requires aggregation. If no explicit scheme is identified this of course transfers the value-weighting to the choice of indicators. In an HAA, by what yardstick does occupancy of a house at 1·7 persons per room in the slums of Glasgow compare with sharing a kitchen in a flat in well-off Chelsea? Common methods of aggregation such as summing rank scores or standardised scores require that data be normally distributed and that variables are statistically independent (Knox, 1978). Is there a causal connection between substandard housing and unemployment? If this is not known, an additive model may be misleading. Studies which press ahead with complex weighting schemes may also run the risk of obscuring the tentative nature of these schemes behind a facade of statistical sophistication. Edwards (1975) argues that debates as to the relative merits of factor analysis, principal components and cluster analysis obscure and mislead by hiding the relative and value-laden nature of aggregation.

Most value-weighting schemes are in fact determined in an *ad hoc* fashion based on political and bureaucratic needs and pressures. This was the case for Educational Priority Areas where the only way to test the composite measure was against the intuitive impressions of local education officers. Knox (1978) warns that the construction of composite measures is open to the pitfalls of cultural imperialism whereby the weighting of indicators reflects more the values of the authors of the system than those whose welfare is under consideration. He goes on to suggest that the values held by the public need to be articulated through citizen participation programmes and the leadership of major community institutions.

Finally, there is the related danger that politicians or planners may use indicators as 'vindicators' of their particular philosophy or ends. This is the accusation of a number of critics against locally based positive discrimination programmes. They argue that the concentration of such programmes on measures of social pathology, like mortality, truancy, deliquency and crime, introduces 'red herrings' which divert attention away from the true nature of urban deprivation (Edwards, 1975). In this argument social pathology, and mental and physical personal handicap, are only symptoms of *structural* inequality, that is, economic and social inequality at the national and even international levels. Proponents of this structural inequality model argue that such factors as unemployment, low wages and low income cannot be explained by social pathology, and are due to a lack of power of some individuals and families to influence their lives (Hirschfield, 1978, p. 36). Given a structural perspective, positive discrimination programmes offer no more than minor soothing of deep-seated disease. They are based on a 'person-blame' rather than 'system-blame' perspective, and have a concept of a 'culture of poverty' as a philosophical base.

According to this culture of poverty concept (or theory of social pathology) deprivation reflects personal inadequacy and an inability to cope with urban life. Coupled with this is the notion of a 'cycle of deprivation' which is transmitted from one generation to the next by family structure and limiting aspirations, and, in the case of urban deprivation, concentrated into discrete and identifiable pockets. Some critics suggest that positive discrimination at a local level was espoused by politicians and policy-makers because it was simpler, cheaper and administratively more attractive than dealing with 'real' structural problems. Ironically some of the employees of locally based positive discrimination programmes came around to the view of the structuralist critics. In Coventry, for example, the Community Development Team found themselves becoming increasingly aware of the extent to which the fortunes of their local priority area were influenced by forces outside local control (Coventry CDP, 1975). This community, the home of Chrysler UK (now Citroen-Talbot), was far more influenced by decisions taken in Detroit, London and Paris than any made locally. No local positive discrimination programme could counteract the effect of Chrysler's fortunes in the international auto market. The final report of the Coventry CDP, entitled 'Gilding the Ghetto', expressed clearly the structuralists' opinion of locally based positive discrimination programmes.

On the other hand, few critics opt for a wholly structural analysis. Lawless (1979, p. 149) suggests that it would not be correct to assume that cultures of poverty and structural arguments are mutually exclusive, because one can envisage them working in tandem. Nor would it be right to assume that these are the only factors which have been invoked to explain deprivation and its generation: life cycles of poverty, regional inequalities and poor local authority service delivery are amongst the more obvious alternative candidates.

Holterman (1978), whose research on the concentration of deprivations was some of the earliest to question the assumptions of priority areas, argues that although area action cannot be the whole answer to deprivation there are a number of cases where it is appropriate and most cost-effective. These include programmes in environmental improvement, housing improvement, recreational facilities and transport facilities – no small list. As in most complex policy problems, flexible and complex solutions embodying a number of partial if valid perspectives are often the best, if not the simplest, answer. Urban deprivation is no exception.

Local urban indicators – what future?
As with most applications of social indicators, their use in determining local priority areas for positive discrimination has not been a matter of simple application of technical instruments but one of political contention. This is inevitable as the allocation of limited resources by government is always a matter of contention. Value-judgements enter into problem definition, indicator choice and locality or group selection. No single approach or system of social indicators will tell us in an objective fashion to what locales and to whom resources should be directed, and indeed the concept of priority areas itself is obviously the product of a particular value-set.

Do the many limitations to using social indicators for local area analysis preclude policy usefulness? No, because every decision about priorities and the allocation of resources requires unambiguous and legible information of both a quantitative and qualitative nature about both equity and efficiency. Social indicators, properly constructed, and presented without technical jargon obscuring their methodological limitations and value-stance, can help define and clarify important issues and fuel the political debate necessary for democratic resource allocation. In the priority area case we found that social indicators have entered into the debate from a number of perspectives: to define local areas and to show that deprivation is not very concentrated in those areas. Research into urban deprivation via social indicators has 'presented an enormous amount of detailed analytical and prescriptive material which must provide a major informational input into urban debates at all scales'

(Lawless, 1979, p. 12). And given the very real problem of information overload, social indicators can serve to classify and highlight the important aspects of policy problems and to identify target groups for service provision.

Where urban problems do have an important spatial component social indicators can identify those factors, and where the spatial component is lacking that fact can also be made clear, as in Holterman's research. Social indicators are also useful for evaluating current policies and programmes, both in terms of progress over time and in terms of testing the underlying assumptions of the programmes. Later in this chapter we will examine social indicators as measures of performance in the delivery of urban services.

Finally, it is worth stressing that indicators will only be useful if they are set at a scale appropriate to the problem. We have seen that some policy actions are appropriate at the neighbourhood level: recreation, housing, some transport and environmental improvement. Other problems are best dealt with at city, county, or national levels. If the initial cut at the social indicator set shows that the problem is best redefined at another level it is most important that researchers be prepared to discard what is no longer appropriate rather than to cling to it because time and resources, or even reputation, have been invested in it. Finally, given the (low) state of the art of social indicator development, indicators are most likely to be relevant to policy when they relate to a single domain or area of concern, such as housing, transport, health, income, and so on. Inter-domain comparisons, trade-offs and weighting schemes, although often necessary to meet the needs of policy-makers, should be approached with explicit caution.

Indicators for inter-urban analysis

Quality of life in US cities
A somewhat different approach to the use of areal social indicators is to use them to compare and contrast cities and counties on a variety of measures. This is especially true in the USA where Flax (1978) has identified twenty-five such studies. The apparent aim of such exercises seems to be to point out which cities or jurisdictions are deficient on certain indicators as a way of stimulating decision-makers to improve the performance of their area on the deficient indicators as a means to improved quality of life. Sometimes the indicators are aggregated, usually by an explicit value-weighting scheme, and then the areas are ranked as to their performance on the overall quality-of-life measure.

One very large study of this type was undertaken by Liu and his associates and reported in *Quality of Life Indicators in the US*

Metropolitan Areas and in numerous academic journal articles (Liu, 1976a, 1976b, 1977, 1978a, 1978b). The basis of this study is a production function model which hypothesises that the quality of life, or satisfaction of wants, is an output which is the function of two factor inputs, the physical and psychological, or in Liu's notation:

$$QOL_{it} = F(PH_{it,} PS_{it}).$$

The physical inputs are seen as consisting of quantifiable material goods and services which satisfy most of the basic needs of human beings. The psychological inputs include subjective spiritual factors such as love, affection, esteem, self-actualisation and community belongingness, and so on (Liu, 1977). It is argued that physical and psychological inputs can, to a certain extent, substitute for each other and vary in proportion to produce a given level of quality of life, but that at some point overemphasis on one factor input can degrade the quality of life. The function is set out in a series of capability curves which represent varying degrees of the capability of society to satisfy wants.

The statistical analysis was done by way of approximately 150 indicators selected by the researchers and drawn from five goal areas: economic, political, environmental, health and education, and social. The researchers chose those goal areas, and subsequent indicators, which they felt represented the major concerns of most people with the objective of developing as common as possible a concept of well-being. A list of some of the 150 selected indicators is found in Table 7.5. Unfortunately Liu (1977, p. 229) takes the line that psychological factors are not quantifiable and thus may be held constant, so *QOL* becomes 'a function of those economic (*EC*), political and welfare (*PW*), health and education (*HE*), and social (*SO*) inputs which are quantifiable, or

$$QOL_{it} = F(EC_{it}, PW_{it}, HE_{it}, SO_{it}/PS_{it}).$$

Therefore only physical inputs were included as indicators; the psychological (i.e. attitudinal) inputs are not included because they are considered unavailable or unquantifiable. Certain environmental inputs are substituted in their place. The indicators were all, in fact, objective cardinal data. Various runs were made on the 1970 census data used. One of the first considered QOL for 243 urban census areas termed Standard Metropolitan Statistical Areas (SMSAs).* Another

---

*An SMSA is a county or group of contiguous counties which contains at least one city of 50,000 inhabitants. The contiguous counties are included if they are socially and economically integrated with the central city.

study ranked sixty-five large metropolitan SMSAs having populations greater than 500,000. A third did much the same for medium metropolitan SMSAs having populations between 200,000 and 500,000 (Liu, 1976a, 1977, 1978a respectively).

Table 7.5   Social indicators in a quality-of-life study

Factor Effect and Weight	Factors
	I Individual Development
	A Existing opportunity for self-support
+ (0·018)	1 Labour force participation rate
+ (0·018)	2 Percentage of labour force employed
+ (0·018)	3 Mean income per family member ($)
+ (0·018)	4 Percentage of children under 18 years living with both parents
− (0·018)	5 Percentage of married couples without own household
+ (0·018)	6 Individual education index
	B Promoting maximum development of individual capabilities
+ (0·028)	1 Per capita local government expenditures on education ($)
+ (0·028)	2 Percentage of persons 25 years old and over who completed 4 years of high school or more
	3 Persons aged 16 to 64 with less than 15 years of school but with vocational training
+ (0·014)	a Percentage of males
+ (0·014)	b Percentage of females
+ (0·028)	4 Individual health index
	C Widening opportunity for individual choice
	1 Mobility
+ (0·007)	a Motor vehicle registrations per 1,000 population
+ (0·007)	b Motorcycle registrations per 1,000 population
+ (0·007)	c Percentage of households with one or more automobiles
	2 Information
+ (0·007)	a Local Sunday newspaper circulation per 1,000 population
+ (0·007)	b Percentage of occupied housing units with TV available
+ (0·007)	c Local radio stations per 1,000 population
	3 Spatial Extension
− (0·011)	a Population density in SMSA, persons per square mile

Factor Effect and Weight	Factors	
– (0·011)	*b*	Percentage of population under 5 and 65+ living in central city
+ (0.022)	4	Individual equality index
+ (0·022)	5	Individual and institutional environment index

Source: Liu, 1978.

The actual indicators used in the analysis range from the usual 'income per capita' (economic) or 'number of hospital beds' (health) to the somewhat more value-laden 'percentage of occupied housing units with TV available' (social) and the decidedly odd 'number of days with thunderstorms occurring' (environmental). The researchers assigned a positive or negative factor effect and a weight to each indicator (e.g. thunderstorms – negative, –0·05) and then went on to tabulate and rank the scores for each goal area. In each case standardised 'Z' values* were computed, and based on the percentile distribution of the 'Z' values the SMSAs were divided into groups and assigned values of 5, 4, 3, 2, 1, for, respectively, outstanding, excellent, good, adequate, or substandard performance on the indicators. Factors within subcategories were weighted equally to derive a subcategory score, and the subcategory scores were weighted equally to obtain a subcomponent score. Then the average of the subcomponent scores was taken to show a composite index for each SMSA, which were then ranked by the indexes in comparison to other SMSAs (Table 7.6).

There exists a wide conceptual gap in this research between the production function model and the actual tabulation of very detailed (to the point of ranking cities) 'quality-of-life' analysis. First, the lack of any data on one of the two factor inputs to the model equation, the psychological variables, constitutes a serious problem with this research. The work of such people as Schneider (1975) and Kuz (1978) has demonstrated that quality-of-life research using only objective variables is highly suspect and that subjective realities are equally important to overall quality of life. Further, the research of Campbell, Converse and Rodgers (1976) and Andrews and Withey (1976) belies the assumption that psychological variables are not measurable. To postulate that $QOL = F(PH, PS)$ and then to ignore the PS does little to suggest that the hypothesis of a production

* $Z = \dfrac{X - \overline{X}}{s}$ where X is the value of an ordinate variable, $\overline{X}$ is the mean and s is the standard deviation.

function model will be validated. Liu (1977, p. 236) admits this to a certain extent when he notes that the lack of psychological variables is 'the weakest point in the study'. Secondly, no actual testing of the hypothesis embodied in this model occurred. Rather the indicators were selected, arbitrarily weighted as to direction and magnitude according to the researchers' value-judgements on the components of well-being, and then the individual indicators were combined to give an alleged composite indicator of life quality. The proposed model was not tested, and the research consisted of a tabulation and aggregation of the indicators resulting in a ranking of US cities as to this overall quality-of-life measure.

At the very detailed, disaggregated, one-domain level, some of Liu's tabulations are of interest. For example, it is useful to learn that in Charleston, South Carolina, 11·4 per cent of housing units do not have minimum plumbing facilities compared with a figure of 5 per cent for the USA as a whole. It is also interesting that mean income per family member in Charleston was only $2,317·0, $775·0 short of the US average. This is interesting information, with useful policy implications. Unfortunately, many of the indicators are very ambiguous and reflect only the researchers' value-judgements. To suggest, for example, that 'motorcycle registrations per 1,000 population' is positively related to quality of life requires a 'leap of faith' far beyond that of most citizens, and we have seen how such vehicle registration figures may also reflect a woeful lack of public transport which especially hits the poor and the aged. Similarly, the argument that 'population density' is negatively related to QOL will be refuted by many people happily ensconced in Manhattan, or downtown Chicago, or San Francisco.

The situation approaches absurdity as composite scores are ranked. It is difficult to accept, given the state of the art of QOL research admitted by most researchers, that Liu's measurements are accurate and valid enough to declare Portland, Oregon, as the big US city with the highest QOL and poor Birmingham, Alabama, as the city with the worst! Rankings in the middle of the scale, say, between city number ten and number eleven, are even more difficult. This is surely aggregation to the point of absurdity and of no policy usefulness.

Social well-being in US counties
Similar to the previous study but far less aggregated is research carried out by the US Department of Agriculture (USDA) and directed at 'policy makers and scientists working in the social indicator field' (Ross *et al.*, 1979, p. i). This study developed four separate composite indicators of well-being: socioeconomic status, health, family status and a measure of alienation. These were

Table 7.6 Ranking of cities in a quality-of-life study

SMSA	Economic Value	Rating	Political Value	Rating	Environmental Value	Rating	Health and Education Value	Rating	Social Value	Rating
1 Akron, Ohio	1·87	C	2·63	C	−0·56	C	1·12	C	0·18	E
2 Albany-Schenectady-Troy, NY	1·32	D	3·74	A	−1·29	D	1·86	B	0·58	B
3 Allentown-Bethlehem-Easton, Pa–NJ	1·42	D	2·47	C	−0·61	A	0·38	D	0·21	D
4 Ansheim-Santa Ana-Garden Grove, Calif.	2·17	B	3·04	B	−1·05	C	2·01	A	0·47	C
5 Atlanta, Ga.	2·47	A	1·87	E	−1·28	D	0·83	D	0·28	D
6 Baltimore, Md	1·34	D	2·52	C	−1·26	D	0·36	D	0·13	E
7 Birmingham, Ala.	1·05	E	1·69	E	−1·42	E	−0·02	E	0·09	E
8 Boston, Mass.	1·17	E	3·38	A	−1·25	D	2·01	A	0·60	B
9 Buffalo, NY	1·83	C	3·88	A	−1·20	D	1·42	B	0·70	B
10 Chicago, Ill.	2·36	A	2·96	B	−1·81	E	0·66	D	0·30	D
11 Cincinnati, Ohio–Ky–Ind.	2·34	A	2·84	B	−1·03	C	0·62	D	0·07	E
12 Cleveland, Ohio	2·51	A	2·78	C	−1·42	E	1·08	C	0·58	B
13 Columbus, Ohio	1·78	C	3·02	B	−1·09	C	1·48	B	0·76	B
14 Dallas, Texas	2·75	A	1·46	E	−0·90	B	0·76	D	0·45	C
15 Dayton, Ohio	2·12	B	2·56	C	−1·31	D	1·06	C	0·34	D
16 Denver, Colo.	1·83	C	3·09	B	−0·99	C	2·50	A	0·96	A
17 Detroit, Mich.	1·89	B	3·22	B	−1·72	E	0·96	C	−0·02	E
18 Fort Lauderdale–Hollywood, Fla	2·31	A	2·13	D	−1·08	C	0·20	E	0·58	B
19 Fort Worth, Texas	2·47	A	1·79	E	−0·85	B	0·35	D	0·43	C
20 Gary–Hammond–East Chicago, Ind.	1·39	D	2·27	D	−1·17	D	0·70	D	0·21	D

SMSA	Economic Value	Economic Rating	Political Value	Political Rating	Environmental Value	Environmental Rating	Health and Education Value	Health and Education Rating	Social Value	Social Rating
21 Grand Rapids, Mich.	2·26	B	3·63	A	–1·03	C	1·53	B	0·55	C
22 Greensboro–Winston–Salem– High Point, NC	1·15	E	1·83	E	–1·30	D	0·10	E	0·23	D
23 Hartford, Conn.	2·03	B	3·61	A	–1·12	C	2·27	A	0·59	B
24 Honolulu, Hawaii	1·13	E	2·14	D	–0·45	A	1·53	B	0·44	C
25 Houston, Texas	2·70	A	1·91	E	–1·00	C	1·08	C	0·55	C
26 Indianapolis, Ind.	2·51	A	2·42	D	–1·52	E	0·65	D	0·43	C
27 Jacksonville, Fla	0·89	E	1·75	E	–1·25	D	0·11	E	0·31	D
28 Jersey City, NJ	0·58	E	2·12	D	–1·01	C	–0·52	E	–0·16	E
29 Kansas City, Mo–Ka.	1·68	C	2·04	D	–1·12	C	1·11	C	0·80	A
30 Los Angeles–Long Beach, Calif.	2·05	B	2·52	C	–1·05	C	1·73	B	0·83	A
31 Louisville, Ky–Ind.	1·90	B	2·34	D	–1·41	E	0·31	E	0·26	D
32 Memphis, Tenn.–Ark.	0·94	E	1·82	E	–1·20	D	0·61	D	0·11	E
33 Miami, Fla	1·28	D	1·90	E	–0·41	A	0·60	D	0·76	B
34 Milwaukee, Wis.	2·17	B	3·27	A	–1·04	C	1·70	B	0·84	A
35 Minneapolis–St Paul, Minn.	1·93	B	3·47	A	–0·90	B	2·23	A	0·83	A
36 Nashville–Davidson, Tenn.	1·72	C	2·08	D	–1·08	C	0·63	D	0·72	B
37 New Orleans, La.	0·78	E	1·56	E	–1·26	D	0·42	D	0·17	E
38 New York, NY	1·95	B	2·20	D	–1·33	D	1·21	C	0·51	C
39 Newark, NJ	1·25	D	2·99	B	–1·20	D	1·26	C	0·10	C
40 Norfolk–Portsmouth, Va	0·85	E	1·93	E	–0·86	B	0·06	E	0·25	D

	Col1		Col2		Col3		Col4		Col5	
41 Oklahoma City, Okla	2·11	B	2·80	B	−0·82	B	1·37	B	0·88	A
42 Omaha, Nebraska–Iowa	2·27	B	2·58	C	−1·30	D	1·75	B	0·99	A
43 Paterson–Clifton–Passaic, NJ	1·93	B	1·85	E	−1·00	C	1·46	B	0·13	E
44 Philadelphia, Pa–NJ	0·95	E	2·43	D	−1·02	C	0·30	E	0·22	D
45 Phoenix, Ariz.	1·27	D	1·90	E	−0·59	A	1·60	B	0·72	B
46 Pittsburgh, Pa	1·59	C	3·11	B	−1·86	E	0·78	D	0·35	D
47 Portland, Oreg.–Wash.	2·67	A	3·54	A	−0·65	A	2·13	A	1·02	A
48 Providence–Pawtucket–Warwick, RI–Mass.	1·07	E	3·03	B	−0·76	B	0·17	C	0·16	C
49 Richmond, Va	2·33	A	2·47	C	−1·13	D	0·45	D	0·11	D
50 Rochester, NY	2·32	A	3·66	A	−0·70	B	2·00	A	0·21	D

Source: Liu, 1977.

analysed for geographical variation but no attempt was made to produce any overall QOL measure. There are 3,097 counties in the USA and the analysis was carried out at this level because many public services are provided by county governments and because the researchers felt that aggregation to the state level, for example, masked considerable substate variation in well-being. They suggest that state level indicators may be misleading and have limited usefulness to policy-makers, and they argue that national development policies are best conceived at a county level.

The study used 1970 Census of Population county data on a wide array of socioeconomic characteristics, and 1965–9 US Vital Statistics on mortality. To compare differences in types of counties, the data were grouped into ten residence categories based on previous USDA research (Hines *et al.*, 1975). These included four types of metropolitan or SMSA counties – three according to size, and one based on the central city/suburban split. The six non-metropolitan county types were classified on a rural–urbanised continuum and on whether they were adjacent or not to a metropolitan county. The most urban classification was counties with SMSAs having a population of at least 1 million, and the most rural classification was counties not adjacent to SMSAs and having no urban population.

From the census data and the vital statistics an initial pool of indicators was selected reflecting conditions of income, employment, labour force participation, education, health, family life and social disorganisation. From this pool an initial set of thirty-five indicators was chosen for further study based on the following criteria:

- *Redundancy:* only one measure of each variable of a social condition was retained. For example, of mean wage rate and mean family income only the latter was kept.
- *Complexity:* simple measures were selected over mathematically complex measures.
- *Instability:* measures reflecting long-run rather than short-run conditions were retained.
- *Interrelatedness:* some highly correlated measures were dropped.

A principal component analysis was then used to identify patterns of relationships among the thirty-five indicators. This suggested twelve indicators which were grouped into the four composite measures. These were:

- *Socioeconomic status:* median family income, employed male heads not in poverty, school attainment level and dwelling units with complete plumbing.

- *Health:* overall mortality, infant mortality, mortality from influenza and pneumonia.
- *Family status:* proportion of children living with both parents, ratio of males to females in the labour force, percentage of families with female heads.
- *Alienation:* suicide rate, mortality from cirrhosis of the liver.

The composite indicators were then constructed based on the numerical scores for each indicator standardised to a common scale.

The conclusions of the study are displayed in tabular form (Table 7.7) and in four colour-coded maps, with a commentary on the geographical variations. The study found, not surprisingly, that low socioeconomic, health, and family status had similar distributions, namely, in southern and western counties with high percentages of minorities (blacks, American Indians) and among the predominantly white areas of the Ozarks and Appalachia. More interesting, however, is the variation along the urban–rural axis. For socioeconomic status they found virtually a direct relationship with the level of urbanisation on all four indicators (Table 7.8). The same situation exists for the health status index (Table 7.9), with the exception of the core area of the largest SMSAs which had relatively lower status than other urban (but not rural) areas. In addition the fringe (suburbs) classification enjoyed proportionally better health than any other classification. For other indicators, the results display little urban–rural variations, or when they do it is not surprising, as in the male–female labour indicator which shows relatively more female employment in urban areas. Finally, one interesting indicator is mortality from cirrhosis of the liver which is considerably higher in the north-east and west than elsewhere. It is also higher in urban areas than rural, and is of course a severe problem in city centres.

The authors of this report urge us to be careful in the interpretation of their results. They warn us that they have not tapped many important dimensions of well-being and that the composite scores of individual counties are to be 'interpreted with caution' (Ross *et al.,* 1979, p. 14). The indicators are designed to monitor some areas of well-being and to expose geographical variation, for example, in the different scores on health indicators between urban and rural areas. The authors stress that the indicators are not to be used to allocate resources nor to evaluate any programmes. They are wise to urge caution, as dangers associated with geographically based social indicators are at work here. For example, one must watch out for the ever-present ecological correlation and not assume that the characteristics of any county are necessarily those of any resident. Also, as with priority neighbourhoods, the statistics can and do mask

Table 7.7 Conclusions of a four-index study of social well-being in US counties

County group and region	Number of counties	Socio economic status	Health status	Family status	Alienation
		US index = 100			
United States	3,097	100·0	100·0	100·0	100·0
Metro	612	115·7	106·1	99·3	99·2
Greater metro	175	122·6	108·6	102·4	97·8
Core	48	123·5	99·0	80·0	87·0
Fringe	127	122·2	112·1	110·8	101·9
Medium metro	258	113·9	105·3	99·4	99·8
Lesser metro	179	111·5	104·7	96·1	99·6
Non-metro	2,485	96·1	98·5	100·2	100·2
Urbanised:					
Adjacent to SMSA	191	112·4	103·7	97·2	100·9
Not adjacent to SMSA	137	109·4	99·8	95·3	98·3
Less urbanised:					
Adjacent to SMSA	564	97·8	97·9	97·1	101·5
Not adjacent to SMSA	721	97·1	98·8	98·1	100·2
Totally rural:					
Adjacent to SMSA	246	87·3	96·4	99·1	100·0
Not adjacent to SMSA	626	89·2	97·7	107·7	99·4
North-East	217	118·3	101·2	100·1	98·7
Metro	100	123·6	103·6	98·9	100·3
Non-metro	117	113·8	98·9	101·1	97·2
North Central	1,055	107·5	107·5	112·0	101·1
Metro	178	122·3	110·1	108·8	100·5
Non-metro	877	104·4	107·0	122·6	101·2
South	1,387	87·8	94·0	88·5	103·6

Metro	270	106·4	102·4	93·2	101·3
Non-metro	1,117	83·3	92·0	87·4	104·1
West	437	111·6	100·2	107·5	86·8
Metro	64	124·0	113·8	99·4	84·6
Non-metro	374	109·5	97·9	108·9	87·1

Source: Ross *et al.*, 1979.

Table 7.8 Socioeconomic status for US counties: mean index of socioeconomic status and means of component indicators for metro and non-metro counties, by region

County group and region	Index of socioeconomic status	Median family income	Indicators included in index		
			Male heads not in poverty	Median school years completed	Dwellings with complete plumbing
	Index	Dollars	%	Years	%
United States	100·0	7,493	89·9	10·9	83·3
Metro	115·7	9,362	94·8	11·6	91·7
Greater metro	122·6	10,589	96·5	11·8	94·2
Core	123·5	10,323	96·7	11·9	97·0
Fringe	122·2	10,689	96·5	11·8	93·2
Medium metro	113·9	9,099	94·5	11·5	90·9
Lesser metro	111·5	8,542	93·4	11·6	90·4
Non-metro	96·1	7,032	88·7	10·7	81·3
Urbanised:					
Adjacent to SMSA	112·4	8,542	93·9	11·6	91·1
Not adjacent to SMSA	109·4	8,018	92·8	11·6	89·6
Less urbanised:					
Adjacent to SMSA	97·8	7,236	89·8	10·6	82·5
Not adjacent to SMSA	97·1	7,003	89·1	10·7	82·7
Totally rural:					
Adjacent to SMSA	87·3	6,467	86·4	10·1	74·1
Not adjacent to SMSA	89·2	6,429	85·7	10·5	76·4
North-East	118·3	9,406	96·3	11·9	92·2
Metro	123·6	10,449	97·3	11·9	95·6
Non-metro	113·8	8,515	95·5	11·9	89·4
North Central	107·5	7,995	92·4	11·5	87·3
Metro	122·3	10,191	96·9	12·0	93·9

Non-metro	104·4	7,549	91·5	11·4	86·0
South	87·8	6,497	86·2	10·0	77·1
Metro	106·4	8,235	92·1	11·1	87·7
Non-metro	83·3	6,076	84·8	9·7	74·6
West	111·6	8,490	92·6	12·0	89·0
Metro	124·0	10,113	96·2	12·4	96·4
Non-metro	109·5	8,212	92·0	11·9	87·7

Source: Ross et al., 1979.

Table 7.9 Health status for US counties: mean index of health status and means of component indicators for metro and non-metro counties, by region

County group and region	Index of health status		Indicators included in index		
		Infant mortality	Total mortality	Influenza and pneumonia mortality
	Index		Death rates		
United States	100·0	24·1	95·5	33·6
Metro	106·1	21·9	92·1	30·0
Greater metro	108·6	21·0	89·5	29·5
Core	99·0	22·8	97·7	34·8
Fringe	112·1	20·4	86·5	27·5
Medium metro	105·3	22·2	93·2	29·7
Lesser metro	104·7	22·3	93·0	30·9
Non-metro	98·5	24·7	96·3	34·5
Urbanised:				
Adjacent to SMSA	103·7	22·8	94·9	29·8
Not adjacent to SMSA	99·8	23·7	97·0	33·1

County group and region	Index of health status	Indicators included in index		
	Index	Infant mortality	Total mortality	Influenza and pneumonia mortality
		Death rates		
Less urbanised:				
Adjacent to SMSA	97·9	25·2	96·5	34·7
Not adjacent to SMSA	98·8	25·1	95·9	33·9
Totally rural:				
Adjacent to SMSA	96·4	25·8	96·2	36·7
Not adjacent to SMSA	97·7	24·1	97·0	36·0
North-East	101·2	21·1	98·5	33·0
Metro	103·6	20·6	96·0	31·9
Non-metro	98·9	21·5	100·7	33·9
North Central	107·5	20·3	92·1	29·6
Metro	110·1	20·1	91·5	26·2
Non-metro	107·0	20·4	92·2	30·3
South	94·0	27·5	97·8	36·6
Metro	102·4	24·1	92·9	32·1
Non-metro	92·0	28·3	99·0	37·7
West	100·2	24·2	94·6	34·0
Metro	113·8	19·4	84·1	28·5
Non-metro	97·9	25·0	96·4	35·0

Source: Ross et al., 1979.

wide variations *within* the county. In addition, any study which talks about QOL without reference to attitudinal measurements may be on shaky ground. For example, when it comes to talking about 'quality of life' in terms of socioeconomic status, there is some danger of bias against agriculture as an occupation which, while scoring low on many common QOL indicators, nevertheless may offer satisfaction levels which are highly relevant to QOL. Finally, the question of value judgements cannot be escaped. The 'male–female labour force difference' indicator as *positively* correlated with higher QOL is an example. To some, that may reflect family stability, but it is equally likely that a low score on it represents a negative factor if it reflects a lack of opportunity for female employment in rural areas.

The USDA study gives an interesting 'broad-brush' perspective on geographical and urban-rural patterns of life quality on some selected indicators, given that we take the authors' warnings to heart. Like national social reports, to which it is similar, it is more useful for its general informational content, and the issues it raises, rather than lending itself to any particular policy perspectives. Like many efforts at social indicators, it is most useful in a disaggregated form which highlights interesting variations between relevant variables.

Social indicators for performance measurements

Both the dramatic growth of public expenditure over the past few decades, and the need to get 'value for money' in that expenditure, have given rise to attempts to use objective and subjective indicators to measure tangible improvements and cost-effectiveness in public service delivery. Sometimes termed productivity measurement or performance auditing, at the extreme these various terms define anything from detailed time-budget studies of the activities of individuals or small groups to overall measures of the effectiveness of public policy. In actual practice, performance measurement most often makes use of objective indicators of efficiency in terms of the conversion of organisational inputs to outputs. Effectiveness measures (as opposed to efficiency) are usually citizen assessments, using subjective indicators, of the perceived quality of service delivery.

Areas subject to study include waste collection and street cleansing, recreational services, library services, police and fire services, public transport, and educational and social services. Proponents of performance measurement studies argue that at any governmental level they can (1) help determine progress towards targets or goals set by public administrators, (2) identify problem areas and help set priorities for efforts at improving productivity, (3) help implement worker incentive schemes or so-called self-financing productivity arrangements (Hatry, 1972). Comparison between local govenments or operational units may also help set priorities for allocating resources by central government to local government (as is done, for example, by the UK's rate support grant) and focus attention on those services which perform consistently well so that they serve as examples for other authorities or units to emulate.

Considerable interest has been evinced in these types of studies, especially at the urban government level. In the UK, for example, a study of five district councils has recently been completed by the District Audit Service (Epping Forest District Council, 1976). In the USA the Urban Institute has issued a variety of reports and guides to performance measurement. Also in the USA, Rossi and Gilmartin (1980) have taken the first steps towards a social indicator system useful for monitoring educational performance. In both the UK and North America the need to cut public expenditure and get value for money in service provision has resulted in increased interest in assessing performance and efficiency. The approach is also quite topical given the increased attention in formal collective bargaining agreements to productivity clauses which stipulate changes in work rules and practices with the objective of achieving increased productivity and reciprocal worker gains (Horton, 1976). In this 'productivity bargaining' measurements of performance serve as both *ex ante* bargaining counters and *post facto* checks of contract fulfilment, the latter often linked to varying wage payments.

The Urban Institute suggests the following criteria for selection of performance indicators (Hatry *et al.,* 1977):

(1) *Appropriateness and validity:* indicators must be quantifiable, in line with goals and objectives for that service, and be oriented towards the meeting of citizen needs and minimising detrimental effects;
(2) *Uniqueness, accuracy and reliability:* indicators generally need not overlap, double counting should be avoided, but some redundancy may be useful for testing the measures themselves;
(3) *Completeness and comprehensibility:* any list of indicators should cover the desired objectives and be understandable;
(4) *Controllability:* the conditions measured must be at least partially under government control;
(5) *Cost:* staff and data collection costs must be reasonable;
(6) *Feedback time:* information should become available within the time-frame necessary for decision-making.

Measures of performance take a number of forms. A common indicator is the ratio of input to output, with the amount or level of service delivery as the output measure, and employee hours or unit cost of service provision as the input measure. Examples of such measures in the crime control and recreation fields are: speed of apprehension of criminals after crime per employee-hour, percentage of crimes cleared after x days, number of hours of recreational facility operation per monetary unit, or number of hours of citizen recreational participation per employee-hour, and so on. The assumption in each of these types of measures is that the *quality* of the output is held constant or improved as more efficient ratios are achieved. The output measures generally most easy to develop are those that cover services with the most tangible outputs. For example, refuse collection measures are much easier to obtain than measures of police efficiency or social service effectiveness. In the police case not only does some measure like 'number of arrests per employee-hour' encourage perverse effects like inadequate investigation, but the objectives of policing programmes are undoubtedly subject to political debate. These types of problems, however, may reflect not so much any inadequacy in the general approach as the primitive methodology for measuring some service outputs.

Where output indicators are unattainable it is very common practice to fall back on personnel and equipment utilisation rates as substitute measures. These generally take the form of the ratio of the resource actually used to the amount potentially available, or the change in service level per specified demographic unit. The direction of the sought-after change in this rate will, of course, depend on the subject area. In crime control the participation rate will decrease per unit of population, in recreation the accessibility rate will increase. Crime control measures, for example, might be:

- number of crimes per 100,000 population by type of crime;
- percentage of housholds or businesses victimised;
- per capita value of property losses.

For recreational facilities some participation or accessibility measures include:
- number of visits to recreation sites per 1,000 population in a specified area;
- average peak-hour attendance divided by capacity;
- percentage of citizens living within fifteen to thirty minutes' travel time of a recreational facility, distinguished by mode of transport;
- number of scheduled hours facilities closed for maintenance.

Another common supplement to these measures are those which have some potential for measuring effectiveness – citizen evaluation of the quality of service provision. This generally takes the form of interviews of actual or past clients to ascertain the number satisfied with a service per monetary unit or employee-hour expended. Such measures thus combine the traditional and somewhat suspect number of clients served with satisfaction levels. The Urban Institute (Hatry *et al.,* 1977) suggests that this form of measure will be particularly important to those who believe that citizen, or client, satisfaction with services is a major product of government services. Examples of such measures for recreational facilities include:

- percentage of households using park and recreation facilities who rate them as unsatisfactory;
- percentage of user households rating crowdedness of facilities as unsatisfactory;
- percentage of non-user households giving overcrowded facilities as reasons for non-use.

And for crime control:

- percentage of citizens who feel safe on neighbourhood streets after dark;
- percentage of citizens who feel police are generally courteous in their dealings with them.

Such questions as these are regularly asked, for example, by the Cleveland (UK) Social Monitoring Survey, which sometimes interviews a representative sample of the whole population of Cleveland and sometimes concentrates on service users' feelings about council services (Mobbs, 1975).

Issues in measuring performance
As with some other types of indicators, performance measurements only take on meaning with reference to something – usually other, similar measurements. Hatry (1972) suggests three reference points. First, comparisons over time to provide information on trends and progress – this is the most common approach in government and with productivity deals. Secondly, comparisons can be made across jurisdictions, especially those with similar characteristics. This was the approach of the UK Epping Forest study which compared the activities of five district councils. Thirdly, comparisons can be made among operational units within a particular service, for example, different police districts can be compared to foster learning about productive methods.

There are other problem areas in using indicators to measure performance which need to be considered. Simplest is the fact that in many cases there are no standards for performance, for example, there is probably no such thing as an acceptable rate of crime, and so such measures as are developed reflect value-judgements of some section of the community (Hara, 1976). In many cases, however, this problem may be theoretical – what administrators and the public are concerned with is relative rates of change – rising crime and not any absolute level. Of more importance is the point that increasing the efficiency of an ineffective service may well be counter-productive, and related to this is the fact that most workload or cost-productivity measures are not necessarily about goals at all. Street cleansing might become highly efficient but if the dropping of litter is on the increase the streets may well be dirtier than ever. Another problem is that such measures should serve to motivate workers positively but the opposite is always a danger. An emphasis on tonnes of refuse picked up from the street might encourage workers to favour stones over paper litter. The answer to these dilemmas is to choose appropriate combinations of measures for each service. Street cleansing tonnage and employee-hours figures, for example, would be complemented by studies of actual street cleanliness measured by one of the available formulas, and by occasional citizen evaluation.

In collective bargaining agreements there are additional problems. The most common is the failure to recognise that increasing output per employee-hour is not necessarily desirable if unit cost increases are of such a magnitude as to more than offset productivity gains because of higher salaries or reduced working hours. This can often be the case in the public sector, especially given the recently increased levels of militancy of public sector unions in the UK and the USA. Horton (1976, p. 408) points out, for example, that 'productivity gains may be counter-productive if they are accompanied by or result from too rapid increases in the price of inputs'. This is, of course, the efficiency perspective and unit cost increases in the public sector may be desirable for other reasons. It is important, however, that the relationship between unit labour costs and productivity levels be understood.

Although of considerable importance to evaluation, the use of subjective social indicators of citizen satisfaction must be approached cautiously, for higher levels of perceived performance do not necessarily imply higher actual levels of service. It is not unfeasible for clients to be dissatisfied with a perfectly adequate service because of a variety of unmet needs which that service is not designed to fulfil. For example, police services cannot make up for inadequate social service provision. Conversely, citizens may quite willingly state their feelings about services about which they in fact know little or nothing. For example, the majority of citizens might be quite satisfied with environmental health services (for example, air emission regulations and inspections) which are in fact substandard and inefficient. A third problem is that citizens may express satisfaction or dissatisfaction with service performance with reference to a general orientation towards government and politics. For example, a conservative person may express that the level of police service is inadequate based on general feelings about 'law and order' rather than on his own experience of police or crime. A general rule about such misleading results is that they are possible whenever there are determinants of the subjective indicator other than the service under consideration (Stipak, 1979a). Finally, citizen ratings may not translate easily into work-related activities – citizens may be concerned with the overall level of public transport provision, a highly political issue which a traffic supervisor can hardly do anything about.

The use of subjective social indicators in performance measurement therefore demands some caution and more study. Research in Los Angeles (Stipak, 1977) and Kansas City (Kelling *et al.,* 1976) has been unable to suggest any strong relationship between service characteristics and citizen evaluations. On the other hand, such indicators may tap important psychological feelings in the community that policy-makers cannot ignore. If people perceive the streets as unsafe, or public transport as poor, then that is an issue even if the level of crime is low or the buses are frequent. Subjective social indicators are probably best used as one section of a parcel of social indicators when it comes to assessing individual services, but they also provide a useful 'litmus' or warning sign of something amiss between government and citizen.

A recurring theme in any discussion of performance measurement, as with social indicators generally, is the potential opposition to, or non-utilisation of, the evaluation by management and staff. Sometimes resistance is based on the alienating effect of incomprehensible jargon in the evaluation and information systems. These difficulties are relatively straightforward, but many times the situation is more complex. For elected representatives performance measurement may expose poor or deteriorating urban services, inefficiency, and may provide material useful to opponents at the next election. Bureaucrats are concerned with things other than efficiency, such as keeping their jobs, getting promoted, increasing agency size, power and budget, and minimising organisational conflict, and may not see performance measurement as serving any of these ends. In Cleveland (UK) one chief administrative officer replied to the results of a Social Monitoring Survey with the observation that the clients for his service were 'all liars anyway' (Mobbs, 1975, p. 133). If inter-jurisdictional comparisons are intended, for example, among district councils in the UK, the fear is generated that such evaluation may be simply to provide 'a league table for the general public' or for central government 'to monitor the spending of individual local authorities' (Capps, 1977, p. 109). There is no easy resolution of these dilemmas. Obviously evaluations can easily be written in understandable terminology, and the development of an organisational structure where evaluation is a positive activity, rather than a threatening prospect, is of great value.

As far as the implementation of performance measurement schemes goes, the UK and the US experiences suggest very similar guidelines. The most important prerequisite for a successful scheme is that it is acceptable to management and staff at the onset. This requires that as many people as possible have a hand in the design of the measures, the data collection procedures and the implementation of the scheme. The performance measurement process, as much as possible, must be presented in a positive, constructive and diplomatic manner so as to appear unthreatening. As with any evaluation this may be the most difficult task of all but the co-operative development of the schemes may alleviate this problem somewhat. In any event, individuals must only be held accountable for those aspects of performance which are within their control. As for the measures themselves they should be simple to use to avoid error and distortion, and as cost-effective as possible. The data produced should be flexible in as much as they might be used by different departments but in the main they will have to be tailored to the specific needs of each separate operating unit. Attention should be given to the reporting frequency which may be at short or long intervals depending on the needs of management and the data source. There should be a range of indicators to give a balanced perspective on any particular service delivery and to avoid the distortion and perverse effects that concentration on a single indicator might introduce. Finally, measurement activities could be institutionalised, perhaps by incorporating them into cyclical budget or policy review procedures.

Summary

This chapter examined a variety of urban social indicators, which were presaged by Robert Park's theory of social ecology, and the Shevky–Bell model of social area analysis. Although both efforts were at least partially discredited in theory, they provided the impetus for the systematic empirical study of urban areas.

One type of this urban analysis uses intra-urban social indicators to classify neighbourhoods or to make particular resource allocations. The use of census data and schemes such as that of the PRAG for neighbourhood classification is useful, but faces problems of data availability, a lack of a theoretical base, value-judgements and the need to be clearly linked to political priorities. When such schemes are used as part of 'positive discrimination' or 'affirmative action' programmes to allocate resources, they face additional problems of determining realistic neighbourhood boundaries, and assessing the significance and concentration of measures within an area. In addition, normative decision criteria have to be established which promote both efficiency and equity, and this raises a number of political issues. Finally, such schemes may reflect a 'culture of poverty' perspective rather than a structuralist analysis. The former views deprivation as based on personal inadequacy while the latter sees it as a matter of national and international socioeconomic inequality. In practice, however, these perspectives need not be taken as mutually exclusive. In spite of the problems associated with these issues, intra-urban indicators will continue to play an important role in urban decision-making.

A second use of social indicators is for inter-urban analysis, which compares and contrasts cities across a variety of measures. Such studies must consider important psychological variables, and must be careful that the choice of indicators, the weighting scheme and the 'good/bad' criteria used to assess QOL reflect more than simply the researchers' arbitrary value-judgements. Such studies, however, can highlight interesting variations among relevant variables, for example, in health indicators for urban and rural areas. They are much less useful when aggregated to the overall quality of life level, and no realistic manner of ranking cities as to QOL is likely to be found.

A third use of indicators at the urban level is in performance measurement, that is, measuring tangible improvements and cost-effectiveness in public service delivery. Such studies are undertaken by local government for public transport, police and fire services, education and social services, using both objective and subjective social indicators. The indicators may measure the ratio of input to output, personnel and equipment utilisation rate (input only), or citizen evaluation of the quality of service provision. Comparisons can be made over time, across jurisdictions, or among operational units delivering a particular service. Problems with performance measurement include lack of performance standards, poor relationship of input measures to objectives, a confused relationship between perceived and actual service levels and resistance to such measures by management and staff. Experience suggests that the co-operative development of such performance measurement schemes can help overcome resistance to their use.

8

Conclusion

The aim of this book has been to explore the important political and methodological issues in social indicator research. This has been done to provide a review of research and activity in this field as embodied in the literature, and a forward-looking agenda of issues which must be tackled if the social indicator movement is to fulfil its two-pronged ambition of contributing to social knowledge, and providing useful and policy-relevant information to the public sector decision-making process.

The important political issues in social indicator research might be summarised as follows:

(1) Social indicators are part of the analytic component of the wider policy-making process. This process has an essential, and often paramount, emphasis on such factors as value-judgements, value-manipulation and bureaucratic maintenance.

(2) Just as the policy-making process may be informed by various social indicator studies, so the contingencies of that process must serve to establish some of the parameters which define individual social indicator efforts. Other important parameters are defined by criteria of social scientific research.

(3) Social indicators are never value-neutral but always contain value-judgements, either implicit in problem definition and indicator selection, or explicit in formal value-weighting schemes. Social indicator researchers must be aware of the dangers of cultural imperialism where their own value-sets and assumptions tacitly guide the research.

(4) Unquantifiable information may be as important to the decision process as that which can be readily quantified. Researchers must scrupulously avoid the pitfalls of 'quantificationism'.

(5) There is a potential conflict and tension between the short-term, cost-effective policy information needs of government and the more 'elegant' criteria which define long-term discipline research. In the social indicator field, policy analysis and discipline research should exist in a creative symbiotic relationship.

(6) Politicians and bureaucrats may well resist the development of social indicators which tend to work against any of their multi-

functional objectives and tasks. This problem cannot be avoided and social indicator research must be related to the determinants of information policy in government decision structures. This requires considerable advances in policy-modelling efforts.

(7) Unaggregated quantitative data will strain decision-makers' limited time-resources and will cause 'information overload'. Overly aggregated data, on the other hand, will be accused of hiding information vital to the decision process, and of offering vague generalities. This is a classic dilemma of rational analysis to which the only solution is the judicious presentation of information geared to the particular policy problem at hand.

The important methodological issues in social indicator research can also be summarised briefly:

(1) All social indicators involve an unmeasurable concept (like good health) and measurable surrogates for that concept (like life expectancy). Social indicators, therefore, implicitly or explicitly postulate some theory of social behaviour which serves to relate the variables under consideration.

(2) Some past efforts at social indicators have tended to be a-theoretical and unsystematic, and to imply unsubstantiated causal relationships. This has resulted in some of these efforts being dismissed by politicians and bureaucrats as useless or mis-leading. Although the pressures of government's short-term information needs may weigh against social indicator modelling, no real advances in social measurement can take place without such modelling efforts.

(3) Social indicator modelling faces problems of time-horizon, operationalisation, replication and boundary definition. If a weighting scheme is applied the difficulty of establishing correlation between concept and surrogate will rise considerably.

(4) The social indicator field consists of numerous very diverse efforts. Definitions abound, and trying to define a social indicator precisely tends to exclude many important research programmes. Social indicators efforts are best distinguished by their policy use and by their location in a hierarchy of statistical sophistication.

(5) Objective social indicators are based on counting the occurrences of a given social phenomenon, and subjective social indicators are based on reports from individuals about their feelings, perceptions and responses. Neither type, used alone, has managed to give us an accurate 'window' on reality, and they are best developed and used in conjunction.

This, then, is the formidable list of unresolved issues in social indicator research. If this book has emphasised the difficulties with social indicators, it is because we must scrupulously avoid any return to the days of overoptimism born of an underestimation of the political and methodological difficulties in social measurement. Against these difficulties, however, there is a continually growing need for an improved flow of cogent social information to a decision-making process becoming ever more complex. This suggests enormous potential for institutionalised policy-relevant social indicators, based on improved social indicator models and policy models. The social indicator models will promote the identification of causality and improve predictive capacity, and will distinguish policy manipulable variables from other non-manipulable structural variables. The social policy model incorporates social indicator models into a wider framework which considers value conflict and bureaucratic elements in its conception. These policy models relate social indicators to the needs for information in government, the flows and uses of that information, and the relationship of information to the implementation of policy.

Early efforts at such policy-modelling will no doubt be at a fairly specific or elementary level. Nevertheless, if the proponents of social indicators are to begin to overcome some of the political and bureaucratic dilemmas in social indicators, it is important that the role of information in policy-making be studied systematically. It is in such modelling efforts that discipline researchers and policy analysts can work together creatively to further social knowledge and aid the decision process.

Even as such policy models become more sophisticated, so we will be reminded of the importance of heeding Knox's (1978) warning that social indicators can only be as effective as their presentation. Technical jargon, a lack of comparative and contextual data and the lack of simple graphical and verbal summaries will be replaced by a simple and straightforward presentation. The research may be based on highly sophisticated analysis, but this will not confuse the subsequent and overriding need to communicate useful advice to policy-makers. In turn the myth of value neutrality will be laid to rest by encouraging an understanding of the values *and* limitations of quantitative analysis. In this way social indicators will provide social information which promotes the communication and intellectual pluralism vital to the continual, necessary debate on public policy issues.

Appendix: Notes on Further Reading

History and definition

The first section in Irvine *et al.* (1979) provides a useful compact history of the development of social statistics. Brindley and Raine (1979) look at the history of social area analysis in the light of modern developments. Bunge (1975) takes up other important aspects of a definition of social indicators. A review of the wide variety of articles in the journal *Social Indicators Research* gives an essential overview of the field.

Aspects of quality of life

Hicks and Streeten (1979) review efforts to supplement GNP with social indicators of basic needs. Articles in Wingo and Evans (1978) consider important dimensions of quality of life from a variety of perspectives, including the relationship of QOL to work, the environment, the city, taxation and government policy. Gehrmann (1978) looks at the difficulties which face researchers who hope to measure the quality of life. Andrews and Withey (1976) describe the rationale, construction and results of a major study of life quality. Buttel *et al.* (1977) examine the relationship between ideology and responses to quality-of-life inquiries.

Social theory and modelling

Guttman (1979) raises a number of important issues in theory construction. Chapter 2 of Jeffers (1978) looks at descriptive models, mathematical models, deterministic models and stochastic models and gives definitions and simple examples of each. Brewer (1978–9) concentrates on the key unresolved problems which hinder social modelling. Van Meter and Asher (1973) explain causal path modelling in a straightforward manner with a simple example. Models of objective social indicators are described in Land and Spilerman (1975) – the chapter by Land is most noteworthy. Blalock (1975) looks at the role of subjective variables in social models. Rossi and Gilmartin (1979) is a useful guide to the detailed construction of some types of social indicators from basic data, and contains a helpful glossary of statistical terms. Warren *et al.* (1980) propose multiple-indicator models, and de Neufville (1979) discusses the task of validating social indicators.

Matters of politics and bureaucracy

In a general vein, Michalos (1978) explores the philosophical basis of rationality in decision-making, and Carley (1980) examines the role of various 'rational techniques', including social indicators and cost-benefit analysis, in public sector policy-making. Meltsner (1976) looks specifically at the experience of policy analysts in the US federal bureaucracy. Strauch (1975) describes the dangers of quantificationism, and Ladd (1975) looks at some of the moral dilemmas posed by rational analysis.

On social indicators and policy, de Neufville (1975) offers considerable insight into, and useful examples of, the use and misuse of some macro indicators, including the unemployment rate and the crime rate. Henriot (1970), Meehan (1975), Brand (1975) and Hope (1978) are all worthwhile articles which chart the political dangers in social indicator efforts. Miller (1979) looks at policy-modelling and takes some first steps in this somewhat neglected direction. Meltsner (1979) discusses the relationship between analysis and the communication of results to decision-makers.

Hoinville and Courtenay (1979) is a useful review of different approaches to measuring priorities and preferences, and making trade-offs, for tangible and intangible social goods. The problems associated with implicit value-weighting and preference aggregation in public surveys is examined by Birch and Schmid (1980). Those interested in the Delphi technique will find Linstone and Turoff (1975) a virtual handbook, which should be read in conjunction with Sackman (1974 and 1976) and Hill and Fowles (1975) for a balanced perspective.

Social reporting

Obviously a perusal of *Social Trends, Social Indicators 1976,* and the *World Development Report* would be the first step. Progress in national social reporting is documented in Brusegard (1977). Excellent dialogues on the pros and cons of the US and Canadian efforts can be found in *Contemporary Sociology,* vol. 7 (1978), the *Annals of the American Academy of Political and Social Sciences,* vol. 435 (1978), and in *Social Indicators Research,* vol. 6, no. 2 (1979). On the UK volume only Thompson (1978b) and Bulmer (1979) constitute the debate. Estes (1975) and Grojer and Stark (1979) are both useful guides to corporate, as opposed to national, social reporting.

Urban social indicators

On positive discrimination programmes and urban deprivation

Lawless (1979) is an excellent and complete guide to the UK experience. Edwards (1975) looks at the conceptual difficulties and untenable assumptions which may underpin such efforts. Stegman (1979) shows the difficulty of making area classifications from examples in New York City, and Holterman discusses the statistical (1975) and economic (1978) problems such an approach raises. Hatry *et al.* (1977) is the best guide to performance measurement of urban services and the September 1978 issue of *Social Policy* was devoted entirely to performance measurement. The difficulties and pitfalls in attempting to use subjective social indicators to measure performance are given a most useful examination by Stipak (1979a, 1979b).

References

Abrams, M. (1973), 'Subjective social indicators', in *Social Trends No. 4*, ed. M. Nissel (London: Her Majesty's Stationery Office), pp.35–50.

Abrams, M. (1976), *A Review of Subjective Social Indicator Work, 1971–1975* (London: Social Science Research Council).

Abrams, M. (1978), 'Social indicators and quality of life studies', paper presented to the Conference on Social Indicators in Planning and Policy, Regional Studies Association, London.

Allardt, E. (1977), *On the Relationship between Objective and Subjective Predicaments,* Research Report No. 16 (University of Helsinki: Research Group for Comparative Sociology).

Allnut, D., and Gilardi, A. (1980), 'Inner cities in England', in *Social Trends No. 10* (London: Her Majesty's Stationery Office), pp. 39–51.

Ament, R. H. (1970), 'Comparison of Delphi forecasting studies in 1964 and 1967', *Futures* vol. 2, pp. 15–23.

Anderson, J. G. (1973), 'Causal models and social indicators: towards the development of social systems models', *American Sociological Review,* vol. 38, no. 3, pp. 285–301.

Andrews, F. M., and Inglehart, R. F. (1979), 'The structure of subjective well-being in nine Western societies', in *Social Indicators Research,* vol. 6, pp. 73–90.

Andrews, F. M., and Withey, S. B. (1976), *Social Indicators of Well-Being* (New York: Plenum Press).

Angrist, S., Belkin, J., and Wallace, W. (1976), 'Social indicators and urban policy analysis', in *Socio-Economic Planning Sciences,* vol. 10, pp. 193–8.

Barnes, J. (ed.) (1975), *Educational Priority, Report of Research Project, Vol. 3, Curriculum: Innovations in London EPAS* (London: Her Majesty's Stationery Office).

Bauer, R. (ed.) (1966), *Social Indicators* (Cambridge and London: MIT Press).

Bell, D. (1969), 'The idea of a social report', *The Public Interest,* no. 15, Spring.

Biderman, A. D. (1966), 'Social indicators and goals', in Bauer (1966).

Birch, A. L., and Schmid, A. A. (1980), 'Public opinion surveys as guides to public policy and spending', *Social Indicators Research,* vol. 7, pp. 299–312.

Bisset, R. (1978), 'Quantification, decision-making and environmental impact assessment in the United Kingdom', *Journal of Environmental Management,* vol. 7, pp. 43–58.

Blalock, H. M. (1975), 'Indirect measurement in social science – some non-additive models', in *Quantitative Sociology – International Perspectives on Mathematical and Statistical Modelling,* ed. Blaclock *et al.* (New York: Academic Press).

Brand, J. (1975), 'The politics of social indicators', *British Journal of Sociology,* vol. XXVI, pp. 78–90.

Brent, R. J. (1979), 'Imputing weights behind past railway closure decisions within a cost-benefit framework', *Applied Economics*, vol. 11, pp. 157–70.

Brewer, G. D. (1978–9), 'Operational social systems modelling: pitfalls and prospectives', *Policy Sciences*, vol. 10, pp. 157–69.

Brindley, T. S., and Raine, J. W. (1979), 'Social area analysis and planning research', *Urban Studies*, vol. 16, pp. 273–89.

Brusegard, D. A. (1977), *National Social Reporting: The Elements and the Activity* (Paris: Organsiation for Economic Co-operation and Development).

Brusegard, D. A. (1978), '*Social indicators 1976* and *Perspective Canada II:* elixirs of reason or of sleep?', *The Annals of the American Academy of Political and Social Science*, vol. 435, pp. 268–76.

Brusegard, D. A. (1979), 'Rethinking national social reports', *Social Indicators Research*, vol. 6, pp. 261–72.

Bulmer, M. (1979), review of *Social Trends No. 9, Journal of Social Policy*, vol. 8, pp. 543–6.

Bunge, M. (1975), 'What is a quality of life indicator?', *Social Indicator Research*, vol. 2, pp. 65–79.

Buttel, F., Wilkening, E. A., and Martinson, O. B. (1977), 'Ideology and social indicators of the quality of life', *Social Indicators Research*, vol. 4, pp. 353–69.

Campbell, A., and Converse, P. E. (1972), *The Human Meaning of Social Change* (New York: Russell Sage Foundation).

Campbell, A., Converse, P. E., and Rogers, W. L. (1976), *The Quality of American Life: Perceptions, Evaluations, and Satisfactions* (New York: Russell Sage Foundation).

Cantril, H. (1965), *Pattern of Human Concerns* (New Brunswick, NJ: Rutgers University Press).

Caplan, N., and Barton, E. (1978), 'The potential of social indicators: minimum conditions for impact at the national level as suggested by a study of the use of *Social Indicators 73*', *Social Indicators Research*, vol. 5, pp. 427–56.

Capps, B. (1977), 'Performance measurement: a cautious welcome', *Municipal and Public Services Journal*, vol. 85, pp. 1009–10.

Carley, M. (1980), *Rational Techniques in Policy Analysis* (London: Heinemann Educational Books).

Carlisle, E. (1972), 'The conceptual structure of social indicators', in *Social Indicators and Social Policy*, ed. A. Shonfield and S. Shaw (London: Heinemann Educational Books).

Chartered Institute of Public Finance and Accounting (1979), *Community Indicators* (London: CIPFA).

Christian, D. E. (1974), 'International social indicators: the OECD experience', *Social Indicator Research*, vol. 1, pp. 169–88.

Churchman, C. West (1975), 'On the facility, felicity, and morality of measuring social change', in *Social Accounting: Theory, Issues, and Cases*, ed. L. J. Seidler and L. L. Seidler (Los Angeles: Melville Publishing).

Clark, Terry N. (1974), 'Can you cut a budget pie?', *Policy and Politics*, vol. 3, pp. 3–31.

Coleman, J. S. (1972), *Policy Research in the Social Sciences* (Morristown, N.J.: The General Learning Press).

Coleman, J. S. (1973), *The Mathematics of Collective Action* (London: Heinemann Educational Books).

Converse, P. E. (1968), 'Time budgets', in *International Journal of the Social Sciences,* ed. D. L. Sills (New York: Macmillan and The Free Press).

Coventry Community Development Project (1975), Final Report, Part I, *Coventry and Hillfields: Prosperity and the Persistence of Inequality.*

Craig, J., and Driver, A. (1972), 'The identification and comprison of small areas of adverse social conditions', *Applied Statistics* (Journal of the Royal Statistical Society – Series C), vol. 2, pp. 25–35.

Cullen, Ian G. (1978), 'Measuring the impacts of urban social policies', paper presented to the Ninth World Congress of Sociology, mimeo., Bartlett School of Architecture and Planning, University College, London.

Culyer, A. J., Lavers, R. J., and Williams, A. (1971), 'Social indicators – health', in *Social Trends No. 2,* ed. M. Nissel (London: Her Majesty's Stationery Office).

Danziger, S., and Plotnick, R. (1979), 'Can welfare reform eliminate poverty?', *Social Service Review,* vol. 53, pp. 244–60.

David, H. (1973), 'Social indicators and technology assessment', *Futures,* vol. 5, pp. 236–44.

Davies, B. (1977), 'Needs and outputs', in *Fundamentals of Social Administration,* ed. H. Weisler (London: Macmillan).

Davies, B., and Knapp, M. R. J. (1980), *Old People's Homes and the Production of Welfare* (London: Routledge & Kegan Paul).

de Neufville, J. I. (1975), *Social Indicators and Public Policy* (Amsterdam: Elsevier Publishing Company).

de Neufville, J. I. (1978), 'Validating policy indicators', *Policy Sciences,* vol. 10, pp. 171–88.

Dennis, N. (1978), 'Housing policy areas: criteria and indicators in principle and practice', *Institute of British Geographers Transactions, n.s., vol. 3,* no. 1, pp. 2-22.

Dever, G. E. A. (1979), 'Social indicators, 1976: a critique', *Social Indicators Research,* vol. 6, pp. 153–62.

Dorman, R. (1979), 'Why statistics in the public sector?', *Public Finance and Accountancy,* October, pp. 22–5.

Dumont, R., and Wilson, W. (1967), 'Aspects of concept formation, explication and theory construction in sociology', *American Sociological Review,* vol. 32, pp. 985–95.

Duncan, Otis Dudley (1969), *Towards Social Reporting: Next Steps* (New York: Russell Sage Foundation).

Edwards, J. (1975), 'Social indicators, urban deprivation and positive discrimination', *Journal of Social Policy,* vol. 4, pp. 275–87.

Encel, S., Marstrand, P. K., and Page, W. (eds.) (1975), *The Art of Anticipation* (London: Martin Robertson).

Epping Forest District Council (1977), *Performance Measurement in Local Government* (Epping: EFDC).

Estes, R. W. (1975), 'A comprehensive corporate social reporting model',

Social Accounting, Theories, Issues, and Cases, ed. L. J. Seidler and L. L. Seidler (Los Angeles: Melville Publishing).

Evans, W., and Chen, M. K. (1978), 'The application of quantitative indices for health planning to regional service areas in Vermont', *Social Indicators Research,* vol. 5, pp. 181–94.

Fanchette, S. (1974), 'Social indicators: problems of methodology and selection', in *Social Indicators: Problems of Definition and Selection* (Paris: UNESCO).

Ferriss, A. L. (1979), 'The US federal effort in developing social indicators', *Social Indicators Research,* vol. 6, pp. 129–52.

Fitzsimmons, S. J., and Levy, W. G. (1976), 'Social Economic Accounts System (SEAS) toward comprehensive community-level assessment procedure', *Social Indicators Research,* vol. 2, pp. 389–452.

Fitzsimmons, S. J., and Lavey, W. G. (1977), 'Community: towards an integration of research, theory, evaluation and public policy considerations', *Social Indicator Research,* vol. 4, pp. 25–66.

Fitzsimmons, S. J., and Ferb, T. E. (1977), 'Developing a community attitude assessment scale', *Public Opinion Quarterly,* vol. 41, pp. 356–78.

Flax, M. J. (1978), *Survey of Urban Social Indicator Data 1970–1977* (Washington DC: The Urban Institute).

Forcese, D., and Richer, S. (1973), *Social Research Methods* (Englewood Cliffs, NJ: Prentice-Hall).

Forrester, Jay (1971), *World Dynamics* (Cambridge, Mass.: Wright-Allen Press).

Fowles, Jib (1976), 'An overview of social forecasting procedures', *Journal of the American Institute of Planners,* vol. 42, pp. 253–63.

Fowles, Jib (1977), 'The problems of values in futures research', *Futures,* vol. 9, pp. 303–14.

Fox, K. S. (1974), *Social Indicators and Social Theory: Elements of an Operational System* (New York: Wiley).

Fry, B. R., and Tompkins. M. E. (1978), 'Some notes on the domain of public policy studies', *Policy Studies Journal,* vol. 6, pp. 305–13.

Gambling, T. (1974), *Societal Accounting* (London: Allen & Unwin).

Gehrmann, F. (1978), ' "Valid" empirical measurement of quality of life?', *Social Indicators Research,* vol. 5, pp. 73–110.

Goldstein, M. S., Marcus, A. C., and Rausch, N. P. (1978), 'The nonutilisation of evaluation research', *Pacific Sociological Review,* vol. 21, pp. 21–44.

Goodman, J. L., Jr (1978), 'Causes and indicators of housing quality', *Social Indicators Research,* vol. 5, pp. 195–210.

Gordon P., and Neidercorn, J. H. (1978), 'A procedure for fully evaluating the anticipated impacts of selected public system innovation on various environments using citizen-generated information inputs', in *Socio-Economic Planning Sciences,* vol. 12, pp. 77–83.

Grojer, Jan-Erik, and Stark, Agneta (1979), *Social Accounting* (Stockholm: Business and Social Research Accounting Institute).

Gross, B. M. (1966), 'The state of the nation: social systems accounting', in Bauer (1966).

Guttman, L. (1979), 'What is not what in theory construction', *Quantitative Sociology Newsletter*, no. 22, pp. 5–36.

Hakim, C. (1978a), *Social and Community Indicators from the Census* (London: Office of Population, Censuses and Surveys).

Hakim, C. (1978b), *'Census-derived social indicators in planning and policy'*, paper presented to the Conference on Social Indicators in Planning and Policy, Regional Studies Association, London.

Hall, J. (1976), 'Subjective measures of quality of life in Britain: 1971–1975', *Social Trends No. 7*, ed. M. Nissel (London: Her Majesty's Stationery Office).

Hall, J., and Perry, N. (1974), *Aspects of Leisure in two Industrial Cities*, Occasional Papers in Survey Research (London: SSRC Survey Unit).

Halsey, A. H. (1972), *Trends in British Society since Nineteen Hundred* (London: St Martin's Press).

Hara, L. F. (1976), 'Performance auditing: where do we begin?', *Governmental Finance*, vol. 5, pp. 6–10.

Hatch, S., and Sherrot, R. (1973), 'Positive discrimination and the distribution of deprivations', *Policy and Politics*, vol. 1, pp. 223–40.

Hatry, Harry P. (1972), 'Issues in productivity measurement for local government', *Public Administration Review*, vol. 32, pp. 776–84.

Hatry, Harry P., *et al.* (1977), *How Effective are your Community Services? Procedures for Monitoring the Effectiveness of Municipal Services* Washington, DC: The Urban Institute).

Hauser, P. M. (1968), 'Social accounting', in *The Uses of Sociology*, ed. P. F. Lazarsfeld, W. H. Sewell and H. L. Wilensky (London: Weidenfeld & Nicolson).

Hayden, F. Gregory (1977), 'Toward a social welfare construct for social indicators', *American Journal of Economics and Sociology*, vol. 32, pp. 129–46.

Hedges, B. (1974), 'Time budgets', in *Social Trends No. 5*, ed. M. Nissel (London: Her Majesty's Stationery Office).

Henderson, D. W. (1974), *Social Indicators: A Rationale and a Research Framework* (Ottawa: The Economic Council of Canada).

Henriot, P. J. (1970), 'Political questions about social indicators', *The Western Political Quarterly*, vol. 23, pp. 235–55.

Hicks, N., and Streeten, P. (1979), 'Indicators of development: the search for a basic needs yardstick', *World Development*, vol. 7, pp. 567–80.

Hill, K. Q., and Fowles, J. (1975), 'The methodological worth of the Delphi forecasting technique', in *Technological Forecasting and Social Change*, vol. 7, pp. 179–92.

Hines, F. K., Brown, D. L., and Zimmer, J. M. (1975), *Social and Economic Characteristics of the Population in Metro and Nonmetro Counties 1970* (Washington, DC: US Department of Agriculture, Economic Research Service).

Hirschfield, A. (1978), 'Theoretical approaches to the study of urban deprivation', working paper, School of Geography, University of Leeds.

Hoinville, G., and Courtenay, G. (1979), 'Measuring consumer priorities', in *Progress in Resource Management and Environmental Planning*, ed. T. O'Riordan and R. D'Arge (Chichester: Wiley).

Holmans, A. E. (1979), 'Housing tenure in England and Wales: the present situation and recent trends', in *Social Trends No. 9*, ed. E. J. Thompson (London: Her Majesty's Stationery Office).

Holterman, S. (1975), 'Areas of urban deprivation in Great Britain: an analysis of 1971 census data', in *Social Trends No. 6*, ed. E. J. Thompson (London: Her Majesty's Stationery Office).

Holterman, S. (1978), 'The welfare economics of priority area policies', *Journal of Social Policy*, vol. 7, pp. 23–40.

Hope, K. (1978), 'Indicators of the state of society', in *Social Policy Research*, ed. M. Bulmer (London: Macmillan).

Horn, R. V. (1978), 'From social statistics to social indicators', *Australian Journal of Statistics*, vol. 20, pp. 143–52.

Horton, R. D. (1976), 'Productivity and productivity bargaining in government: a critical analysis', *Public Administration Review*, vol. 36, pp. 407–14.

Illich, I. (1975), *Medical Nemesis* (London: Calder & Boyars).

Imboden, N. (1978), *A Management Approach to Project Appraisal and Evaluation* (Paris: Organisation for Economic Co-operation and Development).

Irvine, J., and Miles, I. (1979), 'Statistics teaching in social science: a problem with a history', in Irvine, Miles and Evans (1979).

Irvine, J., Miles, I., and Evans, J. (eds.) (1979), *Demystifying Social Statistics* (London: Pluto Press).

Jazairi, N. T. (1976), *Approaches to the Development of Health Indicators* (Paris: Organisation for Economic Co-operation and Development).

Jeffers, J. N. R. (1978), *An Introduction to Systems Analysis: With Ecological Applications* (London: Edward Arnold).

Jenkins, W. I. (1978), *Policy Analysis* (London: Martin Robertson).

Johnston, D. F. (1976), *Basic Disaggregation of Main Social Indicators* (Paris: Organisation for Economic Co-operation and Development).

Johnston, D. F. (1978a), 'Social indicators 1976 – a reply to the critics', *Contemporary Sociology*, vol. 7, pp. 722–4.

Johnston, D. F. (1978b), 'Postlude: past, present and future', *Annals of the American Academy of Political and Social Science*, vol. 435, pp. 286–94.

Johnston, D. F. (1978c), 'Social Indicators and Social Forecasting', in *Handbook of Futures Research*, ed. Jib Fowles (Westport, Conn., Greenwood Press).

Kelling, G. L., Pate, T., Dieckman, D., and Brown, C. E. (1976), 'The Kansas City preventative patrol experiment: a summary report', in *Evaluation Studies Review Annual*, ed. G. V. Glass (Beverly Hills: Sage), pp. 605–57.

Kemp, P. (1979), 'Planning and development statistics 1978/1979', in *District Councils Review*, pp. 62–4.

Kennedy, L. W., Northcott, H. C., and Kinzel, C. (1978), 'Subjective evaluation of well-being: problems and prospects', *Social Indicators Research*, vol. 5, pp. 457–74.

Knox, P. L. (1976a), *Social Priorities for Social Indicators*, Occasional Paper No. 4, Department of Geography, University of Dundee.

Knox, P. L. (1976b), 'Social well-being and North Sea Oil: an application of subjective social indicators', *Regional Studies*, vol. 10, pp. 423–32.

Knox, P. L. (1978), 'Territorial social indicators and area profiles', *Town Planning Review,* vol. 49, pp. 75–83.

Knox, P. L. (1979), 'Subjective social indicators and urban social policy: a review', *Policy and Politics,* vol. 7, pp. 299–309.

Kolodny, R. (1978), 'Some policy implications of theories of neighborhood change', in *Papers in Planning* (New York: Columbia University Graduate School of Architecture and Planning).

Kramer, F. A. (1975), 'Policy analysis as ideology', *Public Administration Review,* vol. 35, pp. 509–17.

Kuhn, T. S. (1970), *The Structure of Scientific Revolutions,* 2nd ed. (Chicago: Chicago University Press).

Kuz, T. J. (1978), 'Quality of life, an objective and subjective variable analysis', *Regional Studies,* vol. 12, pp. 409–17.

Ladd, J. (1975), 'Policy studies and ethics', in *Policy Studies and the Social Sciences,* ed. S. S. Nagel (Lexington, Mass.: D. C. Heath), pp. 177–84.

Lakatos, I. (1970), 'Falsification and the methodology of scientific research programmes', in *Criticism and the Growth of Knowledge,* ed. I. Lakatos and A. Musgrave (Cambridge University Press), pp. 91–196.

Land, K. C. (1971), 'On the definition of social indicators', *The American Sociologist,* vol. 6, pp. 322–5.

Land, K. C. (1975a), 'Theories, models, and indicators of social change', *International Social Science Journal,* vol. 27, pp. 7–37.

Land, K. C. (1975b), 'Social indicator models: an overview', in *Social Indicator Models,* ed. K. C. Land and S. Spilerman (New York: Russell Sage Foundation), pp. 5–36.

Land, K. C. and Felson, M. (1976), 'A general framework for building dynamic macro social indicator models: including an analysis of changes in crime rates and police expenditures', *American Journal of Sociology,* vol. 82, pp. 565–604.

Land, K. C., and Felson, M. (1977), 'A dynamic macro social indicator model of changes in marriage, family and population in the United States, 1947–1974', *Social Science Research,* vol. 6, pp. 328–62.

Land, K. C., and McMillen, M. M. (1980), 'A macrodynamic analysis of changes in mortality indexes in the United States, 1946–1975, some preliminary results', *Social Indicators Research,* vol. 7, pp. 1–46.

Lawless, P. (1979), *Urban Deprivation and Government Initiative* (London: Faber).

Lazarsfeld, P. F. (1961), 'Notes on the history of quantification in sociology – trends, sources and problems', in *Quantification,* ed. H. Woolf (Indianapolis: Bobbs-Merrill).

Leik, R. K., and Meeker, B. F. (1975), *Mathematical Sociology* (Englewood Cliffs, NJ: Prentice-Hall).

Lerner, M. (1979), 'A review of *Health: United States 1975',* *Social Indicators Research,* vol. 6, pp. 197–206.

Levy, S., and Guttman, L. (1975), 'On the multivariate structure of well-being', *Social Indicators Research,* vol. 2, pp. 361–88.

Lewis, J., and Flynn, R. (1979), 'The implementation of urban and regional planning policies', *Policy and Politics,* vol. 7, pp. 123–42.

Lichfield, N., Kettle, P., and Whitbread, M. (1975), *Evaluation in the Planning Process* (Oxford: Pergamon).

Lineberry, R., Mandel, A., and Shoemaker, P. (1974), *Community Indicators: Improving Communities Management* (Austin, Texas: University of Texas).

Linstone, H. A., and Turoff, M. (eds) (1975), *The Delphi Method – Techniques and Applications* (Addison, Mass.: Addison-Wesley).

Little, A., and Mabey, C. (1972), 'An index for designation of Educational Priority Areas', *Social Indicators and Social Policy,* ed. A. Shonfield and S. Shaw (London: Heinemann Educational Books).

Little, D. L. (1975), 'Social indicators and public policy', *Futures,* vol. 7, pp. 41–51.

Little, I. M. D., and Mirrlees, J. A. (1974), *Project Appraisal for Developing Countries* (London: Heinemann Educational Books).

Liu, Ben-Chieh (1976a), *Quality of Life Indicators in US Metropolitan Areas. A Statistical Analysis* (New York: Praegar).

Liu, Ben-Chieh (1976b), 'Social quality of life indicators for small metropolitan areas in America', *International Journal of Social Economics,* vol. 3, pp. 198–213.

Liu, Ben-Chieh (1977), 'Economic and non-economic quality of life', *American Journal of Economics and Sociology,* vol. 36, pp. 226–40.

Liu, Ben-Chieh (1978a), 'Variations in social quality of life indicators in medium metropolitan areas', *American Journal of Economics and Sociology,* vol. 37, pp. 241–60.

Liu, Ben-Chieh (1978b), 'Technological change and environmental quality: a preliminary survey of environmental indicators in medium metropolitan areas', *Technological Forecasting and Social Change,* vol. 12, pp. 325–36.

McFarland, D. D. (1975), 'Models involving social indicators of population and the quality of life', in *Social Indicator Models,* ed. K. C. Land and S. Spilerman (New York: Russell Sage Foundation).

McGinnis, R. (1979), *'Science Indicators, 1976:* a critique', *Social Indicators Research,* vol. 6, pp. 163–80.

Maslow, A. (1954 and 1970), *Motivation and Personality,* 2nd ed. (New York: Harper & Row).

Meehan, E. J. (1975), 'Social indicators and policy analysis', in *Methodologies for Analysing Public Policies,* ed. F. P. Scioli, Jr, and T. J. Cook (Lexington, Mass.: D. C. Heath).

Meltsner, A. J. (1976), *Policy Analysts in the Bureaucracy* (Berkeley, Calif.: University of California Press).

Meltsner, A. J. (1979), 'Don't slight communication: some problems of analytical practice', *Policy Analysis,* vol. 5, pp. 367–92.

Merton, R. K. (1967), *On Theoretical Sociology* (New York: The Free Press).

Michalos, A. C. (1978), 'Social indicators research', *Policy Studies Journal,* vol. 6, pp. 393–404.

Michalos, A. C. (1978), *Foundations of Decision-Making* (Ottawa: Canadian Library of Philosophy).

Miles, I. (1975), *The Poverty of Prediction* (Farnborough and Lexington, Mass.: D. C. Heath).

Miles, I. (1978), 'The ideologies of futurists', in *The Handbook of Futures*

Research, ed. Jib Fowles (Westport, Conn., and London: Greenwood Press).

Miles, I., and Irvine, J. (1979), 'Social forecasting: predicting the future or making history', in Irvine, Miles, and Evans (1979).

Miller, M. K. (1979), 'An operational framework for policy modelling in the social sciences', *Social Indicators Research,* vol. 6, pp. 373–88.

Miller, S. M. (1974), 'A critique of US experience', in *Positive Discrimination and Inequality,* Research Paper 314, ed. H. Glennerster and S. Hatch (London: Fabian Society).

Mindlin, A. (1979), 'The use of social indicators in municipal government', in *Social Indicators and Marketing,* ed. R. Clewett and J. C. Olsen (Washington, DC: American Marketing Association).

Mirrlees, J. A. (1978), 'Social cost-benefit analysis and the distribution of income', *World Development,* vol. 6, pp. 131–8.

Mishan, E. J. (1974), 'Flexibility and consistency in project evaluation', *Economica,* vol. 41, pp. 81–96.

Mobbs, T. H. (1975), 'A continuous survey of citizens in Cleveland', in *Corporate Planning Organisation and Research and Intelligence Techniques* (London: PTRC Seminar Proceedings), pp. 126–33.

Moffatt, M. J., and Reid, T. (1976), 'Comment on indicators and policy formation', *Canadian Public Administration,* vol. 19, pp. 633–7.

Moser, C. (1973), 'Social indicators – systems methods and problems', *The Review of Income and Wealth,* series 19, pp. 133–41.

Mullens, N. C. (1973), *Theories and Theory Groups in Contemporary American Sociology* (New York: Harper & Row).

Nash, C., Pearce, D., Stanley, J. (1975), 'Criteria for evaluating project evaluation techniques', *Journal of American Institute of Planners,* vol. 41, pp. 83–9.

Nissel, M. (ed.) (1970–4), *Social Trends Nos 1–5* (London: Her Majesty's Stationery Office).

Nissel, M. (1974), 'Government social statistics', *Statistical News,* no. 25, pp. 3–8.

Nissel, M. (1979), 'Developing *Social Trends*', unpublished research paper (London: Policy Studies Institute).

Okun, A. M. (1971), 'Should GNP measure social welfare?', *The Brookings Bulletin,* vol. 8, pp. 4–7.

Olson, M. (1969), 'The plan and purpose of a social report', *The Public Interest,* no. 15, Spring, p. 86.

Organisation for Economic Co-operation and Development (1973), *List of Social Concerns* (Paris: OECD).

Organisation for Economic Co-operation and Development (1976a), *Measuring Social Well-Being* (Paris: OECD).

Organisation for Economic Co-operation and Development (1976b), *Measuring Social Well-Being: A Progress Report on the Development of Social Indicators* (Paris: OECD).

Organisation for Economic Co-operation and Development (1977), *1976 Progress Report on Phase II* (Paris: OECD).

Organisation for Economic Co-operation and Development (1979),

Inventory of Data Sources for Social Indicators (Paris: Manpower and Social Affairs Committee).

Palys, T. S. (1973), *Social Indicators of Quality of Life in Canada: A Practical Theoretical Report* (Manitoba, Winnipeg: Department of Urban Affairs).

Parke, R., and Seidman, D. (1978), 'Social indicators and social reporting', *Annals of the American Academy of Political and Social Sciences,* vol. 435, pp. 1–22.

Pigou, A. C. (1924), *Economics of Welfare,* 2nd ed. (London: Macmillan).

Pond, C. (1979), 'Numbers game', *New Society,* 20/27 December, pp. 657–8.

President's Research Committee on Social Trends (1933), *Report of the President's Research Committee on Social Trends* (New York: McGraw-Hill).

Radical Statistics Group (1978), *Social Indicators: For Individual Well-Being or Social Control?* Pamphlet No. 4 (London: British Society for Social Responsibility in Science).

Ramsy, N. R. (1974), 'Social indicators in the United States and Europe: comments on five country reports', in *Social Indicators 1973: A Review Symposium,* ed. R. A. Van Dusen (New York: Social Science Research Council).

Resource Allocation Working Party (1976), *Sharing Resources for Health in England* (London: Her Majesty's Stationery Office).

Reynolds, J. F. (1975), 'Policy science: a conceptual and methodological analysis', *Policy Sciences,* vol. 6, pp. 1–27.

Rittel, H. W. J., and Webber, M. M. (1973), 'Dilemmas in a general theory of planning', *Policy Sciences,* vol. 4, pp. 155–69.

Rivlin, A. M. (1971), *Systematic Thinking for Social Action* (Washington, DC: Brookings Institute).

Rivlin, A. M. (1973), 'Social experiments: the promise and the problem', *Evaluation,* vol. 1, pp. 77–8.

Robinson, W. S. (1950), 'Ecological correlations and the behaviour of individuals', *American Sociological Review,* June, pp. 351–7.

Rogers, W. L. (1977), 'Work status and the quality of life', *Social Indicators Research,* vol. 4, pp. 267–88.

Roos, J. P. (1978), *Subjective and Objective Welfare: A Critique of Erik Allardt,* Report No. 18 (University of Helsinki: Research Group for Comparative Sociology).

Ross, P. J., Bluestone, H., and Hines, F. K. (1979), *Indicators of Social Well-Being for US Counties,* US Department of Agriculture; Economics, Statistics, and Cooperatives Service; Rural Development Research Report No. 10 (Washington, DC: US Department of Agriculture).

Rossi, R. J., and Gilmartin, K. J. (1979), *Handbook of Social Indicators* (New York: Garland Press).

Rossi, R. J., and Gilmartin, K. J. (1980), 'Social indicators of youth development and educational performance: a programmatic statement', in *Social Indicators Research,* vol. 7, pp. 157–92.

Sackman, H. (1974), *Delphi Assessment: Expert Opinion, Forecasting and Group Procedure* (Santa Monica, Calif.: Rand Corporation).

Sackman, H. (1976), 'A sceptic at the oracle', *Futures,* vol. 8, pp. 444–6.

Schmid, A. A. (1975), 'Systematic choice among multiple outputs of public projects without prices', *Social Indicators Research*, vol. 2, pp. 275–86.

Schneider, M. (1974), 'The quality of life in large American cities: "objective and subjective social indicators" ', *Social Indicators Research*, vol. 1, pp. 495–509.

Seashore, S. E. (1975), 'Defining and measuring the quality of working life', in *The Quality of Working Life*, ed. L. B. Davis and A. B. Cherns (New York: The Free Press).

Seidman, D. (1978), 'Picturing the nation', *Contemporary Sociology*, vol. 7, pp. 717–19.

Shaw, M., and Miles, I. (1979), 'The social roots of statistical knowledge', in Irvine, Miles and Evans (1979).

Sheldon, E., and Moore, W. E. (eds) (1968), *Indicators of Social Change: Concepts and Measurements* (New York: Russell Sage Foundation).

Sheldon, E., and Freeman, H. E. (1970), 'Notes on social indicators: promises and potential', *Policy Sciences*, vol. 1, pp. 97–111.

Shevky, E. F., and Bell, W. (1955), *Social Area Analysis: Theory, Illustrative Application and Computational Procedures* (Stanford, Calif.: Greenwood Press).

Shonfield, A. (1972), 'Research and public policy', in *Social Science and Government*, ed. A. B. Cherns, R. Sinclair and W. I. Johnson (London: Tavistock).

Shostack, A. B. (1978), 'How long before we get a volume of social indicators?', *Contemporary Sociology*, vol. 7, pp. 719–22.

Simon, H. E. (1957), *Administrative Behaviour*, 2nd edn. (Glencoe, Ill.: The Free Press).

SSRC (Social Science Research Council – US) (1979), *Social Indicators Newsletter*, August, p. 3.

Sondheim, M. W. (1978), 'A comprehensive methodology for assessing environmental impact', *Journal of Environmental Management*, vol. 6, pp. 27–42.

Stegman, M. A. (1979), 'Neighbourhood classification and the role of the planner in seriously distressed communities', *Journal of the American Planning Association*, vol. 45, pp. 495–505.

Stinchcombe, A. L., and Wendt, J. C. (1975), 'Theoretical domains and measurement in social indicator analysis', in *Social Indicator Models*, ed. K. C. Land and S. Spilerman (New York: Russell Sage Foundation).

Stipak, B. (1977), 'Attitudes and belief systems concerning urban services', *Public Opinion Quarterly*, vol. 41, pp. 41–55.

Stipak, B. (1979a), 'Are there sensible ways to analyse and use subjective indicators of urban service quality?', *Social Indicators Research*, vol. 6, pp. 421–38.

Stipak, B. (1979b), 'Citizen satisfaction with urban services: potential misuse as a performance indicator', *Public Administration Review*, vol. 39, pp. 46–52.

Stone, R. (1973), 'A system of social matrices', *The Review of Income and Wealth*, series 19, pp. 143–66.

Strauch, R. E. (1975), ' "Squishy" problems and quantitative methods', *Policy Sciences*, vol. 6, pp. 175–84.

Strumpel, B. (ed.) (1974), *Subjective Elements of Well-Being* (Paris: Organisation for Economic Co-operation and Development).

Thompson, E. J. (ed.) (1975, 1976, 1977, 1978a, 1979), *Social Trends Nos 6–10* (London: Her Majesty's Stationery Office).

Thompson, E. J. (1978b), 'Social Trends: the development of an annual report for the United Kingdom', *International Social Science Journal,* vol. 30, pp. 653–9.

Timms, D. (1971), *The Urban Mosaic: Towards a Theory of Residential Differentiation* (Cambridge: Cambridge University Press).

Tribe, L. H. (1976), 'Ways not to think about plastic trees', in Tribe, L. H., Schelling, C. S., and Voss, J. (1976), *When Values Conflict – Essays on Environmental Analysis Discourse and Decision* (Cambridge, Mass.: Ballinger).

United Nations (1971), *A System of Demographic, Manpower, and Social Statistics Series, Classifications and Social Indicators,* ST/STAT/49 (New York: UN Secretariat).

United Nations (1974), *System of Social and Demographic Statistics (SSDS),* E/CN3/450 (New York: UN Secretariat).

United Nations (1975), *Towards a System of Social and Demographic Statistics,* ST/ESA/STAT/SER.F/18 (New York: Department of Economic and Social Affairs).

United Nations (1976), *National Social Reports: Contents, Methods, and Aims,* SOA/SEM/62/WP5 (Geneva: Division of Social Affairs).

US Department of Commerce (1977), *Social Indicators 1976* (Washington, DC: US Government Printing Office).

US Department of Health, Education, and Welfare (1969), *Toward a Social Report* Washington, DC: US Government Printing Office).

Van Meter, D. S., and Asher, H. B. (1973), 'Causal analysis: its promise for policy studies', *Policy Studies Journal,* vol. 2, pp. 103–8.

Vauzelles-Barbier, D. (1978), 'Public participation in the rehabilitation of urban centres', *International Social Science Journal,* vol. 30, pp. 336–59.

Vigderhous, G., and Fishman, G. (1978), 'Social indicators of marital instability, USA, 1920–1969', *Social Indicators Research,* vol. 5, pp. 325–44.

Wan, T., and Liveratos, B. (1978), 'Interpreting a general index of subjective well-being', *Health and Society,* vol. 56, pp. 531–56.

Ward, P. (1980), *Quality of Life in Residential Care* (London: Personal Social Services Council).

Warren, R. D., Fear, F. A., and Klonglan, G. E. (1980), 'Social-indicator model building: a multiple-indicator design', *Social Indicators Research,* vol. 7, pp. 269–98.

Webber, R. J. (1975), *Liverpool Social Area Study 1971 Data: Final Report,* PRAG Technical Papers TP14 (London: Centre for Environmental Studies).

Webber, R. J. (1977), *The National Classification of Residential Neighbourhoods: An Introduction to the Classification of Wards and Parishes,* PRAG Technical Papers TP23 (London: Centre for Environmental Studies).

Webber, R. J. (1978a), 'The contribution of a national classification of residential neighbourhoods to regional analysis', paper presented to the

Conference on Social Indicators in Planning and Policy, Regional Studies Association, London.

Webber, R. J. (1978b), 'Making the most of the census for strategic analysis', *Town Planning Review*, vol. 49, pp. 274–84.

Webber, R. (1979), *Census Enumeration Districts: A Socio-Economic Classification* (London: Office of Population, Censuses and Surveys).

Weitzman, M. S. (1979), 'The developing program on social indicators at the US Bureau of the Census', *Social Indicators Research*, vol. 6, pp. 239–50.

Wilcox, L. D., Brooks, R. M., Beal, G. M., and Klonglan, G. E. (1972), *Social Indicators and Societal Monitoring* (San Francisco: Jossey-Bass).

Wingo, L., and Evans, A. (eds) (1977), *Public Economics and the Quality of Life* (Baltimore and London: Johns Hopkins University Press).

Wisman, J. D. (1978), 'The naturalistic turn of orthodox economics: a study of methodological misunderstanding', *Review of Social Economy*, vol. 36, pp. 263–84.

World Bank (1979), *World Development Report, 1979* (Oxford: Oxford University Press).

Woudhuysen, J., and Law, H. (1979), 'Underground transport: how to do it right', *Design* no. 371, pp. 42–7.

Zapf, W. (1975), 'Systems of social indicators: current approaches and problems', *International Social Science Journal*, vol. 27, pp. 479–98.

Zapf, W. (1976), *Social Indicators Newsletter,* Social Science Research Council, US, November 1976.

Zapf, W. (1977), *Applied Social Reporting: A Social Indicators System for West German Society,* SPES Working Paper No. 70 (Frankfurt Mannheim: Sozialpolitische Forschergruppe).

Index

Abrams, M. 40
affirmative action (scheme) (US) 131, 142
aggregation (of data) 28, 31, 47, 79-82, 92-3, 147, 154, 158
    in global measures 84-5
    in social reports 127
allocation of resources 9-10, 21, 24, 67, 93, 100, 102, 131, 141-4, 145, 149, 160, 166
    distributional equity 98-100, 146
    part played by censuses 134
    part played by Community Indicators Programme 52
    part played by Planning Research Applications Group 140
    see also affirmative action, positive discrimination and Resource Allocation Working Party
analytic rationality 101, 103
Andrews, F. M. 38-40, 41

budget pies (US) 35
Bureau of the Census (US): part played in social reporting 120
bureaucracy 13, 97, 98, 100-1, 103, 106, 108, 147, 170

Cantril Self-Anchoring Striving Scale, 35-6
Carlisle, E. 26-7
causality 3, 13, 26, 54-5, 72-3, 77, 81, 82, 106, 144, 147
    causal models 51, 54, 61-3, 66, 68, 85-6
    new causalists 70
census data 52, 132-9, 143-4, 158
    Census of Population (1971) (UK) 133 *see also* Small Area Statistics
    decennial census (US) 15
Central Statistical Office (UK):
    part played in social reporting 113, 115, 117
    non-political stance 89, 125
Chartered Institute of Public Finance and Accountancy (CIPFA) (UK) 11
    see also Community Indicators Programme
Chicago Community Inventory 131
Chicago School of sociologists 131
client-groups 52, 54
cluster analysis 132-3

collection of data 14-15, 17, 28, 57-8, 60-1, 70, 76-7, 79, 82, 83, 112, 126-7
    by census 143-4
    by survey 96-8
    see also time-series data
Community Development Project (UK) 143
Community Indicators Programme (UK) 51-4
community profiles (US) 130
component analysis 132, 158-9
corporate social audit (report) 32-4
cost-benefit analysis 15-16, 98, 101
crime 1, 83
    FBI uniform crime index (US) 3, 90
cultural imperialism 93

Delphi technique 94-5
deprivation (urban) 11, 91, 92, 144-9
dimensionality 82-5, 92
    multidimensionality 76, 77, 83
disaggregation 88, 93, 96, 108
    in social reports 127-8
    see also information overload
distributional equity 98-100, 146-7
D-T scale 39-40

economics 1, 32-4, 64, 74-5, 106-7, 115
    economic indicators and econometric models 16, 17-18
Educational Disadvantage Unit (UK) 142
Educational Priority Area programme (EPA) (UK) 80, 142, 147
empirical testing vii, 66, 69-70, 76
enumeration districts 133-4, 139
European Economic Community (EEC): use of indicators 9

Gallup poll 44-5, 83
General Improvement Area programme (UK) 143
geographical area 11, 27, 44, 103, 145, 159-60
government:
    collection of statistics 125-7
    expenditure 9-10, 60, 88, 160
    local government programmes 11, 49, 52, 108, 150